TAUNTON'S

FOR PROS BY PROS ®

BUILDER-TESTED | CODE APPROVED

Foundations & Concrete Work

EDITORS OF
FineHomebuilding

The Taunton Press

The Taunton Press
Inspiration for hands-on living®

The Taunton Press, Inc., 63 South Main Street, Newtown, CT 06470-2344
Email: tp@taunton.com

Editors: Peter Chapman, Christina Glennon
Copy editor: Candace B. Levy
Indexer: Jay Kreider
Jacket/Cover design: Alexander Isley, Inc.
Interior design: Carol Singer
Layout: Rita Sowins/Sowins Design
Front cover photographer: Justin Fink, courtesy of *Fine Homebuilding,* © The Taunton Press, Inc.
Back cover photographer: Roe A. Osborn, courtesy of *Fine Homebuilding,* © The Taunton Press, Inc.

The following names/manufacturers appearing in *Foundations & Concrete Work* are trademarks: Ashlar Blend™, Avongard™, Basement Systems®, Bigfoot Systems®, Bobcat®, CarbonCast®, Chem-Calk®, Dryvit®, ElastiKote®, Goo Gone®, Goof Off®, Hilti®, International Residential Code®, Jackson®, Keystone Country Manor®, Kodak®, Pene-Krete®, Plasti-Grip®, Quikrete®, Renew-Crete®, RomanPisa®, Roxul®, Rub-R-Wall®, Silly Putty®, Simpson®, Sonotube®, SquareFoot™, Stabila®, Styrofoam®, Superior Walls®, Sure Klean®, Tapcon®, Techno Metal Post™, Termidor®, Thermafiber®, Thermal-Krete®, Thermax™, Tu-Tuf®, Typar®, Tyvek®, Versa-Lok®, Vulkem®, YorkShield 106 TS™, Zoeller®.

LIBRARY OF CONGRESS CATALOGING-IN-PUBLICATION DATA
Names: Taunton Press, editor.
Title: Foundations & concrete work / editors of Fine homebuilding.
Other titles: Foundations and concrete work | Taunton's fine homebuilding.
Description: Newtown, CT : The Taunton Press, [2017] | Includes index.
Identifiers: LCCN 2017033157 | ISBN 9781631869136
Subjects: LCSH: Foundations | Concrete footings.
Classification: LCC TH5201 .T38 2017 | DDC 690/.11--dc23
LC record available at https://lccn.loc.gov/2017033157

This book is compiled from articles that originally appeared in *Fine Homebuilding* magazine. Unless otherwise indicated, construction costs listed were current at the time the articles first appeared.

About Your Safety: Construction is inherently dangerous. Using hand or power tools improperly or ignoring safety practices can lead to permanent injury or even death. Don't try to perform operations you learn about here (or elsewhere) unless you're certain they are safe for you. If something about an operation doesn't feel right, don't do it. Look for another way. We want you to enjoy working on your home, so please keep safety foremost in your mind.

ACKNOWLEDGMENTS

Special thanks to the authors, editors, art directors, copy editors, and other staff members of *Fine Homebuilding* who contributed to the development of articles in this book.

Contents

INTRODUCTION

Years ago, when I was just beginning to dip my toes into the world of building, I worked at a local home improvement retailer. My purview included, among other things, the concrete aisle. Occasionally, whether from being caught in a rainstorm or thanks to the haphazard hose work in the nearby garden nursery department, we would have to deal with a bag of concrete that got wet. Often these bags looked no different from the others, but when you grabbed one, you'd find a perfect bag-formed 80-lb. brick of hardened concrete. This was a terrible initiation that set me back far too many years in my building career, because it flew in direct defiance of the instructions printed on the bag.

The instructions were telling me to pour the 80 lb. of dry ingredients into a mortar tub or wheelbarrow, create a depression in the center, pour in 2 qt. of water, and then work the mix with a hoe, gradually adding another quart of water until the mix looked just right, like thick oatmeal. By contrast, my real world experience was telling me that it was just as easy to leave the sealed bag out in the rain, and to hell with the measuring and mixing, never mind the mortar tub or wheelbarrow.

What I didn't know then was that concrete only seemed simple. Yes, if you get concrete wet it will harden. But hardening really isn't the point. Concrete only has three main ingredients—portland cement, aggregate, and water—and by adjusting the ratio of those three ingredients you can tailor the mix to the specific job. Mortar, for example, is commonly mixed in one of five different common proportions, each of which has a specific task. They'll all get hard, but use the wrong one and the stone veneer won't stick, or the bricks you're trying to bond will crack after the first freeze/thaw cycle. The same is true with concrete additives, which can either save the day or make life miserable. The mix spinning around in the back of every cement truck will harden, but order the wrong one and it will harden faster than you can finish the surface, or take so long to set that you'll be forced to set up work lights and babysit the pour well past quitting time.

I didn't have the good sense to read a book like this during my early years as a builder, and I suffered through some painful lessons before finally realizing that simplicity is about as complex as it gets. The mix will always harden, but only with the right research, right tools, and right procedures will it harden the right way.

—Justin Fink
Editor, *Fine Homebuilding*

Foundations and Concrete Basics

Understanding Building Loads

BY ROB MUNACH

A house is more than an assembly of studs, joists, and rafters clad in materials like drywall, tile, paint, carpet, concrete, and asphalt shingles. When built well, a house protects its inhabitants from relentless physical forces.

It is important, then, before sinking a nail into the first piece of framing lumber, to understand how a house frame and foundation perform. To begin, you need to know what a building load is. Here's how it works.

Understanding Loads Improves Framing and Design Skills

A building load is simply a force that a house frame needs to resist. The frame must be designed to withstand eight of these loads—including wind, earth, and snow—without catastrophic stress on the structure. Although not every load consideration is applicable to every geographic region, or even every home within a region, having a collective understanding of building loads will strengthen your view of framing as a general system. That's an asset when designing, building, or remodeling any home, anywhere.

1. THE LOAD: DEAD

- **What it means:** Dead loads are the forces incurred due to the weight of all the materials used in the construction of a home. Dead loads can vary greatly depending on the type of construction and the interior finishes. For example, carpet, sheet vinyl, trussed roofs, 25-year shingles, and vinyl siding are relatively light in weight. Tiled floors, suspended concrete slabs, 40-year shingles, built-in cabinetry, granite counters, plaster walls, fiber-cement siding, and veneered masonry are relatively heavy.
- **What it affects:** Dead loads have an effect on all structural members of a house. The loads are a constant over the life of the structure, and they have a big impact on the long-term deflection or creep of framing members.

2. THE LOAD: LIVE

- **What it means:** Live loads are produced by the users of a home. These loads include the weight of people, their furniture, and their storage items. A live load is most applicable to floors, but it can apply to roofs during repair projects due to the weight of workers and their materials.
- **What it affects:** Live loads exert force on almost all of a house's framing components. The goal is to design floor systems that limit deflection and vibration.

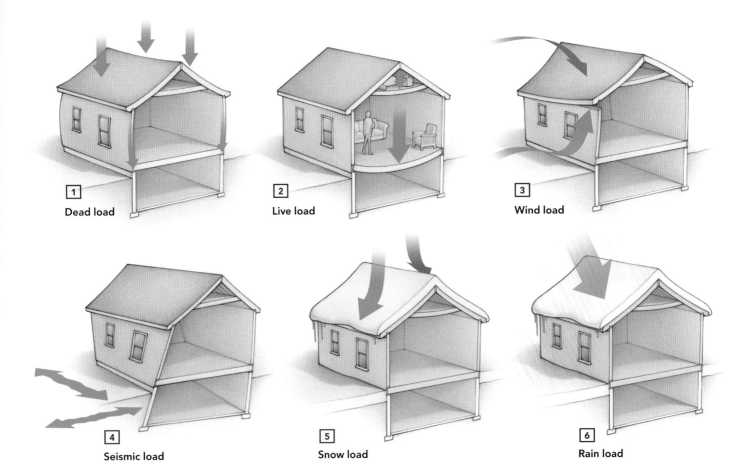

1 Dead load

2 Live load

3 Wind load

4 Seismic load

5 Snow load

6 Rain load

3. THE LOAD: WIND

- **What it means:** Wind loads are the positive or negative pressures exerted on a house when it obstructs the flow of moving air. Wind loads generally act perpendicular to the surfaces of the house.

- **What it affects:** The significance of the load depends on the geographic location of the house, its height, and its roof pitch. Wind loads have the most significant impact on roof framing, overhangs, and large openings, especially those near building corners. On a larger scale, shear-resisting elements, such as the roof, floor framing, and sheathed wall segments (shear walls), are affected by wind loads.

4. THE LOAD: SEISMIC

- **What it means:** Seismic loads are the inertial forces acting on a house due to earthquake-induced ground motions. These forces generally act horizontally on each element of the structure and are proportional to their mass. As such, heavier houses are more susceptible to seismic loads.

- **What it affects:** While all components of a frame feel the effect of seismic loads, shear-resisting elements (see wind loads) that provide stability are most affected.

5. THE LOAD: SNOW

- **What it means:** Snow load is the weight of snow uniformly distributed on the roof or piled into drifts. Snow that slides from an upper roof onto a lower roof can also add significantly to snow load.

- **What it affects:** Roof and wall framing is generally responsible for resisting snow loads. Floor joists and girders also may be affected, depending on the framing configuration.

6. THE LOAD: RAIN

- **What it means:** Rain load is the weight of rainwater that accumulates on a roof. This type of load is typically an issue only on very low slope roofs. In addition, rain can add to snow loads on low-slope roofs.

- **What it affects:** The framing members that support snow loads also resist the forces of rain loads.

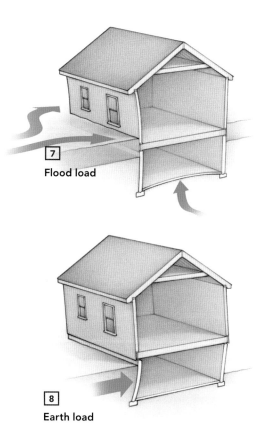

7

Flood load

8

Earth load

7. THE LOAD: FLOOD

- **What it means:** Flood load is the pressure exerted on a house when it obstructs the flow of moving water.
- **What it affects:** Foundations must be designed adequately to resist these forces as well as impact forces from moving debris. Also included are hydrostatic loads due to the difference in elevation between the water inside and outside the structure, which can cause uplift on slabs and floor systems.

8. THE LOAD: EARTH

- **What it means:** Earth load is the lateral pressure on the foundation wall due to the height of the backfill.
- **What it affects:** Foundation walls and their attachment to mudsills and floor joists must be designed properly to withstand this load. Floor diaphragms and lower-level shear walls are also affected; they must resist racking due to the overall pressure of the earth on the structure.

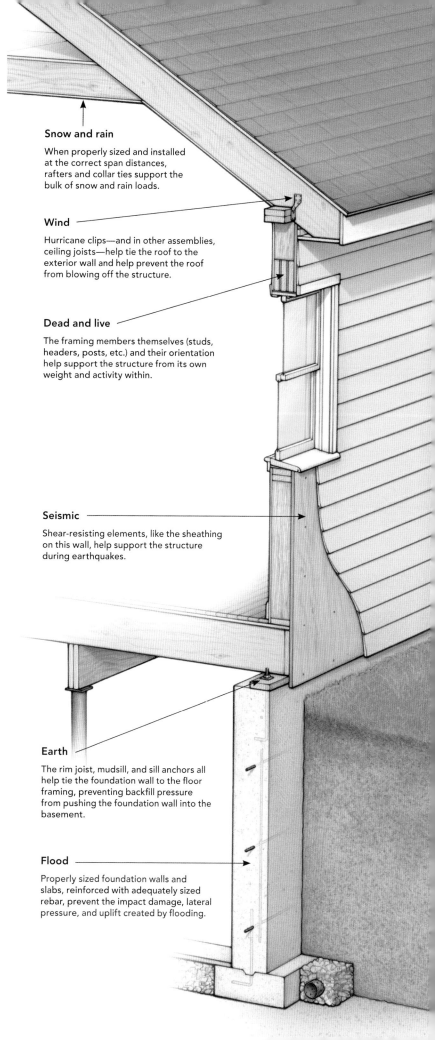

Snow and rain

When properly sized and installed at the correct span distances, rafters and collar ties support the bulk of snow and rain loads.

Wind

Hurricane clips—and in other assemblies, ceiling joists—help tie the roof to the exterior wall and help prevent the roof from blowing off the structure.

Dead and live

The framing members themselves (studs, headers, posts, etc.) and their orientation help support the structure from its own weight and activity within.

Seismic

Shear-resisting elements, like the sheathing on this wall, help support the structure during earthquakes.

Earth

The rim joist, mudsill, and sill anchors all help tie the foundation wall to the floor framing, preventing backfill pressure from pushing the foundation wall into the basement.

Flood

Properly sized foundation walls and slabs, reinforced with adequately sized rebar, prevent the impact damage, lateral pressure, and uplift created by flooding.

Soil: The Other Half of the Foundation

BY ROBERT M. FELTON

Most builders and architects are familiar with the problem of building settlement: the chimney that won't stop going down, the wall cracks that keep opening up, the older home that suddenly begins to exhibit movement for no apparent reason. Everyone in the building industry has a story about a fix that "shoulda done it," but didn't.

Preventing settlement problems begins with the recognition that the soil a foundation rests on is part of the foundation system; it's a building material, just like the 2×4 studs that frame the house. The fact that you can't go to a lumberyard and select this building material—that in most cases you're simply going to use whatever you happen to have—makes it especially important that you recognize differences among soil types, know something of the way soils respond to building loads, and be able to identify potential problems.

Differential Settlement Is the Real Enemy

A few things need to be understood about settlement. First, all houses settle. The amount may be so small as to be undetectable or may be so uniform as to leave no signs, but it unquestionably happens. Second, because of the natural and construction-related variations in soil properties, not every point on a foundation settles the same amount.

To avoid problems with entrances and utility connections, total settlement must be minimized. To avoid racking door frames and cracking walls, you must prevent differential settlement, the difference in settlement between various points on the foundation. The distinction between total and differential settlement is important. The Palace of Fine Arts in Mexico City, for instance, has settled several meters without significant distress to the structure and remains in service because the settlement has been uniform. The Leaning Tower of Pisa, on the other hand, is useless for anything but the Kodak® moments of tourists.

Elementary Research Can Dig Up Most Problems

Fortunately for homebuilders, the loads involved in most residential construction are relatively light. Following time-proven procedures and steering clear of some common misconceptions will keep you out of trouble in most cases.

For starters, you can learn a lot about soil conditions on your site by taking advantage of public-sector resources. The U.S. Department of Agriculture

FINDING OUT WHAT'S DOWN THERE. Taking samples from a series of drillings enables engineers to determine subsurface soil characteristics.

> ## Understanding the stuff the house sits on may prevent cost overruns, callbacks, and neighborhood gossip.

(USDA) has prepared soil maps for most of the country. Available at no cost at any local USDA branch office, these maps superimpose soil-type delineations over aerial photographs (see "Two Ways to Look at the Same Piece of Land" on p. 10). By studying these maps and the soil descriptions that accompany them, you can find out information such as whether your site might have a high groundwater table or whether problematic soils—for example, shrink/swell-susceptible clays—might lurk beneath the surface.

Having been taken 40 years ago or more, aerial photos often reveal evidence of unsuspected devel-

opment or manipulation of the site. An even better source for this type of information is a topographic map from the U.S. Geological Survey. This map may reveal abandoned cemeteries, farm ponds, or wells or even the long-forgotten town dump. A topographic map may be purchased for a few dollars at outdoor-sporting-goods stores or downloaded at no cost (www.trails.com).

Don't forget to check with your community's building and engineering departments; they often have a wealth of local information and experience, which they are usually happy to share. Developers who have built close by and homeowners on adjoining lots are other good sources of information.

Virgin Soil Is Not Always Virtuous

If your research unearths potential problems, then it's time to bite the bullet and consult an expert (see

TWO WAYS TO LOOK AT THE SAME PIECE OF LAND

SOIL MAPS FROM THE U.S. DEPARTMENT OF Agriculture (USDA) are actually aerial photographs with soil types superimposed on them (see the drawings below left). They can alert builders to problem soil conditions before they start digging.

Topographic maps from the U.S. Geological Survey (USGS) can reveal wetlands or intermittent streams (see the drawings below right). Serving as snapshots in time, both maps provide valuable insight into human activity that has taken place on the land.

USDA SOIL MAP

USGS TOPOGRAPHIC MAP

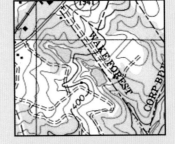

CITY DUMP? The soil descriptions that accompany this map indicate that except for the suspicious area in the center (*Ma* signifies man-made soil), all the soils delineated in this close-up are builder friendly sand. The two straight, bold lines to the left of the dump represent dammed lakes.

WHAT CITY DUMP? Although a topographic map is generally the better indicator of previous development, a builder who relied on only a topo map in this case would not be able to tell that the lakes were man-made and, more important, would have no idea that his or her dream land was once the city dump.

"When Should You Call in a Soils Engineer?" on p. 12). If you uncover no history of activity that may have left behind problems, that's probably good news, but there may still be things that need attention. "Virgin soil" isn't inherently problem free. Muck (decomposed organic material), for instance, may have been undisturbed since Mother Nature deposited it, but building on it is always a bad idea.

Clay can also be troublesome. The strength of clay soils varies inversely with changes in moisture content: The greater the moisture, the weaker the soil. If clay materials underlie your site, the site plan must provide for positive drainage that will direct surface water away from the structure and paved areas; otherwise, water may penetrate and weaken the supporting soil. This is, in fact, a common cause of postconstruction settlement problems. If site constraints make it impossible to direct runoff away from the driveway, you should plan to provide lateral drains alongside the drive to prevent water from accumulating beneath the pavement. Foundation drains must also be carefully designed to carry groundwater well away from the structure. These measures aren't cheap, but they cost less than repairs, ill will, and neighborhood gossip.

Bridging the Gaps

What if there's a wet, loose, soft, low, or mucky spot on the site? Can you bridge it with fill? Geotechnical engineers like me have a couple of easy rules of thumb that we refer to when called to a site and asked what to do. After that, it gets complicated.

- *Rule one:* Never fill a low spot with surface strippings, shrubs, or woody debris, no matter how much clean fill will be placed on top of it. It might take years, but the organic material will inevitably decompose and cause settlement.
- *Rule two:* Muck must be removed. Although it's possible to force sand and gravel fill into the muck and create a stable mixture, that's not a reliable solution. What usually happens is that pockets of weak material become scattered throughout the

reworked material, and those areas slowly compress over the years.

To control settlement problems, soils engineers want the foundation to rest on stable, compacted material that extends at least half of the influence depth, the distance beneath the footing that its weight is still "felt" by soil particles (see "The Other Half of the Foundation" on p. 13).

Square foundations (such as those beneath a Lally column) stress the soil to a depth equal to about 2 times the foundation width. A 2-ft. by 2-ft. pedestal, for example, is felt by soil particles to a depth of about 4 ft. below the foundation.

A strip foundation, one whose length is 10 or more times greater than the width (for example, a wall foundation), stresses the soil to a depth equal to about 4 times the foundation width. Thus an 18-in.-wide foundation is felt by soil particles as much as 6 ft. below the foundation. The maximum stress for either type of foundation occurs at a depth of about one-quarter of the influence depth.

What all this means to the builder is that for the pedestal I just described, you must provide at least 2 ft. of competent support; for the strip, you must provide at least 3 ft. If that can't be done with the existing soil, you should plan to remove and replace the undesirable material and restore the site to grade with engineered fill.

Self-Compacting Soil Has Not Been Invented Yet

One of the misconceptions I often encounter is the belief that soil will densify and strengthen if it's merely dumped on a site and left undisturbed for several months—that fill dumped in a low area in the fall will be ready to support construction in the spring without any compaction. To this opinion, I always respond: " 'Fraid not." To understand why, think back to your high-school physics class: "An object at rest tends to remain at rest unless acted on by an outside force." Loosely dumped soil does not densify and strengthen by itself.

WHEN SHOULD YOU CALL IN A SOILS ENGINEER?

MANY BUILDERS AND ARCHITECTS are reluctant to hire engineers to perform subsurface investigations, and that's easy to understand: The cost of a house can go up a few thousand dollars. Despite the cost, there are circumstances in which consulting a soils engineer is a wise investment.

- If you're wondering how on earth (to belabor the point) you're supposed to build a house on a lot with a steep slope, then you need an engineer to determine the soil properties and to evaluate the stability of the incline.
- Evidence of previous earthwork at the site, especially filling, requires careful investigation. The site may host buried organic materials such as muck, debris such as demolition rubble or abandoned vehicles, or simply dumped fill. Any of these things can cause severe settlement problems.

- A local history of the presence of clay soils that are susceptible to shrinking and swelling with changes in moisture content also requires careful investigation and, usually, specialized design services and the use of an out-of-the-ordinary foundation.
- Encountering groundwater or weak soil while excavating for foundations may indicate a potential for future settlement or instability. The problem area should be carefully delineated by an expert and remedied after close consultation.
- Consult your experience. If you're crossing your fingers and hoping the soil conditions won't cause a problem, you're probably right to be uneasy. Call in a specialist.

To locate an engineer in your area, contact the American Society of Civil Engineers (www.asce.org) at (800) 548-2723.

NOT EXACTLY WINE TASTING. Soils engineers inspect core samples they've taken using the split-barrel sampler on the left.

Failure to compact is what leads to cracking sidewalks and uneven driveways.

It is particularly important that fill be placed in thin layers so that the densification effect of the compaction equipment is felt all the way to the bottom of each layer (see "Proper Fill Placement" on p. 14). The maximum thickness for each layer depends on soil type: Ordinarily about 12 in. for sand and 6 in. to 8 in. for clay. The required degree of densification is usually set forth by the local building code and specified as some percentage of maximum dry density as determined by one of several standard methods.

The moisture content of the fill material must also be controlled. If the moisture is too low, it is difficult for individual soil grains to realign themselves into the densest configuration; adding moisture lubricates the grains and makes realignment easier. But if there is too much moisture, the soil becomes unstable under the influence of compaction equipment because a portion of the compactive effort will be borne by the water between the soil grains and result

THE OTHER HALF OF THE FOUNDATION

TO PREVENT SETTLEMENT PROBLEMS, soil that is stable and compacted must extend at least half the distance from the base of the footing to the influence depth (the farthest distance beneath the footing that its weight is felt by soil particles). Strip foundations (such as the wall in the drawing below right) stress the soil more than square foundations (such as the pedestal in the drawing below left) and thus have greater influence depths.

Square foundation

Stable, compacted fill extends half the influence depth.

B

Only the soil grains inside this stress bulb "feel" the weight of the foundation.

Stress bulb

Influence depth (ID) = $2 \times B$

Strip foundation

This formula applies when the length of the foundation is 10 or more times greater than its width (B).

B

Stable, compacted fill extends half the influence depth (ID).

Influence depth (ID) = $4 \times B$

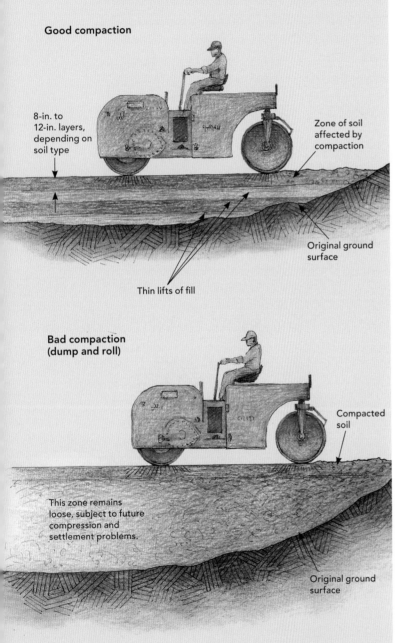

To MINIMIZE SETTLEMENT and to ensure that the foundation is properly supported, fill must be placed in thin layers, and each layer must be individually compacted.

Good compaction

8-in. to 12-in. layers, depending on soil type

Zone of soil affected by compaction

Original ground surface

Thin lifts of fill

Bad compaction (dump and roll)

Compacted soil

This zone remains loose, subject to future compression and settlement problems.

Original ground surface

in a water-bed-like rolling of the soil. Granular soils such as sand are most desirable for use as fill because their moisture content can be easily tweaked.

Keep Heavy Equipment away from Foundation Walls

Compacting soil against below-grade walls also requires special care, lest the horizontal load imposed by the compaction equipment damage the walls. A good rule of thumb is to keep heavy equipment away from the wall a distance of at least two-thirds the unbalanced height of the fill (see "Compacting Soil against Foundation Walls Takes Care" on the facing page). In other words, if the fill on the outside of the wall is 6 ft. higher than the fill on the inside, the big rollers should be kept at least 4 ft. away from the wall.

The strip of ground adjoining the wall should be compacted using small, hand-operated equipment. But make no mistake: It should be compacted; failure to compact is what leads to cracking sidewalks and uneven driveways. It is equally important to ensure that fill placed in utility-line excavations be properly placed and compacted. Improper placement of fill by the plumbing contractor, for instance, not only causes drain problems but frequently leads to exterior-wall settlement and cracking over buried drain lines.

Troubleshooting

In spite of your best efforts, what if the new homeowners call your office and demand that you come over right away to inspect a crack they've just noticed? You have not only a public-relations problem, because previously unnoticed hairline cracks suddenly become subjects of concern to the buyer, but a real technical problem too: You've got to figure out what has happened.

Most cracks are minor and insignificant, a consequence of the settlement and shifting that all houses undergo. In these cases, you need to explain a few things to the homeowners. Ideally, you would have prepared them for these possibilities beforehand:

COMPACTING SOIL AGAINST FOUNDATION WALLS TAKES CARE

TO AVOID DAMAGE from the horizontal loads imposed by compaction, heavy equipment should be kept away from the wall a distance of at least two-thirds the unbalanced height of the fill.

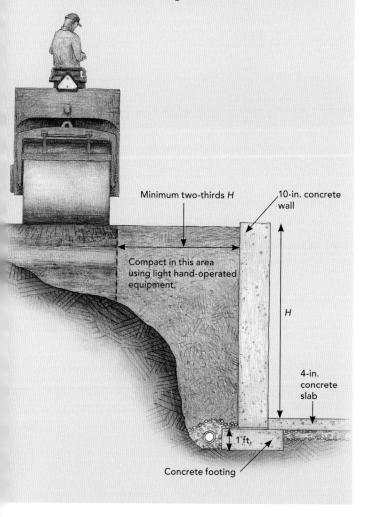

Minimum two-thirds *H*

10-in. concrete wall

Compact in this area using light hand-operated equipment.

H

4-in. concrete slab

1 ft.

Concrete footing

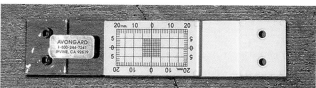

HAIRLINE CRACK OR STRUCTURAL DISASTER?
A crack monitor is used to track crack movement over a period of time. The pattern of movement enables an engineer to determine when and what remedial action may be necessary.

- The act of building the house changed the local groundwater conditions. In particular, the shallow soil zone beneath the house is drying. The minor settlement that results can be enough to cause hairline cracking.
- When you painted the house, it was empty. When the owner took possession and brought in the home gym, water bed, and baby grand, this stress caused flexing of virtually all the structural members. This too can cause hairline cracking.

Of course, there may be times when simple explanations don't suffice, when something strange seems to be happening. The best way to identify the cause of the problem is to install a crack monitor (Avongard™ Products; www.avongard.com), a two-piece, specialized ruler that is mounted over a crack (see the photo at left). Using a crack monitor spares you the work of trying to decide by eye and memory whether a crack has grown or changed. If it appears you've got a real problem, the data will be invaluable to whoever is trying to figure out what's causing the crack and what ought to be done because different settlement mechanisms leave distinctive signatures, which become apparent when the data are graphed.

The correction of foundation problems requires thorough investigation by experts. You should not hire a grouting contractor to mud-jack (pump concrete beneath a distressed area) until the cause of the distress has been positively identified. If a house corner is settling due to the presence of buried, compressible organic material, for example, pumping a yard or two of concrete into the soil immediately beneath the foundation will increase the load over the soft material and thus *increase* settlement. The wall may look fine when the contractor cleans up the job site and leaves, but more irate-homeowner phone calls are inevitable.

When making repairs, just as when beginning a project, you should be guided by a single rule: The best defense against future problems is doing it right the first time.

Getting the Right Concrete

BY RICK ARNOLD

Concrete is the most versatile construction material you can work with. It can be formed to any shape and can be used for just about any purpose: footings, walls, roofs, floors, walkways. It can be poured from a wheelbarrow, a truck, or a pump. It can be placed during freezing or hot temperatures, dry conditions, pouring rain, and blinding snow. The beauty of concrete, though, is that you can manipulate and control its physical properties to create the perfect combination of strength, durability, workability, and cost for each particular use and condition.

Having a basic knowledge of the ways that the concrete mix can be altered to suit certain use requirements and to compensate for the various weather and pouring conditions you may encounter is crucial to making sure you have a successful project. If you've ever watched an experienced crew pour and work concrete, they make it look easy. That's partly because they understand concrete; they know that they can adjust the mix to suit the job and the conditions. For example, a patio that's poured in a cold climate on a damp 35°F day should have a different mix than a patio that's poured in a hot climate on a dry 85°F day. The problem is that the consequences of an improper mix are not evident until it's too late.

Even inexperienced builders, though, can have success with concrete if they know the available options and can communicate their needs to the batch operator at their local ready-mix concrete plant. Don't worry; knowing the actual ingredients and ratios is not necessary. That's the batch operator's job. In fact, the batch operator is the best source of guidance in creating the ideal mix for the job because it's in his or her best interest to ensure that your project goes well.

When I order concrete, I specify the strength, aggregate size, and slump, and then I discuss any physical limitations of the job, the weather conditions, and my desired level of quality. This allows the batch operator to give me a mix that suits all my needs.

Cement Is the Glue of Concrete

When mixed with water, cement forms a paste that coats the aggregate in the mix. The cement cures and binds the ingredients together. Cement is available in five different types, but most are intended for large-scale or specialized projects. Type I cement is the most widely used, especially for residential projects.

The strength of concrete depends on its water-to-cement ratio: the lower the ratio, to a point, the

stronger the concrete. The primary characteristic that you need to consider is the required strength for the use, which is measured in pounds per square inch (psi). Concrete with a psi of 3,000, for instance, will withstand 3,000 lb. of compression per square inch before breaking.

In many cases, building codes dictate the required strength of concrete. The IRC (International Residential Code®) calls for concrete used in footings, foundations, and interior slabs (basements and garages, for example) to have a strength of 2,500 psi. The concrete for exterior slabs (patios, for example) must be at least 3,000 psi.

You may hear a seasoned concrete worker call in an order and identify the strength that he or she wants by stating a mix ratio ("1:2:2," for example) or a number of cement bags per yard ("five-bag mix," for instance). A good batch operator knows that the worker wants concrete with a certain psi strength, which he or she will provide, but not necessarily with those exact ingredient measurements. A more accurate approach is to identify the desired strength of the concrete in terms of its psi, which reduces the chance of misinterpretation.

Increasing the strength of the concrete above its specifications is perfectly acceptable, but if you are

A THREE-PART RECIPE

CONCRETE IS MADE BY COMBINING three main ingredients: portland cement, water, and aggregate (both fine and coarse). The ratio of those combined ingredients determines the concrete's strength, durability, workability, and cost.

CEMENT

Cement acts as the glue in a concrete mix. Combined with water, it forms a paste that coats the aggregate and binds together the mixture.

WATER

Without water, cement and aggregate would be just a dry, uncured mixture. Water triggers a chemical reaction in the cement; known as hydration, this reaction is what makes concrete harden.

AGGREGATE

The job of aggregate—gravel and sand—is to increase the strength of concrete while reducing its cost. Think of it as cement filler. The individual stones (coarse aggregate) interlock with each other, and the sand (fine aggregate) fills in the voids.

considering it because of job-specific structural concerns, then consult an engineer. About the only time that I increase the strength beyond what is required is when I plan to add water at the job site (which decreases the strength) to improve the concrete's ability to flow for a hard-to-reach pour. Admixtures, however, are better than water in many cases, especially when it comes to flatwork like slabs or patios.

Aggregate Is the Filler

Aggregate, which makes up 60% to 80% of concrete, adds strength while reducing cost. Most ready-mix plants offer stone from around ⅜ in. to 1½ in. in diameter. The smaller the aggregate, the more cement is needed to coat the total surface area (smaller stones add up to more surface area), and the greater the chance that the cured concrete will crack. That's because it's the cement in the concrete that cracks, not the stones.

The stone size is sometimes driven by the type of project. In general, the size of the aggregate shouldn't exceed one-fourth the thickness of flatwork or one-fifth the thickness of walls. For example, 1½-in. stone is too big to use in a 4-in.-thick slab such as a garage floor. For this application, ¾-in. stone is fine, but I usually call for ⅜-in. stone for slabs because the smaller stones are easier to move and require less work to float. The workability of the concrete is the other driving factor in aggregate size. Smaller stone makes the concrete easier to work with and finish, which is especially important to consider for areas like basements or garage floors, which have a large surface area.

When specifying larger sizes of aggregate, request that a gradient mix of smaller stones be added to the batch. This helps to fill in the gaps between larger stones, reducing your reliance on sand, which is typically added to every mix regardless of stone size. Remember, the more sand and cement used in a mix, the higher the risk of cracking.

Water Activates the Curing Process

The amount of water used in a batch of concrete depends on several things: the required strength of the concrete, the ratio of aggregate to cement, and the desired slump of the batch. The slump is a measure of the consistency of concrete; the lower the number, the stiffer the mix. In addition to specifying the strength of the concrete, you also must specify the slump at which you want that strength.

For pouring footings or foundation walls, a slump of 5 or 6 is typical. If access on the site is limited and I know that I'll be manually pushing the concrete through the forms rather than being able to drive the discharge chutes where needed, I figure on a looser slump of about 6 or 7. If I want a slump higher than 7, I don't want to get it by increasing the amount of water in the mix because that also means reducing the amount of aggregate and increasing the amount of cement to maintain the desired strength. For footings or foundations that require a slump higher than 7, I ask for a water-reducing admixture, which lets me get a higher slump without adding more water. For slab work, I order up to about a 5 slump with water; for anything beyond that, I ask for an admixture. If a job has strict specifications about required strength and slump, be careful about using water to adjust slump.

The concrete truck carries water on board; that water can be added to the mix at the job site to increase the slump and to make the concrete easier to pour. Be careful about adding too much water at the job site, though, because that will change the design of the mix. In general, adding 1 gal. of water to 1 yd. of mixed concrete can reduce the strength by about 200 psi. It also will increase shrinking potential—and therefore cracking potential—and decrease freeze–thaw resistance. At a certain point, the mix can become so loose that the large aggregate will separate from the rest of the mix, producing an inferior final product.

During cold-weather conditions (40°F and below), the plant uses hot water to warm up the ingredients

TWEAK THE LOAD WITH ADMIXTURES

IN ADDITION TO MANIPULATING the concrete's three main ingredients, ready-mix plants rely on an array of chemical and mineral additives, called admixtures, to customize a load of concrete. Admixtures typically are added to concrete to compensate for difficult jobs and uncooperative weather, and their beauty is that they don't adversely affect the strength of the concrete.

1. WATER REDUCERS

The name says it all: Water reducers reduce the need for water. Generally speaking, you can add a water reducer to a mix without reducing the water, and you can create concrete that has a higher slump while still retaining its strength. If you add a water reducer and reduce the amount of water in the mix, the slump can stay the same while the strength of the mix increases.

Midrange water reducers are generally used for slumps of 4 to 7, such as in flatwork, and they help to provide better workability.

High-range water reducers, also known as superplasticizers, help on jobs where a high slump—say, around 8 or higher—is required. For instance, a foundation wall that contains a lot of steel rebar,

especially around the openings, can easily get clogged by a stiff mix; this creates problematic voids in the concrete. These water reducers are especially handy for stay-in-place forms such as insulated concrete forms (ICFs), which are more prone to voids because of their internal structural webbing and because there is no way visually to inspect the concrete wall within.

2. AIR ENTRAINERS

Air entrainers add air to the mix, forming microscopic voids throughout the cured concrete that allow for the expansion of water as it freezes.

They're a critical ingredient for the durability of exposed flatwork in regions that experience freeze/thaw cycles and deicing salt applications, and it's required by code in many areas. If air entrainment is not added to exposed flatwork, the consequence is often a weak surface susceptible to spalling or scaling, by which the top 1/8 in. or so of cured concrete pops off in chunks.

Air entrainers aren't necessary for interior slabs and should be avoided on jobs that will receive a smooth trowel finish. This admixture also can lead to finishing difficulties if you plan to use a power trowel.

3. RETARDERS

Retarders are used to delay the setting time of concrete. The warmer the ambient temperature, the more quickly the concrete will set up and the smaller the window of opportunity you'll have to work it properly. It's a sure bet that on a hot day when you're pouring a large slab in direct sunlight, one of your workers won't show up. This situation is when a retarder is a lifesaver.

Quick set times can be anticipated on very hot days, and the retarder can be mixed in at the plant. Alternatively, it can be added to the truck before the pour as conditions require. A retarder also can be used as a water reducer.

4. FIBERS

Small synthetic fibers are mixed into the concrete to help prevent microscopic cracks from developing during the concrete's plastic state, when cracking is a risk. These fibers can provide a more durable finished product that is less prone to problems. Some workers use fibers as a substitute for 6×6 welded-wire mesh in exterior flatwork, but I still include wire mesh because it helps to keep any cracks that do form from opening up.

5. FLY ASH

Fly ash is the residue produced from coal combustion, and in concrete, it's kind of like high-performance filler. Fly ash can replace a portion of the cement and/or sand in a mix with no detrimental effect on strength. In fact, fly ash can improve the performance of concrete. This is a great way to use industrial waste that would otherwise be headed for a landfill. Keep in mind, however, that fly ash usually acts as a retarder.

6. ACCELERATORS

Accelerators are used to reduce the setting time of the mix without lowering the concrete's intended strength.

For those cool-weather pours (temperatures in the 40s and 50s) when you don't want to hang around for hours waiting to work the concrete after it has been poured, an accelerator cuts the wait time considerably. For pours when the temperature doesn't get above freezing, it's a good idea to add an accelerator to prevent the water in the mix from freezing. An accelerator shouldn't be used in place of thermal blankets or other freeze-protection methods that typically are used to aid in the curing process of concrete poured in cold weather. I have also used an accelerator to give the mix early strength when I have needed to remove forms prematurely.

A warning: If the job contains steel rebar or wire mesh, you should avoid chloride-based accelerators because they can corrode the steel.

7. INTEGRAL COLORING

Integral coloring, which changes the color of the entire batch of concrete mix, is an alternative to broadcasting a color across the surface after the concrete has been placed or using stains or dyes after the concrete has cured. The advantage to integral coloring is that because the color runs throughout, surface wear won't be as evident. Also, most integral coloring pigments are resistant to damage from exposure to weather and UV light.

Some ready-mix plants have dispensing systems for integral coloring; others often add a customer-supplied colorant to the batch as it is being mixed at the plant. Avoid adding color to the mix when the truck arrives. There's a good chance of uneven distribution, and this will be evident only after the concrete is placed. Also, the extra on-site mixing needed to distribute the color may accelerate the setting of the concrete, which will reduce your work time once the concrete is poured. Finally, avoid adding water to a colored batch of concrete partway through the pour, because this can alter the shade of the remaining mix.

so that hydration (curing) will occur in a timely manner. Be aware that hot water accelerates the setting of concrete. Once winter weather starts in cold climates, most ready-mix plants continue to use hot water even though there may be unseasonably warm days at the beginning and at the end of the season. Accelerated curing times can be countered if you use the proper admixture in your concrete.

Conversely, if the temperature is unseasonably cold and the ready-mix plant hasn't switched over to mixing loads with hot water, the curing time of the concrete may be painfully slow. While it's nice to have a little extra time, waiting around with a crew for an extra 3 hours or 4 hours can get expensive. In both cases, an admixture can be used either to accelerate or to slow down the curing time.

ESTIMATE ACCURATELY SO YOU DON'T GET CAUGHT SHORT

CONCRETE VOLUME IS MEASURED and ordered in cubic yards. A simple example is a 10-ft. by 10-ft. patio formed for a 4-in.-thick slab:

10 ft. × 10 ft. = 100 sq. ft.
100 sq. ft. × 4 in. (or 0.333 ft.) = 33.33 cu. ft.
33.33 cu. ft. ÷ 27 cu. ft. (1 cu. yd.) = 1.23 yd.

One sure way to create havoc and possibly ruin a job is to come up short on concrete. There are lots of ways to lose concrete: Forms can spread, holes can be overexcavated, chutes can overflow, concrete can be spilled, or there can be a change in volume from loss of air entrainment or settling in a wet mixture. Unless your job site is next to the ready-mix plant, chances are that the short load of concrete you just poured will have set up by the time the makeup load arrives. It's nearly impossible to meld the new concrete into the old without a structural or visual flaw.

I usually order at least a half yard more than I need, but if I'm using an overhead boom pump, I order a full yard extra.

When scheduling, try to give the plant as much warning as possible, particularly if you want to pour first thing in the morning. Four or five days' notice is usually sufficient, and a follow-up call the day before is always a good idea. For a large pour involving more than one truck, make sure to discuss the timing of the deliveries. For easy-access foundations and slabs, close intervals are preferred, but for difficult jobs or when using a pump, plan on spacing out the deliveries. Otherwise, unless you've included a retarder in the mix, the concrete in the waiting trucks will set quickly after placement.

WHEN IS IT WORTH MIXING YOUR OWN?

ALL THE CONCRETE PLANTS that I've dealt with have a minimum order, which ranges from 1 yd. to 5 yd. depending on the plant.

For jobs requiring less than a yard, I often buy ready-mix bags (80 bags per yard) and mix my own batches in a portable job-site mixer or a wheelbarrow. If I need 1 yd. to 3 yd., I rely on companies that specialize in the delivery of small loads; they mix the on-board ingredients on site. Because their trucks are smaller, they are handy at getting into areas too small for regular concrete trucks. For any job requiring more than 3 yd., I call the ready-mix plant. Most concrete trucks can hold 10 yd. to 12 yd.

Some ready-mix plants have additional costs that should be considered before setting the budget for a job. Extra fees are often charged for exceeding the time allotted for emptying a truck (be ready when the truck pulls up) and for using concrete from the same truck for multiple small jobs on different sites. Always check with the individual ready-mix plant to find out its specific charge schedule.

Efflorescence and Spalling

BY ROB YAGID

Concrete work and masonry work are stressful. If you've tackled either, you know that a lot can go wrong quickly. While efflorescence and spalling may not trump immediate concerns over the weather, of having the right mix, or of running out of material before the job is done, they contribute to results that can turn a promising project into a headache.

Efflorescence, the white, chalky residue that sometimes appears on the surface of a concrete or masonry project, can simply be a frustrating cosmetic issue, or it can be an indication of moisture problems that might eventually lead to serious structural issues as a result of spalling. Before you can adequately address either, you first need to understand how they work.

The Process

Concrete, brick, stone, and mortar all contain mineral salts, as do the soils they routinely come in contact with. All of these porous building materials also absorb water (see "Capillary Limit" on p. 27). As water moves through the porous structure of these materials due to capillary action, it draws salt with it. This capillary pressure is relatively low—between 300 psi and 500 psi. The water makes its way to the surface of the material, evaporates, and leaves the white, powdery salt behind. The moisture that fuels this process most often comes from groundwater, but in some cases, it is caused by snow and rain. Efflorescence alone does not pose a problem, other than an unpleasant appearance in areas of high visibility.

The Concern

As more salt accumulates on or just beneath the surface, more water migrates through the material to dilute the salt in a process known as osmosis. This process can create incredibly strong hydrostatic pressure within the building material—anywhere from 3,000 psi to 5,000 psi. Concrete typically has a structural strength of 2,000 psi to 3,000 psi. Hydrostatic pressure that exceeds the strength of the building material can blow the surface off the material. This flaking is known as spalling, and if it is not addressed, it can eventually compromise the structural integrity of the project. While spalling can occur on concrete, it's especially a concern on stone, brick, and block, where portions of the assembly can degrade to a point where they crumble. Hydrostatic pressure is not the only cause of spalling. Spalling also can be caused by freeze/thaw cycles in concrete and masonry products that have a high moisture content.

HOW IT WORKS

EFFLORESCENCE

SALT AND WATER. The brine migrates through the porous structure of concrete.

SPALLING

How to Prevent It

Efflorescence and spalling can be prevented in concrete by stopping moisture migration. This can be accomplished with a capillary break, such as subslab polyethylene sheeting or liquid-applied elastomeric waterproofing. Although the same is true for masonry work, efflorescence is sometimes tolerated, and spalling is often anticipated by using sacrificial mortar. The mortar used in these assemblies is intentionally softer than the masonry, and it degrades first. The mortar joints, or in some cases the mortar parge coating, are simply repointed or reapplied every 20 years or so.

CAPILLARY LIMIT

THE ABILITY FOR CONCRETE to absorb water through capillary action is remarkable. According to the Building Science Corporation, the theoretical limit of capillary rise in wood is roughly 400 ft. In concrete, however, the capillary rise can approach 6 miles.

6 mi.

400 ft.

Working with Rebar

BY HOWARD STEIN

Why should you have a spare tire in the bed of your truck? It's not required by law, and the truck will run just fine without it. Using essentially the same logic, some people might ask why we use rebar in our residential foundations. Many houses are built without it (East Coast building codes don't require it), and if a house is built with rebar, building inspectors often don't inspect its placement.

The simple answer is that rebar is cheap insurance against the potential problems that can develop after concrete is poured or, worse, after the foundation has been backfilled. A foundation that has gone wrong is extremely expensive to repair. Just to be safe, my crew and I reinforce concrete in footings and walls, in piers and columns, and in structural slabs, and we also use rebar to tie new work to old.

Concrete used in residential construction is usually specified in a range of compressive strength in 500-lb. increments between 2,500 psi and 4,000 psi. It's obvious that concrete can support phenomenal compression loading. However, when it is under tension or shear forces, concrete has lower values compared with other common construction materials. If the underlying soils are of uneven densities, differential settling beneath the foundation can cause large cracks in the walls. Concrete is also subject to shrinkage cracks, especially when poured with a high water to cement ratio. When properly sized and embedded in concrete, rebar partially compensates for these deficiencies. (Remember that excess water produces lower-pounds-per-square-inch concrete, which is weaker and more prone to shrinkage. Even reinforced with rebar, concrete with a high water to cement ratio shouldn't be used.)

Sizes and Grades of Rebar

Rebar comes in many sizes and grades (see "Know Your Rebar" on p. 30). In residential work, we mostly use bar sizes #3, #4, and #5. These sizes translate to the diameter of the stock, measured in $\frac{1}{8}$-in. increments; #3 bars are $\frac{3}{8}$ in. in dia., #4 bars are $\frac{4}{8}$ in. ($\frac{1}{2}$ in.), and #5 bars are $\frac{5}{8}$ in. The grades 40 and 60 refer to the yield (tensile) strength (40,000 psi and 60,000 psi, respectively). Grade 60 is harder to cut and bend. Both grades are priced the same. The designer usually specifies which one to use for a particular purpose. If the grade is not specified, I buy the softer grade 40 for short lengths and bends, and grade 60 for long straight runs with few or no bends.

CUTTING AND BENDING REBAR is a matter of leverage and muscle. The cutter/bender's head provides a lever and fulcrum that makes simple bends; more complex bends can be made from individual pieces lapped together.

Make Sure the Rebar Is Delivered Where You Want It

Rebar is available at some lumberyards and from most masonry suppliers. However, 9 times out of 10, I order it from a steelyard that stocks both grades, that always has #5 bars, and that delivers to the site. If the site has good access and if we have an excavating machine available during the delivery, the machine can lift the rebar from the truck with a chain sling. If we don't have equipment on site, I let my suppliers know so that they can deliver my order on the outside edge of the truck bed, where it can be levered off and onto the ground.

If the delivery is early or late or if the machine is unavailable, we drop the bundles off the side of the truck onto blocks of wood; it's easier to maneuver the chain and slip hooks under the load when we

ALTHOUGH CHOPSAWS OR TORCHES can make quick work of cutting rebar, at a site without electricity, the stock can be cut with the cutter/bender.

KNOW YOUR REBAR

#8, grade 60

#5, grade 60

#4, grade 60

#3, grade 40

DECIPHERING THE CODE
The series of letters and numbers stamped along a length of rebar contains a great deal of information.

S: type of steel (billet)

L: production mill symbol

Country of origin: Latvia

60: tensile strength in psi × 1,000

4: size measured in ⅛-in. increments

are ready to move it to the foundation area. We also store the rebar off the ground at its staging area so that it doesn't get muddy or sit in puddles. Dirty rebar must be cleaned before use.

The Concrete Reinforcing Steel Institute (CRSI; www.crsi.org; 847-517-1200) has something to say about clean rebar in its manual *Placing Reinforcing Bars*: "The surface condition of reinforcing bars may affect the strength of the bars in bond. The main factors affecting bond are the presence of scale, rust, oil and mud." Scale is caused by the manufacturing process; loose scale usually falls off when the bar is handled or bent. Tight scale and light rust are acceptable and actually enhance the bond with concrete because they add more surface area. Too much form oil on rebar can adversely affect the bond, according to the CRSI manual.

The Grunt Work of Cutting and Bending Rebar

If there's power on site, steel can be cut using a circular saw outfitted with a metal abrasive wheel or a 14-in. chopsaw with the same blade. The latter cuts the bar more easily, but we need to bring the steel to the saw. Using either saw, we can cut three to six pieces of rebar to common lengths simultaneously. Incidentally, wearing goggles and earplugs is a must when cutting steel with a saw.

Without electricity, rebar can be cut to length with an oxyacetylene torch or a cutter/bender (see the bottom photo on p. 29). Lacking a torch, we use the slower cutter/bender, mounted on a 2×8 for stability, and cut one piece at a time. Available from masonry-supply houses and some tool catalogs, cutter/benders have cast-steel heads, feature replaceable cutters and cost $250 to $300. Many cutters have a 52-in.-long handle that gives you plenty of leverage. Even so, the process is slow, and if we're cutting #5, grade-60 bar, we really have to throw our weight into it.

We've found that the best way to mark steel for cutting is with a quick shot of spray paint (see the photo on p. 33) from a can designed to work upside down. With anything else, the marks can be pretty

TWISTED WIRE HOLDS
THE REBAR IN PLACE

PRELOOPED WIRE TIES are twisted around the junction of two pieces of rebar to hold them in place until the concrete is poured. The wooden-handled hook (see photos below left), known as a twister, speeds up the process. On longer runs or in place of multiple bends, rebar can be lapped. The overlap should be a minimum of 36 bar diameters and tied together with wire in two places (see photo at right).

REBAR MAKES THE AVERAGE FOUNDATION BETTER

IN A TYPICAL SITUATION, rebar is placed in a foundation wall to prevent cracking and to strengthen the wall. The exact type and placement of the rebar varies from job to job and is always determined by the structural engineer.

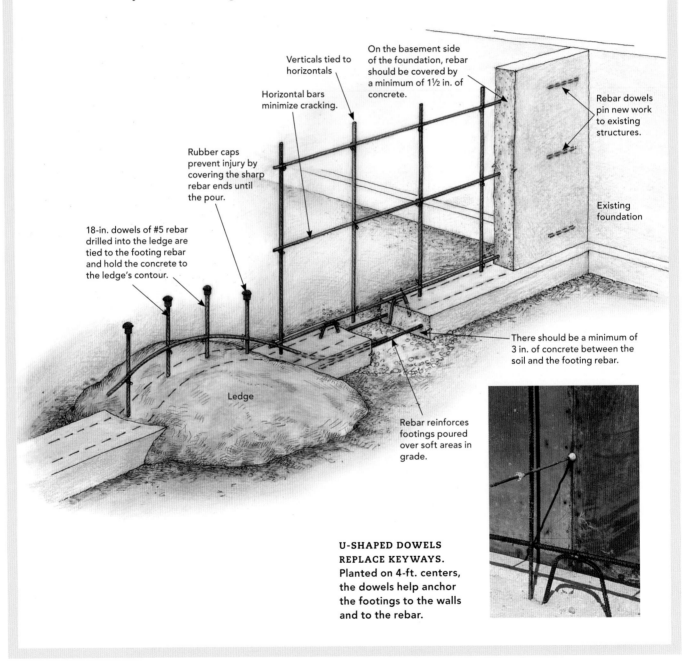

Verticals tied to horizontals

Horizontal bars minimize cracking.

On the basement side of the foundation, rebar should be covered by a minimum of 1½ in. of concrete.

Rebar dowels pin new work to existing structures.

Rubber caps prevent injury by covering the sharp rebar ends until the pour.

Existing foundation

18-in. dowels of #5 rebar drilled into the ledge are tied to the footing rebar and hold the concrete to the ledge's contour.

There should be a minimum of 3 in. of concrete between the soil and the footing rebar.

Ledge

Rebar reinforces footings poured over soft areas in grade.

U-SHAPED DOWELS REPLACE KEYWAYS. Planted on 4-ft. centers, the dowels help anchor the footings to the walls and to the rebar.

SPRAY PAINT MARKS THE SPOT. A spray can that's made to shoot upside down marks the position of bends or cuts on a piece of rebar. The mark is waterproof, easy to read, and nearly indelible.

hard to see. Exact length is seldom critical with rebar. Because it's designed to overlap, if you're off by 1 in., it usually doesn't matter.

The easiest way to bend rebar is with the cutter/bender (see the top photo on p. 29). After measuring and marking bends with paint, we lay the stock under the head and lever it into shape, using the tool head as a fulcrum. The stock has to be in a straight line when bent. Although some of the newer models have stops at 90° and 180°, we just eyeball the bend and adjust as needed. We're careful not to overbend an angle, though, because you can't use the bender to bend it back and because it's hard to do using your hands and feet. To save time, we'll often bend corners while we're waiting for the forms to be completed. If we need more than one bend in a piece of rebar, we've found it's easier to lap with another bent

bar; it's awkward to make multiple bends on site, especially with long lengths. In a pinch (such as when we don't have the cutter/bender), we have bent bars around the pintle on my truck's hitch plate, but I wouldn't want to do more than a few bends this way.

Wiring the Rebar Together until the Pour

To lap or cross rebar, we use prelooped wire ties (see "Twisted Wire Holds the Rebar in Place" on p. 31). Commonly available in lengths of 6 in. and 8 in., the latter are handy for tying together pairs of #4 or #5 bars. A bag of 5,000 8-in. ties will last for several residential-size foundations. Wire is also available on spools, but we find that less convenient.

The simplest tie requires merely bending it diagonally over the bars and, using a tool called a twister, hooking the loops and spinning the wire. Over-twisting the wire will simply break it. (The wire adds no strength or integrity once the concrete has been placed.) The twisted wire is then wrapped around the bar so that it doesn't extend toward the exterior surface of the concrete. The wire might rust if it remains exposed to the elements or could lead water into the embedded rebar if exposed below grade. Incidentally, spools of wire are also handy for hanging the rebar at a consistent height in the footings (see the photo at right on p. 36). Because the footing is covered later by the waterproofed foundation wall, the wire is never exposed to the elements.

Rebar Maintains Control of Concrete Shrinkage

In addition to solving problems related to shear or tension, rebar is also specified for shrinkage control of concrete (see "Rebar Makes the Average Foundation Better" on the facing page). Because the water in poured concrete is lost by evaporation as it cures, concrete shrinks in volume. Rebar doesn't prevent shrinkage but binds both sides of the eventual cracks into a single wall plane.

WELDED-WIRE MESH VS. REBAR: WHAT'S THE DIFFERENCE?

CONCRETE HAS GREAT STRENGTH under compression. Under tension, however, concrete doesn't fare so well. For example, as concrete cures, it loses water, which causes it to shrink and crack. Similar cracks open as concrete endures the rigors of changing seasons. Reinforcing concrete ensures that the cracks that do develop don't go far, thus preventing substantial failure.

To reinforce concrete, you can use rebar or welded-wire mesh. Either material can be engineered to work in almost any application. With a few exceptions, there is no difference in the tensile strength of the materials as long as they're installed correctly. Choosing the reinforcement becomes a matter of the job-site conditions, the availability of the product, and the way you prefer to work.

REBAR

Rebar is nothing more than common steel rods that come in sizes ranging from #3 (⅜ in. dia.) to #18 (2¼ in. dia.). For residential use, #6 rebar is usually the largest size used.

Rebar's use depends on its application. In a sidewalk, driveway, or slab, rebar is wire-tied into a grid pattern, usually 12 in. or 18 in. on center, then is supported above grade on small piers so that it ends up in the center of the slab. Building codes dictate what size rebar should be used for which job as well as the appropriate grid spacing.

In walls, rebar specifications also are determined by code. In some areas and uses, you need to install a grid pattern over the entire wall; in others, you need only a few lengths of rebar.

Rebar clearly outperforms welded-wire mesh in one application: When reinforcing piers or columns, rebar offers superior strength and maneuverability.

WELDED-WIRE MESH

Welded-wire mesh is a steel grid that can be used in many of the same applications as rebar. Because welded-wire mesh is usually made of lighter-gauge steel, the grid patterns have to be much tighter than with rebar. Mesh can be purchased in either rolls or sheets, but sheets are commonly available only in heavier gauges for commercial work and might not be readily available.

For slab work, mesh performs in much the same way as an assembled grid of rebar. The mesh is unrolled and fixed in place—using small piers—so that it stays in the center of the finished slab. The upside of using mesh is that it's less labor intensive because the grid is already welded together; no wire-tying is required. The downside of using rolled mesh is that it tends to curl back up, so controlling its location in the slab can be a challenge. Also, because it's not as heavy, it's easy to pull it up with rakes during the pour, so it could end up being in the wrong position in the slab.

—Matthew Teague, contributing writer

According to Val Prest, a structural engineer from Harvard, Massachusetts, "This shrinkage will result in ¹⁄₁₆-in. to ⅛-in. cracks at about every 20 ft. at the top of an unreinforced wall. Add more water to the concrete, and you get more shrinkage—cracks that are perhaps every 10 ft. to 15 ft.—and the concrete is weaker. Horizontal bars will minimize the cracking by causing multiple fine line cracks instead."

Prest also says, "Temperature- and shrinkage-designed steel for the average 10-in.-thick residential foundation is commonly spaced on 12-in. centers, or every 10 in. horizontally for #4 bars and every 15 in. for #5 bars." For horizontal placement in wall forms, we almost always tie rebar to the tie rods (or form ties) that hold the outer and inner concrete formwork together. After the concrete subcontractor sets up the outer wall and pushes the tie rods through, we place the steel on these tie rods and wire the rebar to them (see the drawing on p. 32). The verticals are tied to the horizontal bar and to U-shaped dowels in the footing (see the photo on p. 32).

Although steel is specified for its temperature and shrinkage control, Prest says, "99% of the time, steel is designed for shrinkage, not temperature." Some exceptions are bridges, concrete roadbeds, and large retaining walls built on highways exposed to direct sun.

That said, there are some general rules about placing rebar that can be applied to most situations:

- In footings and walls below grade, rebar should be covered with at least 3 in. of concrete to protect it from groundwater and soil.
- Inside a wall, rebar is positioned on the tension or inner (basement) side with approximately 1½ in. of concrete cover.
- The horizontal shrinkage-control steel is placed in the wall first, followed by shorter vertical bars placed to the inner unrestrained side of the wall.

One note: If there is a dense mat of steel in a slab or wall, it may be necessary to vibrate the concrete with a pencil vibrator to consolidate the concrete without leaving voids.

KEEPING REBAR AT A CONSISTENT HEIGHT

REBAR PLACED IN FOOTINGS should always be above grade. To prevent the bars from sinking in the wet concrete, foundation crews often suspend rebar from strapping that spans the tops of the forms (see photo at right). Any exposed wire is trimmed after the concrete sets up and is covered by the foundation wall. Manufactured supports known as chairs offer another option for locating rebar (see photos below). Available in different sizes, chairs are usually made of plastic or heavy-gauge wire; plastic feet help insulate the wire from corrosion that results from ground contact.

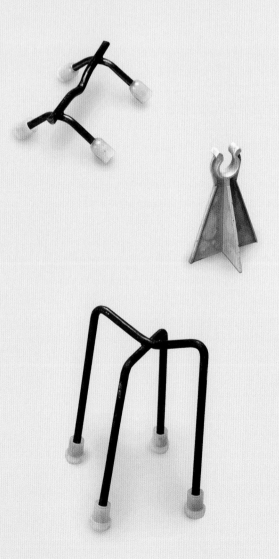

Start with Batter Boards

BY JIM BLODGETT

You're finally ready to build that new deck, porch, patio, or addition. With a permit in your pocket, money in the bank, and a shovel in your hand, it hits you: Now what? How do you make the transition from concept to concrete? Batter boards. Batter boards are like bookmarks. They're placeholders for string lines that describe the dimensions of a structure. You can use batter boards as a job progresses to reduce compounding error.

Build with Screws, Brace with Stakes, and Walk Away

To keep batter boards accurate, place them safely away from construction traffic, and build them sturdily. Use braces. I usually place batter boards within a couple of feet of the foundation and discourage the flow of foot traffic with strategically placed piles of demolition debris, dirt, or lumber.

I use two types of batter boards for most small projects: a three-legged freestanding type for outside corners, and a single 2×4 screwed horizontally (and level) to the side of the existing house. Rather than nails, I use screws so that I don't loosen the braces on freestanding batter boards, which lessens accuracy. Deck screws are great for this, but drywall screws are fine.

ENSURE A SQUARE AND LEVEL building project right from the get-go with strings and a few scraps of wood.

Use a Builder's Level Once, Then Leave It in Its Case

Installing batter boards that are level with each other allows me to use a level string line to set the grade on excavations, footings, and foundations. I generally use an elevation higher than where the top of the foundation will be. I level batter boards with a water level or a builder's level.

37

FIVE STEPS TO SQUARING SUCCESS

ONE GOAL OF BATTER BOARDS is to define a footprint with square corners. Most people use the Pythagorean theorem ($a^2 + b^2 = c^2$) to check that the corners are square. They do so by measuring 3 ft. along one side, 4 ft. along the other, and checking for a 5-ft. diagonal (or hypotenuse) between those two points. But those dimensions (3–4–5) are too small to square up a larger corner accurately. It's better to use multiples of 3–4–5 (see the chart below left) that define a right triangle that's close to your building's dimensions.

Step 1: Choose your triangle from the chart of multiples (below). Select the triangle nearest to your project's footprint; bigger is better.

SHORT	LONG	HYPOTENUSE
3	4	5
6	8	10
9	12	15
12	16	20
15	20	25
18	24	30
21	28	35
24	32	40
27	36	45
30	40	50

Step 4: Measure the hypotenuse. Pull a tape measure from point *B*, and find where the 30-ft. mark intersects the reference string line (mark this point with ink). Now run a string from point *A* through this mark and fasten the string to the batter board.

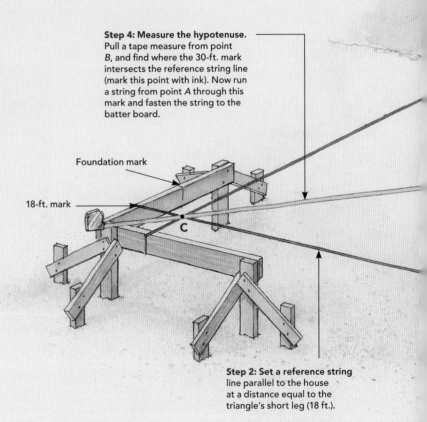

Foundation mark

18-ft. mark

C

Step 2: Set a reference string line parallel to the house at a distance equal to the triangle's short leg (18 ft.).

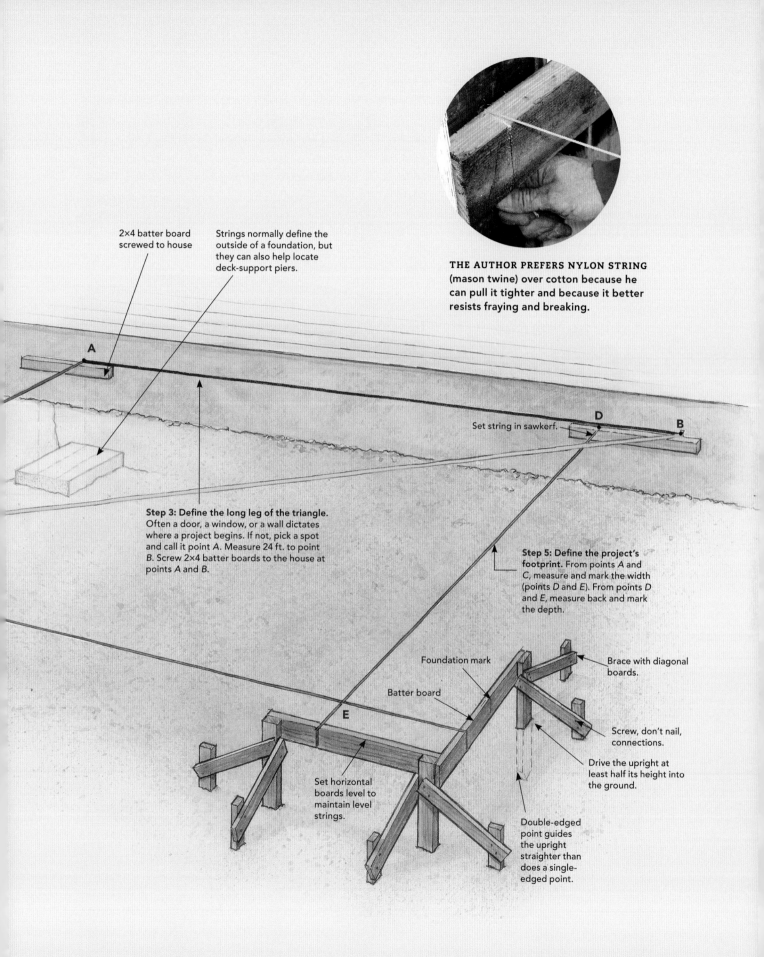

2×4 batter board screwed to house

Strings normally define the outside of a foundation, but they can also help locate deck-support piers.

THE AUTHOR PREFERS NYLON STRING (mason twine) over cotton because he can pull it tighter and because it better resists fraying and breaking.

A

Set string in sawkerf.

D

B

Step 3: Define the long leg of the triangle. Often a door, a window, or a wall dictates where a project begins. If not, pick a spot and call it point *A*. Measure 24 ft. to point *B*. Screw 2×4 batter boards to the house at points *A* and *B*.

Step 5: Define the project's footprint. From points *A* and *C*, measure and mark the width (points *D* and *E*). From points *D* and *E*, measure back and mark the depth.

Foundation mark

Brace with diagonal boards.

Batter board

E

Screw, don't nail, connections.

Drive the upright at least half its height into the ground.

Set horizontal boards level to maintain level strings.

Double-edged point guides the upright straighter than does a single-edged point.

After the building lines and levels are determined and double-checked (and verified and triple-checked), I use a handsaw to score just deep enough through the top edge of the batter board to hold the string. No matter how many marks, arrows, offsets, or elevation notes are written on the batter boards (and over the course of a job, there can be a lot), I can find the building lines quickly.

I take all measurements from these sawkerfs, and I mark them on the batter boards. In addition to the inside and outside faces of the footing and foundation walls, I lay out offsets from the building lines so that I can set up a parallel string quickly. These offset lines allow me to climb in and out of the excavation without doing the limbo to avoid lines all day.

QUICK-RELEASE KNOT HOLDS STRING TIGHT

LOOP STRING AROUND ONE FINGER, twisting that finger several times as you pull your hands apart.

PLACE THE LOOP OVER A NAIL, pulling on the free end of the line while feeding the fixed end toward the nail.

WHEN THE STRING IS BANJO-TIGHT, pull the free end back toward the nail. The twists will ball up into a knot. To loosen, pull the free end in the opposite direction.

A Solid Deck Begins with Concrete Piers

BY RICK ARNOLD

Dig a hole and fill it with concrete. How hard can that be? I've seen old decks built on top of little more than a shovelful of concrete, cinder blocks up on end, and even 8-in. by 12-in. patio blocks. I've also seen old decks—not to mention a couple of new ones—sink and pull away from a house, heave up with the same results, and even both sink and heave from one end to the other.

An insufficient design or a bad installation of this simple foundation system can have disastrous consequences in terms of safety, aesthetics, and a builder's reputation. That's why I approach piers with the same care as I do a house or addition foundation.

Determining Pier Size and Spacing

Because piers perform the same job for the deck that the foundation does for the house, it's critical to size and space them properly (see "How Many and What Size?" on p. 45). I begin by figuring out how many piers I'm going to need. This decision depends mostly on deck design. For this project, I was building a simple 12-ft. by 16-ft. rectangular deck with a double rim joist to act as a beam that could span about 8 ft., with posts running down from the beam to the piers. In this type of application, I start with two piers on the corners and divide the 16-ft.

double-rim joist until I get a figure of 6 ft. or less. Here, I found that dividing the rim joist into three sections gave me a span of roughly 5 ft. 4 in., which came out to four piers. Even though my double-rim joist could span 8 ft., I chose to use a 5-ft. 4-in. pier spacing to minimize the pier diameter.

After calculating the number of piers I need, I determine the size they need to be. The size of builder's tube dictates the size of the bottom of the pier, which is the area that will be in contact with soil at the bottom of the excavation. To figure this out, I calculate the maximum weight each pier must be designed to bear (by code). For the deck in this chapter, I figured a 1,600-lb. load on each of the two inside piers (see "How Many and What Size?" on p. 45). Then I compared that to the bearing capacity of the soil at the bottom of the hole. I was building on hard-packed gravel, which easily has a bearing capacity of more than 3,000 lb. per sq. ft. (psf).

The bearing capacity of a 10-in.-dia. tube in 3,000 psf soil is 1,650 psf ($0.55 \times 3,000$). The design load of each inside pier is 1,600 lb., so a 10-in. tube will work. However, by jumping up to a 12-in. tube, the bearing capacity becomes 2,370 psf ($0.79 \times 3,000$), which can carry the 1,600-lb. load more easily. For just a bit more concrete, I ensure the pier is well designed. I typically ignore the pier

BEING ACCURATE WHEN PLACING PIERS and inserting anchor bolts ensures a safe, long-lasting, and professional-looking deck.

weight because there is enough fat in these calculations to justify this simplification.

The two outside-corner piers are required to bear only half the weight, but to simplify the work process, I use the same-size tubes for all four of the piers.

The depth you set the piers at depends a lot on the region of the country you're working in. In climates where frost is an issue, the minimum depth is established by code. For this project, the bottoms of the piers have to be 36 in. below finished grade.

Wherever you live, it is important to dig past soil that contains organic matter (topsoil) and any uncompacted fill. Organic matter decomposes over time and settles; loose fill also settles over time. In most cases, the depth of undisturbed soil is not known until the excavation is well under way.

Begin Layout with Deck Dimensions

Once I know the size and the number of piers I'm going to use, the next step is to lay them out on site. If the deck details aren't drawn on the plans, I sketch the outside deck framing to determine exactly where the center of the supporting posts are in relation to the outside dimensions of the deck. Then I use those locations to form a layout rectangle. I use batter boards and string to locate the exact center of the post, which is also the location for the anchor bolts that hold the post hardware in place.

Once the post locations are identified and marked with surveyor's paint, I remove the strings and dig the pier holes. When the holes are deep enough, I rough-cut the builder's tubes, drop them in, and replace the string lines. I keep the tubes centered on the string lines while they are backfilled, and I double-check the measurements with a tape measure.

PIERS TRANSFER THE DECK'S WEIGHT TO THE SOIL

To effectively transfer the weight, the piers need to be sized and spaced according to the deck's design load and the soil's bearing capacity (see "How Many and What Size?" on p. 45). In cold climates, piers should always sit below the frost line to prevent frost heaves. Check your local code for pier-depth requirements.

FOOTINGS SPREAD THE WEIGHT OVER A LARGER AREA

If the piers will be used in soil with poor bearing capacity or if the deck has a heavy design load, use a spread footing to distribute the load over a greater surface area. The more expensive, labor-intensive way to do this requires a relatively large excavation for each pier. After forming and pouring the footings, you have to install the tubes and backfill around them, then complete a second pour for the piers. But plastic footing forms bring this process down to just one pour.

For most of these systems, a builder's tube is fastened to the top of the form; then the assembly is lowered into the hole, backfilled, and poured in one shot. See the manufacturer's website for sizing and load requirements.

SQUAREFOOT™
www.sqfoot.com
Available from 22 in. dia. to 32 in. dia.

BIGFOOT SYSTEMS®
www.bigfootsystems.com
Available from 20 in. dia. to 36 in. dia.

THE FOOTING TUBE
www.foottube.com
A builder's tube and spread footing in one. Top diameter sizes range from 6 in. to 12 in.

REDIBASE
www.redibase-form.com
Available in 24 in. dia.

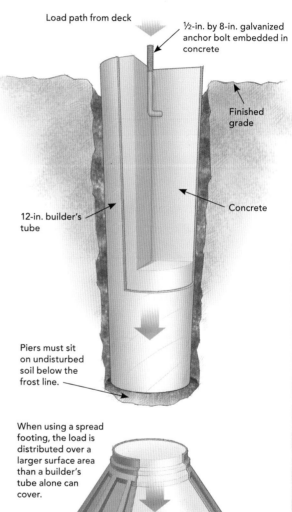

Load path from deck

½-in. by 8-in. galvanized anchor bolt embedded in concrete

Finished grade

12-in. builder's tube

Concrete

Piers must sit on undisturbed soil below the frost line.

When using a spread footing, the load is distributed over a larger surface area than a builder's tube alone can cover.

24-in.-wide spread footing

Rather than try to cut tubes to the exact height, I leave them long and pour concrete to the desired height inside the tube. In most cases, I like the pour to come a couple of inches above the finished grade. If the piers are on a pitched elevation, the tops of the piers won't be level with each other. On this job, the finished grade was level, so I used a long level to carry the elevation across the piers.

After marking each pier with a small nail pushed through at the right height, I again remove the string lines so that I can pour the concrete into the tubes. Once they're filled to the right height, I float the concrete smooth with a scrap of wood. Then I replace the string, and using a slight up-and-down motion to prevent air from becoming trapped, I insert the anchor bolts in their proper locations.

EVERYTHING YOU NEED

A FEW TOOLS, even fewer materials, and a little sweat will get most deck foundations out of the ground in less than a day.

- Builder's tubes
- 80-lb. bags of ready-mix concrete
- Garden hose
- Foundation spikes
- Batter boards
- ½-in. by 8-in. anchor bolts, nuts, and washers
- Adjustable post bases
- Post-hole digger
- Digging bar
- Electric concrete mixer
- Stabila® plate level

HOW MUCH CONCRETE DO I NEED?

TO POUR THE PIERS for an average-size deck, I use 80-lb. bags of concrete and an electric mixer, which rents for about $45 a day or sells for $250 or so.

For major pours, I have a concrete truck deliver a 2,500-lb. mix. Either way, the basic formulas below will help you estimate the number of bags or cubic yards of concrete required based on pier size and depth.

EXAMPLE
- Size of tubes: 8 in.
- Number of tubes: 8
- Average depth per tube: 4 ft.
- 0.53 (8 × 4) = 17 bags

TUBE SIZE	NUMBER OF 80-LB. BAGS PER FOOT	CUBIC YARDS PER FOOT
8 in.	0.53	0.13
10 in.	0.8	0.02
12 in.	1.2	0.03
14 in.	1.6	0.04

HOW MANY AND WHAT SIZE?

THREE THINGS AFFECT THE NUMBER and the size of piers you use: the way you frame the deck, the weight the deck is designed for, and the load-bearing capacity of the soil. For the deck I'm building, I chose to support the double-rim joist with piers instead of a cantilevered approach that uses piers beneath a beam. I use the design load for decks suggested by the International Residential Code (IRC), which is 50 lb. per sq. ft. (psf) (40 psf live load, 10 psf dead load). Different soils have different bearing capacities (measured in psf); consult Table 401.4.1 of the IRC for the bearing capacities of different soil types.

STEP 1. SPACE PIERS EVENLY BENEATH THE DOUBLE-RIM JOIST

Because I'm using a double-rim joist to support the floor joists, I support this 16-ft. deck with four piers.

STEP 2. DISTRIBUTE THE DECK'S WEIGHT ONTO THE PIERS

A 12-ft. by 16-ft. deck is 192 sq. ft. Multiply by 50 psf to determine the design load, 9,600 lb. Half of that weight (4,800) is carried by the ledger; the other half is carried by the piers. Because the corner piers carry only half the weight that the inside piers carry, dividing 4,800 lb. by three tells me the two inside piers must each bear 1,600 lb.

STEP 3. TRANSFER THE WEIGHT TO THE SOIL

For this project, I was working in hard-packed gravel, which I estimate to have a bearing capacity of 3,000 psf. Using the chart below, I multiply the square-foot equivalent of each tube by 3,000 psf to find one that will work in this soil. A 10-in. tube will bear 1,650 psf, which is close, but I chose to bump up to 12-in. piers for peace of mind. To keep things simple, I made the corner piers the same size.

Tube diameter	8 in.	10 in.	12 in.	14 in
Square feet	0.35	0.55	0.79	1.1

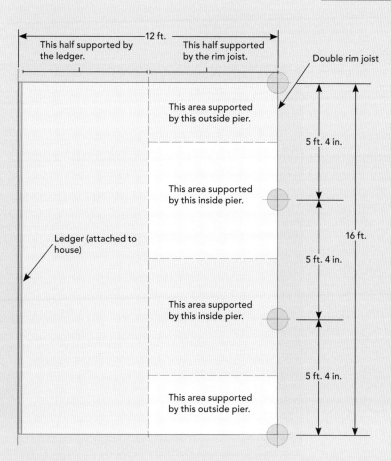

This half supported by the ledger.

This half supported by the rim joist.

Double rim joist

This area supported by this outside pier.

This area supported by this inside pier.

This area supported by this inside pier.

This area supported by this outside pier.

Ledger (attached to house)

12 ft.

16 ft.

5 ft. 4 in.

5 ft. 4 in.

5 ft. 4 in.

USE TWO LINES FOR A DEAD-ON LAYOUT

WITH THE LEDGER LOCATION TRANSFERRED to grade level, I can measure out from the house foundation and run a string line to represent the center point of the piers. A single line parallel to the house intersecting a line perpendicular to the house locates the center of the far-corner pier. Measurements for the rest of the piers are taken from this intersecting point. Batter boards help set the lines accurately.

1 **PLUMB DOWN FROM A HIGH LEDGER.** With a Stabila plate level (www.stabila.com), I carry one end of the ledger down to the grade. I drive a stake into the ground here to anchor a line that will run perpendicular to the house.

2 **THE PIER CENTERLINE RUNS PARALLEL TO THE HOUSE.** The batter boards I use make it easy to adjust the string line until it's exactly the right distance from the house foundation. I set the batter boards a couple of feet beyond the corner-pier locations so that the boards won't be disturbed when holes are dug.

3 $A^2 + B^2 = C^2$. Pulled diagonally from the foundation, my tape forms the hypotenuse of a right triangle. A helper shifts the line that extends from the house to intersect with the right measurement, identifying the center of the far-corner pier.

4 **MARK PIERS WITH PAINT.** Measure the remaining piers from the far-corner pier. A dot marks the center point, and a rough circle highlights where to dig. Pull the string lines and prepare to dig, but keep the batter boards in place.

TOOL TIP
If excavating multiple holes, consider renting a gas-powered auger. A one-person auger, shown here, costs about $50 a day. The two-person version rents for about $70.

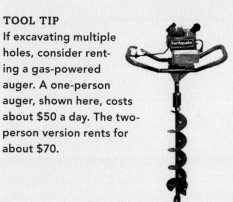

5 **THE BEST HOLES HAVE NO ROCKS.** But just in case you encounter a few, make sure to have a long digging bar in addition to a post-hole digger. Take care not to disturb the batter boards or their settings because you'll have to reattach the string lines later. Dig down deep enough so that the bottom of the pier rests on undisturbed soil below the frost line.

FINE-TUNE THE LAYOUT BEFORE AND AFTER THE POUR

ONCE THE HOLES ARE DUG, put the string lines back on the batter boards. When setting each builder's tube, use the lines and a tape measure to center them according to layout, adjusting the hole locations as needed. Take the time to check the tube locations often as you backfill to keep them on layout. After all the fill is in place and the final layout check is made, fill the tubes with concrete, and insert the anchor bolts.

1 BACKFILL WITH MEASURING TAPE AND SHOVEL. I cut the builder's tubes so that they stick out a few inches above grade when placed in the hole. To make sure a tube is placed precisely, I hold it on its layout while a helper backfills. Pack the soil around the tube every so often as you go.

2 DOUBLE-CHECK THE CORNERS. I spend a little extra time checking the location of the final corner pier to make sure that it's in the right spot because I won't get a chance to move it once the concrete is poured. Use a nail to mark the finished height of the piers, keeping it a couple of inches above the finished grade. If you need to have piers all at the same height, use a long level or a transit to locate their finished height.

TOOL TIP
A mixer does the most difficult work of mixing the concrete. Just dump in the mix, turn it on, then add water.

3 **A SHOVEL MAKES UP FOR BAD AIM.** Fill the tubes with concrete until it reaches the nail. The concrete should be just slightly on the wet side, about the consistency of thick oatmeal. As the concrete is poured into the tube, a helper uses a shovel to agitate the mix every 8 in. to 10 in. to work out air pockets.

4 **PLACE ANCHOR BOLTS ACCURATELY.** Once all the piers are poured, I go back and insert anchor bolts in the center of the piers. I measure from the line running perpendicular to the house to set anchor bolts accurately. Be sure to leave the threads high enough so that a post base, washer, and nut can be added later.

5 **ADJUSTABLE POST BASES ALLOW FOR FINAL TWEAKS.** After the concrete is cured completely, I attach adjustable post bases. I like to use Simpson® ABA-style bases because they allow me to fine-tune the post location after the post is attached.

Mix Concrete by the Bag

BY SCOTT GRICE

A COMMON GARDEN RAKE is the ideal tool for mixing small batches of concrete.

Some people might assume that mixing concrete is an obvious task: Buy a bag of premix, dump it in a wheelbarrow with some water, and mix it up. Sounds simple, right? As a fence and deck contractor, I have learned otherwise. I often have to mix 5 bags to 10 bags in an afternoon, and then have to push around wheelbarrow loads of wet concrete. This chore was a strong motivator for me to come up with an efficient, reliable mixing system.

The first step to smarter concrete mixing is to use my truck's tailgate as a platform for emptying the concrete premix into the wheelbarrow. This setup limits the number of times I have to move the bags of concrete and keeps them at a comfortable working height. Second, I put the water in the wheelbarrow before the concrete. This step helps keep down the dust and prevents dry pockets in the mix. Third, I use a stiff rake to mix the concrete. A rake mixes more efficiently and is easier to work with than a hoe or a shovel. Finally, to keep from straining the operator (me), I mix only one 90-lb. bag at a time. I don't think mixing two bags at once is any faster, and I know it tires me out sooner.

After I've finished, I pour any excess concrete into a compact lump to be removed once it hardens. Then I wash out the wheelbarrow so that it's ready to work another day.

STURDY, STABLE, AND SIZED RIGHT

WHEN IT COMES TO WHEEL-BARROWS, bigger is not always better. A medium-size 6-cu.-ft. tray is large enough to hold as much wet concrete or rock as I can move comfortably but is not so big that it's unwieldy. I prefer a tray made of heavy-gauge steel that, unlike plastic, is not affected by UV rays and won't crack if the temperature dips into single digits. Nice extras on any wheelbarrow are solid hardwood handles for easy gripping and anti-tilt-back supports on the feet to reduce the chance that I'll end up with a load of concrete exactly where I don't want it. All this adds up to a wheelbarrow that can take the abuse of a full-time professional. For information about the Jackson® wheelbarrow, visit www.jacksonprofessional.com.

MIXING CONCRETE: STEP BY STEP

COMBINE WATER AND CONCRETE AT THE TRUCK

1 **PUT IN THE WATER FIRST.** For this size wheelbarrow, add water to a depth of about 1 in. Too little water is better than too much. You always can add more later.

2 **ADD THE CONCRETE.** Place the unopened bag in the water. Then use a utility knife to open the bag with a single cut along the end. Grab the bottom of the bag and tip it up so that the concrete slides out rather than pours out. This technique minimizes dust.

3 **MOVE THE MIX TO WHERE IT'S NEEDED.** To maneuver through tight areas without hanging up the rake, put the working end of the rake in the wheelbarrow with the handle pointing ahead.

(Continued on p. 52)

MIXING CONCRETE (CONTINUED)

MAKE A LAGOON IN THE ISLAND OF CONCRETE

4 STAND IN FRONT TO MIX. Pull the concrete to the front, and water will flow in behind it. Because I'm standing at the front of the wheelbarrow, I now can work the concrete without having the wheelbarrow move as I push back and forth. Let the water flow in after each push-and-pull stroke. Keep mixing until most of the water is absorbed.

5 ADD WATER IN SMALL AMOUNTS. Too much will weaken the concrete, so add a little water at a time, then mix. Aim for the texture of dry cottage cheese.

6 THE FINAL TEST. I'm done when all the concrete is wet and I've scraped the rake along the bottom and sides to remove any dry pockets. The mix passes my personal slump test when it's all wet but still firm enough for the rake's furrows to hold their shape.

PART 2

Building Foundations

Placing a Small Concrete Slab

BY ANDY ENGEL

Although the amount of concrete used is small, the forming and finishing techniques for a slab such as a deck-stair landing—or in this case, a propane-tank pad—aren't much different from those used for larger slabs. First and foremost is subgrade preparation. Get that wrong, and the slab will crack. The underlying ground needs to be compacted evenly. In most cases, slabs shouldn't be placed next to new buildings until the backfill around them has settled for several years. After digging out the slab location, compact the soil directly below so that there's no loose dirt.

Use a Gravel Base

One step that's called for but rarely done on small jobs is to place gravel between the slab and the subgrade. The usual explanation is that the gravel provides drainage to prevent soil saturation and the resulting frost heaving. But unless you drain that gravel somewhere with pipes, where's the water going to go?

There are two reasons to use gravel. First, concrete moves because of thermal expansion and contraction. Restricting this movement will crack the concrete. A gravel base allows the slab to move freely.

Second, slabs need a flat base to ensure uniform thickness, and gravel is easier to grade than many soils.

Choosing Concrete

For a slab that's 40 sq. ft. or more (about ½ cu. yd. of concrete for a typical 4-in.-thick slab), it's easiest to order truck-mixed concrete. This 3-ft.-sq. slab was small enough that mixing bagged concrete by hand made sense. At 9 sq. ft. and 4 in. thick, the project called for 3 cu. ft. of concrete. An 80-lb. bag of concrete mix makes $3/5$ cu. ft., so this slab took five bags.

I used a crack-control concrete, which includes reinforcing fibers. The slab was small enough that no steel reinforcement was needed, and that little extra strength from the fibers cost me only $5. Larger slabs, say 5×5 and up, will benefit from reinforcement with rebar or wire mesh to control cracking.

Concrete needs moisture to cure. After finishing the slab, cover it with plastic and keep it damp for at least a day. A week is better, and 28 days ensures the best cure.

1 PREPARE THE SUBGRADE. Dig 6 in. beyond where you want the slab edges and 8 in. deeper than where you want the top of the slab. Make sure the subgrade pitches away from the building, and tamp down loose soil.

2 GRADE THE GRAVEL. Fill the excavation with 4 in. of gravel. Rake it flat, and use a level to make sure it's pitched about ¼ in. per foot so that the slab, which will parallel the base, drains water.

3 MAKE AND SET THE FORM. Most 4-in. slabs are actually the 3½-in. depth of standard 2×4s. Nail the corners together, and place the form on the graded gravel, making sure it doesn't rock. Drive 12-in. lengths of rebar to just below the top of the form to keep it from moving.

4 MIX THE CONCRETE. Dump two 80-lb. bags of mix in a wheelbarrow for each batch. Add 3 qt. of water per bag, and mix thoroughly with a hoe. Add small amounts of additional water if necessary to bring the concrete to a consistency that's about the same as thick cake batter.

5 SETTLE THE CONCRETE. After dumping the mixed concrete in the form, jab into it all along the edges with a shovel. This helps ensure the mix fills the form without leaving voids.

6 TAP THE SIDES OF THE FORM. Lightly hammer the form all around the slab until you see bubbles rising from the concrete. This step makes for a smoother slab edge that won't collect water, which can freeze and spall the concrete.

7 SCREED THE SLAB. Flatten the concrete using a straight 2×4 that's about 1 ft. longer than the form width. Move the board forward with a back-and-forth sawing motion while keeping it on the form.

8 TAMP THE SURFACE WITH A RAKE. Gently tamp the entire surface of the slab. The rake pushes down the gravel that's part of the concrete mix, and brings up a mixture of cement and sand that's easier to smooth.

9 SMOOTH THE RAKE MARKS WITH A MAG FLOAT. Keep the leading edge of the float up. When the surface water dissipates, float the slab again. This is the final finish for exterior slabs. For a smooth interior slab, work it again with a steel float when the surface begins to lose its wet sheen.

10 ROUND THE CORNERS. This leaves smooth, friendly edges that are less likely to chip. Use an edger once after each mag floating; on interior slabs with exposed edges, use it after the steel float. After the slab hardens for a day or more, pry the joints apart and remove the form.

CONCRETE TOOLS

MAG FLOAT
Used in the initial tooling to bring up a creamy mix that's easy to finish. As a final finishing tool, it leaves a coarse, slip-resistant surface that's good for exterior slabs.

STEEL FLOAT
A finishing tool that leaves a smooth, compacted surface that repels water but that also can be slippery when wet.

EDGER
Rounds over the exposed edges of slabs, leaving a surface that's more resistant to chipping than a simple square edge would be.

Pouring Concrete Slabs

BY CARL HAGSTROM

L iquid stone. It's an image you might think describes placing concrete, and to some extent, it does. But there's more to it than backing up the ready-mix truck, opening the spigot and letting the concrete flow out until the forms are full.

The applications of concrete are almost limitless, but here I'll focus on residential slabs. About half of the new homes currently built in the United States start with full-basement foundations, and virtually all of these basements have concrete floors. For the most part, these floors consist of 4 in. of concrete placed over 4 in. or more of crushed stone. Concrete floors in garages are similar, except they are sometimes reinforced with wire mesh or steel. But whether it's a basement or a garage slab, the way you place the concrete is the same.

Ordering Concrete

Concrete is sold by the cubic yard, and calculating the amount you need is simple: length times width times depth (in feet) divided by 27 equals cubic yards. Most concrete trucks max out at 9 yd., and if your floor will require more than nine (the average floor uses about 19 yd.), tell your supplier to allow 1 hour to 1½ hour per truckload so that all the trucks don't arrive at once.

But a word of caution. Running out of concrete is like running out of champagne at a wedding: If you can't get more real soon, you're headed for trouble. Don't be stingy with your concrete estimate. You're a lot better off with half a yard left over than a quarter yard short.

Once you've told your concrete supplier how much concrete, you'll have to tell them what kind. Concrete is made up of four basic ingredients: cement, sand, stone, and water. Depending on the proportions of the ingredients, the strength can vary considerably. Compressive strength, measured in pounds per square inch (psi), is the method used to evaluate the performance of a given mix. Generally speaking, the higher the cement content, the higher the compressive strength. Most residential concrete has a compressive strength between 2,000 psi and 3,500 psi.

You'll also need to specify the slump, or the wetness, of the mix. A slump of 4 to 5 is about right for slabs, whereas a slump of about 2 to 3 is normal for piers, which don't need to be worked, so the concrete can be stiffer.

Placing the Slab

Arrive early on the day of the pour and use a water level or a transit to snap chalklines on the founda-

FIRST MUD. With the vapor barrier in place and the chalklines snapped, the first load of concrete is dumped in the far corner of the foundation. The mason dumps the concrete away from the wall so that he won't cover the chalkline.

Running out of concrete is like running out of champagne at a wedding: If you can't get more real soon, you're headed for trouble.

ESTABLISHING A PERIMETER SCREED. A magnesium hand float is used to push the concrete up to the chalkline. This strip of wet concrete, placed along the foundation walls, is a perimeter screed.

USING A SCREED RAIL. Two workers use a magnesium straightedge, or screed rail, to level freshly placed concrete. The ends of the rail glide over previously leveled concrete strips, called wet screeds. A third worker rakes the concrete behind the screed rail to adjust for high and low spots.

tion wall at finish-floor height (usually 4 in. higher than the stone). The lines help you level the concrete along the walls.

You should also lay out the vapor barrier at this time. Six-mil polyethylene works well, but if you're concerned about punctures from traffic during the pour, a puncture-resistant, cross-laminated product is available, called Tu-Tuf® (Sto-Cote Products, Inc., 888-786-2683).

If you elect to use wire-mesh reinforcement, this is also the time to lay it out. Wire mesh doesn't prevent cracking, but it will help keep hairline cracks tight, even as the temperature varies. Typically, a basement slab isn't subjected to wide temperature swings. Therefore, a basement slab placed over a properly prepared stone base doesn't require wire mesh. Garage slabs, on the other hand, typically experience harsher weather conditions, and wire mesh

may be used as temperature reinforcement. But wire mesh won't be effective unless it's placed midway in the thickness of the slab, so be sure to use wire high chairs, which hold the reinforcement up off the stone during the pour.

The ready-mix truck arrives, and the driver asks, "How wet do you want it, Mac?" Drivers routinely ask about adding water to soften the mix. When a mix is too stiff, it's physically difficult to work and presents problems when it's time to float and finish the slab. To get a smooth, hard, dense finish on top of the slab, the mix has to be workable. As mentioned earlier, however, the wetness was determined when you specified the slump of the mix. And as any structural engineer will tell you, when you add water to concrete, you lower the final strength. The issue of water content in concrete is critical; many concrete

> **BE PREPARED FOR THE POUR**

BE PREPARED FOR THE DAY the concrete is scheduled to arrive by first surveying your situation.

Do you have a grade-level door or will you need to chute the concrete through a basement window? Will the ready-mix truck be able to get next to the house, and if not, will the manpower be available to transport the concrete in wheelbarrows? Pushing one wheelbarrow full of concrete uphill is possible for some, but making 30 trips uphill is a job for the John Henry type. It never hurts to have more help than you might need because concrete is always a rugged day's work.

A little rain the night before can turn a dry approach into a muddy nightmare. I call my supplier several days in advance and say that I'm shooting for next Thursday, for example, but that I'll call first thing Thursday to confirm. If conditions are terrible, I reschedule.

Remember, concrete waits for no one. From the minute it leaves the plant, it has a finite time before it sets up, and just about any builder can come up with a horror story describing a pour that got away.

techniques they use. If you have placed a few slabs, don't be afraid to try a different method; you may discover a system that you're more comfortable with. But whatever approach you take, follow a logical progression: Don't trap yourself in a corner. I prefer to use wet screeds as guides to level the slab (see the photo on p. 59).

Wet screeds are wet strips of concrete that are leveled off at finish-floor height and used to guide a straightedge, or screed rail, as you level the slab. If you've ever watched a sidewalk being placed, you've seen concrete placed between two wood forms, a screed rail placed on top of those forms and sawed back and forth to strike the wet concrete down to the level of the forms. Wet screeds guide the screed rail in places where there are no wood forms, such as against an existing concrete wall or in the middle of a slab.

Where you start with your wet screeds depends on the layout of the slab. In a typical rectangular basement with the walls already in place, a wet screed is placed around the perimeter of the foundation, and a second wet screed is placed down the center of the foundation (see the photo on the facing page), parallel to the longer dimension of the foundation. On a bigger slab you might need more wet screeds; the determining factor is the length of the screed rail you'll be using.

Placing the wet screeds around the perimeter of the foundation is simple. Use the chalkline you snapped at finish-floor height as a guide to level the concrete at the wall (see the bottom photo on p. 58). As the concrete is placed, either from a wheelbarrow or directly from the chute, use a magnesium hand float to push and level the concrete to the line. Be sure you don't cover up your chalkline as you place the concrete. Dump it near the wall and bring it up to the line with the float (see the top photo on p. 58).

Establishing the level of the center screed requires that you drive pins about 8 ft. apart at the level of the finish floor; 16-in. lengths of ½-in. rebar work well. Try to set these pins immediately before the pour, using a transit or a string line, and cover them with

companies require that you sign off on the delivery slip when requesting additional water so that they have a record of your compromising the rated strength of the mix.

If the first few wheelbarrows of concrete are difficult to work, have the driver add water to it—but in small amounts. You can always soften the mix by adding water, but you can never dry it if it becomes too wet.

Leveling with Wet Screeds

There are many ways to place a basement slab. If you've never placed one, ask some masons about the

RAKER'S ROLE. As the screed rail levels concrete between the perimeter screed (right) and the center screed (left), the raker pulls away excess concrete or fills low spots. A rebar spike set at finish-floor height and subsequently driven below the concrete's surface establishes the center screed's level.

TIP: If you're pouring a garage slab, you'll probably use wire mesh as temperature reinforcement. Be sure to use wire high chairs during the pour to hold the reinforcement up off the stone.

upturned buckets so that no one trips on the pins. Place and level a pad of concrete around each pin, then fill in the area between the pads with concrete and use a screed rail, guided by the pads, to level the area between them. As you complete each portion of this center screed, drive the pins a few inches below the surface with a hammer and fill the resulting holes with a little concrete.

Raking and Striking

To fill in the areas between screeds, place and rake the concrete as close as possible to finish level before striking with a screed rail. Placing too much material makes it difficult to pull the excess concrete with the screed rail as you strike off, and the weight of

OPERATING A BULL FLOAT. After the concrete is screeded, a bull float pushes stones down and brings up the fines—sand and cement—that make a smooth, finished surface. To use a bull float, lower its handle as you push it away, and lift the handle as you pull it back.

the excess concrete can distort a wooden screed rail. If you starve the area between the screeds, you'll constantly be backtracking through freshly placed concrete, filling in low spots and rescreeding.

Using a screed rail, strike off the concrete with the perimeter screed and the center screed as guides. Your path of escape will determine the placement and the size of your screeds, but generally speaking, you progress in about 10-ft. or 12-ft. sections of slab.

The person raking the concrete can make or break the pour. As the wheelbarrows are dumped, the raker should nudge the concrete to the plane of the finish floor, eyeing the placed concrete like a golfer lining up a putt, and noting any mounds or valleys that will create problems as the screed rail works across. As the concrete is struck off, an alert rake person will pull away any excess concrete accumu-

Teamwork is the name of the game. Establish each person's role well ahead of the pour, and do your best to stick to the plan.

lating ahead of the screed rail (see the photo on p. 61) and push concrete into any low spots.

At this stage of the pour, with five or more people working, teamwork is the name of the game. Establish each person's role well ahead of the pour, and do your best to stick to the plan.

Striking off the concrete with the screed rail is the last step in placing the concrete and the first step in finishing it. A good, straight 2×4 will work well, but magnesium screed rails, available in a variety of

Bull Floating

As the pour progresses, it's necessary to smooth the surface of the leveled concrete with a magnesium bull float (see the photo on the facing page). What size bull float you use is determined by the length of the tool's handle and how comfortable you are operating the tool. For example, a bull float with an 18-ft. handle will easily float a 10-ft. or 12-ft. section of a slab. Bull floating levels the ridges created by the screed rail, but more important, it brings cement and sand to the surface of the slab and pushes stones lower.

Water is the lightest ingredient in concrete and quickly finds its way to the surface as you jostle the mix around with a bull float. As the water rises to the surface, it also brings some cement and sand with it. These are the fines (sometimes called fat or cream) that provide a stone-free medium for troweling to a smooth finish.

Although its size is intimidating, a bull float works about the same as a hand trowel. The trick is to keep the leading edge of the bull float inclined above the surface of the slab by lowering the bull float's handle as you push it away and raising the handle as you pull it back. Some masons jiggle the handle as they move it out and back to jostle more fines to the surface. The ease of final troweling depends on how well the slab has been bull floated.

Floating from Knee Boards

Once the bleed water has evaporated, work the slab. Some slabs (in crawlspaces, for example) are acceptable with just a coarse, bull-floated finish. But these finishes tend to dust over time; that is, concrete particles come loose from the coarse slab surface whenever it's swept. Additional finishing compacts the surface so that the slab won't dust.

You may have seen professionals using a power trowel to float and finish larger slabs. A power trowel works like a lawn mower without wheels. It rides on rotating blades that smooth the surface of the concrete. If you're inexperienced, however, or if the slab is small, you're better off finishing it by hand. And

CEMENT SHOES. Knee boards—pieces of plywood with strips of wood on one edge—allow you to move around on fresh concrete without sinking in because the boards distribute weight over a large surface area. Concrete finishing is done from knee boards while the concrete is in a plastic state, meaning it's neither liquid nor solid.

lengths, will perform better. No matter which you choose, working a straightedge back and forth is a lot like running a two-man saw. The work is done on the pull stroke, and you have to be aware of your partner's progress. Wear rubber boots because, standing alongside the wet screeds, you'll often be wading through concrete. (For anyone tempted by the prospect of a barefoot frolic in concrete, be warned that concrete is caustic and will corrode your skin.)

As you saw the screed rail back and forth, let it float on top of the wet screeds, keeping an eye open for low spots and stopping when excess concrete dams up ahead of the screed rail so that the raker can pull off the excess.

ONCE THE SLAB IS PLACED and bull floated, it's time to sit and wait. The first stage will be the evaporation of the bleed water, water that rises to the surface as the slab sets up. Depending on the weather conditions and the consistency of the mix, this time can vary from 1 hour on a hot, dry day to 10 hours on a cool, damp day.

But keep in mind that when concrete starts to set, it waits for no one. There is a small window of opportunity in which you can work the slab, and if you happen to be out for coffee when the concrete starts to set up, you'll learn an expensive lesson. Unless you're a veteran finisher, don't ever leave the pour; you may return to a problem whose only solution is a jackhammer.

even professionals still use hand floats and trowels at the edges of the slab and around projections because a power trowel will finish only to within a few inches of these spots.

Hand finishing is commonly done from knee boards, which are like snow shoes for the still-wet slab (see the photo on p. 63). They let you move around on the slab without sinking. To make a simple pair of knee boards, cut two pieces of ¾-in. plywood 2 ft. square, and tack a 2×2 strip at one edge of each piece.

It's difficult to describe just when the slab is ready for hand floating, but it may help to think of the slab as drying from the bottom up. If you set a knee board on the slab, and it sinks ¾ in. when you step on it, you're too early; if it fails to leave a mark, you're too late. As soon as you can easily smooth over the tracks the knee boards leave behind, the slab is ready for the first hand floating.

Test the concrete at the area where the pour started because it tends to be ready first. If any areas of the slab are in direct sunlight, you can bet they'll be ready long before the shaded areas are. At any rate, your first pass will be with a magnesium hand float (see the top left photo on p. 66).

Like a bull float, a magnesium hand float works the fines to the surface, and you fill in any low spots or knock down any high spots during this pass. The goal when using the magnesium float is to level the concrete, preparing a surface that is ready for smoothing with the steel trowel. You can generally work the entire slab with the magnesium float before it's time to trowel with steel.

The difference between a magnesium float and a steel trowel is easy to recognize on the slab. You can work the slab all day long with magnesium, but you'll never get beyond a level, grainy surface. But when the slab is ready, and you lay a steel trowel to it, the results are impressive.

Hit the Slab with Steel

Keeping the image in your mind of the slab drying from the bottom up, picture the top ⅛ in. of the concrete, which is all cement, sand, and water. While the top section is in a plastic state—neither liquid nor solid—the steel trowel will smooth this layer and compact it into a dense, hard finish. Now the preparatory work pays off; if the concrete was placed and leveled accurately, the final finish goes quickly.

Obtaining an exceptionally smooth finish is a practiced technique that takes years to develop. The steeper the angle of the trowel to the slab, the more trowel marks will occur. If you hold the trowel at an extremely slight angle, you're liable to catch the slab and tear out the surface.

Your troweling technique will be dictated by how loose or tight the surface of the slab is. When the surface is wet, you can hold your trowel fairly flat, but as the fines tighten up, you'll have to increase both the angle and pressure of your trowel. As the slab dries you might have to use both hands on the trowel to muscle some fines to the surface

TIPS FOR POURING IN ANY WEATHER

TEMPERAMENTAL IS AN APT DESCRIPTION of concrete. Temperature, along with humidity, influences the pour more than any other factor.

HOT-WEATHER POURS

When it's hot, and the humidity is low, every minute is important. If you spend time fussing around, when the last wheelbarrow of concrete is finally off the truck, the first section of floor you placed will probably be hard enough to walk on.

HERE ARE SOME STRATEGIES THAT HELP IN HOT WEATHER:

- Even if a polyethylene vapor barrier is not required, use one. It blocks the moisture from dropping through the subgravel.
- Have lots of help available. The sooner you get the truck unloaded and the concrete leveled, the better your chances will be of getting a good finish.
- Have two finishers working the slab: one with a magnesium float, and another following behind with a steel trowel.
- Although it compromises compressive strength, consider using a wetter mix to buy a little more working time.
- If more than one truckload is needed, coordinate the arrival times carefully. If a fresh truckload of concrete has to sit and wait 1 hour while you finish unloading the first truck, you may find that concrete from the second truckload will set up before you're ready for it.
- Areas that receive direct sunlight set up much more quickly than shaded areas.
- Start wetting down the slab as soon as the final finish has set. Few things will weaken concrete as much as a "flash" set, by which the concrete dries too quickly.

COOL-WEATHER POURS

When the temperature is cool, concrete initially reacts in slow motion. After the slab is placed, and the bleed water slowly evaporates, you'll wait hours for the slab to tighten up enough to start hand troweling. When it's finally ready to be troweled, you'd better be there because that window of opportunity for finishing doesn't stay open much longer on a cool day than it does on a warm day.

HERE ARE A FEW COOL-WEATHER TIPS:

- Don't wet the mix any more than necessary.
- If a polyethylene vapor barrier isn't required, don't use one. Any moisture that drains out of the slab will speed the set.
- Pour as early as possible to avoid finishing the slab after dark.

COLD-WEATHER POURS

When the temperature is cold, a whole new set of rules comes into play. Concrete cannot be allowed to freeze. That tender, finely finished surface you just troweled on the slab will turn to mush if it's allowed to freeze. Fortunately, the chemical reaction that takes place when concrete hardens generates heat.

HERE ARE SOME STRATEGIES THAT HELP IN A COLD-WEATHER POUR:

- Ask your concrete supplier about using warm mixing water to prevent problems during transit on days when the temperature is well below freezing.
- Having the supplier add calcium to the mix accelerates the initial set of the concrete, and the concrete achieves the strength to resist freeze–thaw stress faster. The amount of calcium is measured as a percentage of the cement content and ranges from ½% to 2%. Talk to a veteran concrete finisher before deciding when and how much calcium to add to the mix. Too much calcium produces the same problems as hot, dry weather. It's important to note that calcium is corrosive to steel and should never be used in steel-reinforced concrete.
- Always be sure that all components of the subbase are frost free.
- Provide supplemental heat to keep the building above freezing.
- Cover the slab with polyethylene and then spread an insulating layer of straw or hay at least 4 in. thick on top, or use an insulating tarp.
- The best strategy: Pour when cold temperatures are not an issue.

START WITH A MAG; FINISH WITH STEEL. After bull floating, use a magnesium float (left) to smooth out bumps and fill in low spots. The resulting finish will be coarse. Later, use a steel trowel (right) to get a smooth, dense finish that won't crumble when it's swept.

TWO HANDS! TWO HANDS! As the concrete sets up, working it with a steel trowel may require the strength of two hands. The back of the trowel is angled up as you push it away (left), and the front of the trowel is angled up as you pull it toward you (right).

(see the bottom photos above). Once the fines have emerged, switch back to one hand and polish the area with your trowel (see the top right photo above). If you've waited too long, and you're losing the slab, sprinkle water on its surface to buy a little more finishing time. After that, there isn't enough angle, pressure or water anywhere on earth to bring a lost slab back to life. If it's important that the final finish be first rate, consider hiring a professional. Remember, you get only one try.

Curing the Finished Slab

While it's true that you can walk on the floor the day after it's placed, concrete actually hardens very slowly. The initial set represents about a quarter of the total strength; it takes about a month for con-crete to cure fully. The goal during this period is to have the concrete cure as slowly as possible.

Keeping the slab soaked with water for 4 days or 5 days will keep it from drying too quickly, but continual hosing down involves a lot of time and effort. Slabs can require a soaking every half hour in the heat of summer. A masonry sealer applied the day after the pour will keep the slab from drying too quickly and protect the floor from stains that might otherwise wick into the slab.

When you consider that the material cost of a basement slab is less than $1 per sq. ft., it's difficult to imagine a more economical finished floor system. But when you consider the cost of removing and replacing an improperly finished concrete floor, the importance of knowing how to handle two or three truckloads of concrete becomes apparent.

Forming and Pouring Footings

BY RICK ARNOLD AND
MIKE GUERTIN

Over the years, we've built homes on almost every type of foundation imaginable. However, a concrete foundation always seemed to provide the best base for a home built in Rhode Island, our part of the country. In 1996, Rick bought a concrete-forms company, and our firsthand knowledge of footings and foundations increased exponentially.

With every project, we do everything in our power to keep the house and its foundation from settling and cracking, which can cause problems ranging from drywall cracks and sloping floors to doors that won't close. The best preventive medicine is putting the foundation on top of poured-concrete footings (see "Why Footings?" on p. 69).

The price for this medicine is usually reasonable. On a 26-ft. by 38-ft. house, footings add only about $800 to $950 to the cost of the house. Prospective homeowners will spend that much in a blink to upgrade a kitchen. We figure that it makes more sense to upgrade the whole house by adding footings to ensure that the new kitchen stays put.

Laying Out the Footings

Most of the footings called for in our work are 1 ft. high and 2 ft. wide. We normally reinforce footings with a double row of $\frac{1}{2}$-in. (#4) steel rebar unless plans specify otherwise. For the project featured here, the soil at the bottom of the excavated hole was like beach sand, so footings were a must. We went with standard-size footings to support the 10-in. wide by 8-ft. high foundation walls that would be poured on top.

But before we can think about footings, we have to lay out the location of the foundation. We begin by establishing two starting points, the corners at both ends of one foundation wall. With most houses, there are a couple of surveyor stakes (see photo 1 on p. 70) outside the hole with the offsets (the distance to the edge of the foundation wall) written on them.

For most jobs we find corner points by running a string line between the stakes. We measure in the offset amount and then drop a couple of plumb lines to the floor of the foundation hole.

We drive stakes (usually foundation-form rods) into the ground at the two points; the measurement between the two rods should be the length of the wall as indicated on the plans (see photo 2 on p. 70). If the points are off an inch or so, we adjust them until the measurement is correct. If there is a large gap between our measurement and the plan, we call the surveyor back. For the house shown here, setbacks were tight, so the surveyor set two exact foundation corner points on the floor of the hole.

FILL UP A TRENCH WITH CONCRETE—WHAT'S TO KNOW? If a house is going to stand on those little sidewalks, they'd better be straight, level, and correctly placed.

ON THE DIAGONAL

The best way to locate the rest of the corners or points from the two reference points is to use diagonal measurements, just like we learned in high-school math. Unlike in high school, however, we depend on a calculator to do the math.

Before jumping into the hole, we sit down with the blueprints and the calculator. In about 10 minutes we figure out our diagonals so that every corner on the plans has two reference measurements. Then it's just a matter of measuring those distances from the original two points to find the other foundation corners. The quickest method is to have two crew members hold tapes at the original reference points. A third crew member pulls the tapes tight and crosses them, moving the tapes until the calculated measurements from the corners meet each other

> We always double-check our measurements between the corners to make sure the foundation dimensions are right on.

(see photo 3 on p. 70). A stake is then driven into the ground to mark the point. We always double-check our measurements between the corners to make sure the foundation dimensions are right on.

The project house has a garage with a connecting breezeway that meets the house at an angle. To locate the corners of the breezeway, we triangulate from the foundation corners we've just found for the main body of the house. Again, we double-check all our dimensions to be sure they jibe with the plan. Once stakes have been driven at every corner, we run a string line from one to the other, sort of like a giant connect-the-dots game. The result is an outline of the entire foundation.

Setting Up the Forms

With the outline in place, we're ready to start setting forms. We use 2×12s connected by steel form brackets that hold the inside and outside forms exactly 2 ft. apart (see photo 5 on p. 71). Rick had these brackets custom made.

We locate the forms so that the foundation walls will be centered on the footings. The foundation walls for this house were 10 in. wide, so we subtracted 10 in. from the footing width of 24 in. To leave equal amounts of footing on both sides of the foundation wall, we divided the remaining 14 in. in half to give us 7 in. of exposed footing on both sides of the walls.

Because the string line we've set indicates the outside of the foundation wall, we start by nailing two 2×12s together to form an outside corner. We then set our corner 7 in. away from the string line (see photo 4 on p. 71). A form bracket locks the inside form plank at the proper width (see photo 5 on p. 71). We continue this process around the perimeter of the foundation. Form brackets are dropped every 4 ft. or so. Where two planks butt, we toenail the tops together and put form brackets on both sides of the butt joint.

We keep many different lengths of form stock on hand, so we rarely need to cut a piece. When we come to a small jog, such as the inside corner of the angled breezeway, we simply form the whole area off. The extra concrete used is negligible. When two planks don't quite meet, we bridge the gap with a short piece, and if a plank is a little long, we just run it by the adjacent plank and tack the two together. Forming footings is forgiving because the finished product is buried. The major concern with footings is strength and function, not how they look.

When we need a footing that is wider than 2 ft. or if we're forming a large area such as a bulkhead pad, we secure the forms in a different manner. We run ¾-in.-wide perforated-steel strapping beneath the planks across the bottom of the footing. The strapping is run up the outside of the form planks and nailed to keep the bottoms of the planks from spreading. The tops are then held at the proper width with a length of 1×3 nailed between the two planks.

Setting the Footing Height

Once all the forms are in place, we backfill against potential weak points such as butt joints or the larger areas where we couldn't use form brackets. Backfilling prevents the concrete from getting underneath the planks and lifting them up during the pour. At this point we transfer the foundation lines to the tops of the forms for future reference. The string line is removed, but the stakes are left in the ground as a visual reference to make sure that the forms don't shift during the pour.

SURVEYOR STAKES INDICATE WALL LOCATION.
1 Measurements are taken from surveyor stakes and transferred to the floor of the excavated hole to locate one foundation wall. 2 The ends of the wall are then located precisely with a measuring tape.

3 **DIAGONAL MEASUREMENTS LOCATE THE OTHER WALLS.** All other corners are located by triangular measurements from those points. Three people and two tapes make the process go quicker.

The major concern with footings is strength and function, not how they look.

Next, using a builder's transit, we set the grade to make sure the top of the footing is poured to the same level. First, we find the lowest point on the forms by checking the height of the planks at every corner and at several points in between. The low point becomes the grade for the footing. We mark a yardstick to the measurement at the low point on the forms. Then we work our way back around the footing, installing grade nails every few feet on the inside of the forms. To mark the grade, we hold a 6d nail against the bottom of the yardstick and move it up or down until it's at the right height. The nail is then hammered in about halfway.

4 OUTSIDE FORMS ARE SET UP FIRST. Starting at one corner, the outside forms are set at a given distance off the foundation line.

5 BRACKETS SET THE FOOTING WIDTH. Brackets are then slipped over the forms that keep the inside form exactly 2 ft. away from the outside. The footing height is then set with a transit and marked on the inside of the form.

SUMMER VS. WINTER CONCRETE MIXTURES: WHAT'S THE DIFFERENCE?

WHEN IT'S SLIGHTLY OVERCAST and temperatures are consistently in the 70s, pouring concrete comes with few surprises. That's seldom the case when the truck backs down the driveway and the temperature is below freezing or in the high 80s. Different seasons demand a little extra planning and work. Understanding the differences in each type of concrete mixture ensures that your slab, patio, or walkway cures correctly.

KEEP HOT CONCRETE WET

Concrete needs water to cure properly, and the slower it cures, the better. But on hot summer days, the water in the mix begins evaporating as soon as it comes off the truck, causing concrete to dry too quickly. Admixtures such as water reducers or superplasticizers can be added to help retard the cure and reduce water demand, and both types increase workability and strength. Once the concrete is set and finished, keeping it wet is the best way to strengthen the curing process. A lawn sprinkler set to go off at regular intervals can help ensure that the concrete doesn't dry too quickly.

KEEP COLD CONCRETE FROM FREEZING

Cold weather creates an opposite set of problems. The amount of water in the cement mix is greatly reduced, which in turn reduces the setting time and gain of strength. If concrete freezes, it can become damaged.

The best way to increase the setup time of concrete is to add hot rather than cold water to the mix. While most companies switch to hot water automatically when it's below 40°F, it's a good idea to double-check. Another option is to use a finer cement, type III, which generates more heat and has a higher early strength. Admixtures like calcium chloride (salt) also work as accelerators with reinforced concrete.

Concrete generates heat as it cures, which works to your advantage in the winter. However, you may still need to cover the work with thermal curing blankets to retain heat. A layer of plastic and straw also works.

—Matthew Teague, contributing writer

6 **REBAR IS INSERTED INTO THE WET CONCRETE.** The footing forms are filled to grade, and the concrete is worked with the flat side of a shovel until the footings are level. Then ½-in. rebar is pushed down into the fresh concrete.

7 **THE TOP IS TROWELED SMOOTH,** and 8 a keyway is formed by dragging a 2×4 down the center of the footing.

The excavators we work with usually leave the foundation hole less than 2 in. out of level. But if we see that some parts of the footing are too shallow because the bottom of the hole is too high after we shoot the grade, we dig out inside the forms until the proper depth is reached. If we undermine the planks in the process, we backfill the outside of the form. We also spray a light coat of form-release oil on the inside of the 2×s.

Pouring the Footings

Now we're ready for the concrete. The best foundation holes have clear access for the cement trucks all the way around the hole. Good access makes the pour go more quickly because the truck can shoot concrete into the forms without our having to drag it with shovels. If access is a problem, we usually start the pour at the most difficult spot for the truck to reach and work our way out.

The concrete chute is moved slowly along the forms, allowing the concrete to fill up to the grade nails. For sections that can't be reached with the truck's chute, we drag the concrete along the forms until those areas are filled. When the pour is finished, we begin installing a double row of ½-in. steel rebar around the footing (see photo 6, above).

Although rebar is not required for residential footings here in the Northeast, we believe that its added strength is cheap insurance. For commercial footings that are required to take many times the load of

9 FOUNDATION CORNERS ARE MARKED ON TOP. While the concrete is still green, the corner of the foundation is marked on the footing.

a typical house, we wire the rebar together and set it on chairs that keep it at a specific height during the pour. However, the additional cost of the labor and the materials usually rules out this option when we're doing residential projects.

Instead, rebar is placed atop the wet concrete about 6 in. in from each form. For angles or 90° corners, we bend the rebar around a knee until it's at the desired angle. Rebar is then inserted under the brackets and pushed down about 8 in. into the concrete, using the shovel as a gauge. As rebar is pushed in, we jiggle it with the shovel to remove any trapped air.

We level the concrete by vigorously pushing it with the flat of the shovel until the concrete is at finish grade. We add or remove a shovelful of concrete to adjust the level and to rework the concrete until the grade nails are exactly half-exposed.

After the concrete is leveled to the grade nails, we gently lift up all the form brackets a couple of inches, which makes our last two jobs easier. The first job is troweling the top of the footing (see photo 7 on p. 73)

to provide a smooth surface for snapping chalklines for the foundation walls. The smooth surface also makes it easier to sweep off the dirt that always gets on the footing while the forms are being stripped.

A 2×4 CUTS THE KEYWAY

The final part of the pour is making a keyway, centered on top of the footing, that will lock the foundation walls in place. We usually make our keyway 1½ in. deep and 3½ in. wide, or the size of a 2×4 laid flat. We simply press a short piece of 2×4 into the concrete and drag it down the center of the footing (see photo 8 on p. 73). By now the concrete should have cured enough for the 2×4 to leave a significant depression.

Cutting a keyway this way causes a slight buildup of displaced concrete, and we've found that concrete built up in the corners can interfere with setting the foundation forms plumb. To avoid this problem, we end the keyway short of each corner or angle in the foundation. Because corners and angles are the strongest parts of a foundation wall, we aren't worried about compromising integrity at these points.

Before stripping the forms, we square off the foundation-line marks on the forms and mark the foundation corners in the green concrete (see photo 9, above). A long steel bar makes short work of popping the brackets, and with the duplex nails, removing the forms is a breeze.

Forming and Pouring Foundations

BY RICK ARNOLD AND
MIKE GUERTIN

The lime green neon sign flashed "Learn your future today." Our crew, skeptics all, filed in through the purple door in the tiny storefront and listened expressionless as the gypsy inside delivered eerily detailed portraits of each of us as well as glimpses into what was in store for our lives. Rick shrugged off her bizarre prophecy that his future would involve "packaging the earth." Then, a couple of years later, he decided to buy a concrete-form business from a friend. On hearing the news, Rick's wife said, "My God, Rick, that lady was right: You are going to be packaging the earth."

There are over a dozen different types of forming systems for poured-concrete walls, but the basic concepts of laying out, squaring, leveling, pouring, and finishing are common to any good foundation job. So whether you're pouring a foundation yourself or paying someone to do it for you, it's important to understand the process because things can go wrong in both subtle and dramatic ways.

The Foundation Hole Must Be Level

The key to raising foundation forms quickly and securely is having a good base to set them on. We always prefer to put a foundation on concrete footings (see "Forming and Pouring Footings" on p. 67), as we did for the job featured here. The footing surface is flat and level, so the forms go up as quickly as we can move them.

The alternative to using footings is setting the forms on a gravel or crushed-stone base on the floor of the foundation hole. A good foundation hole is usually within 2 in. of level. Any more than that means a lot of labor for us scratching down or filling up to level as we set the form panels.

The excavator is also responsible for the amount of overdig, or the area that is dug beyond the actual perimeter of the foundation. Ideally, there should be 4 ft. to 5 ft. left between the forms and the hole sides to give us the room we need to handle the forms and to work on the outside of the walls. For safety's sake, the sides of the hole should not be excavated vertically or undercut. Instead, there should be some sort of slope or pitch to the hole walls.

Another critical duty of the excavator is making sure the concrete trucks have good access to the foundation (see the photo on p. 76). If they don't have access, we end up having to push the concrete by hand along the forms, sometimes 40 ft. or more. Some conditions require a concrete pump truck, to the tune of an extra $700 to $800. Once the hole is satisfactory and the footings are ready, we give the tops of the footings a final sweep before layout.

THIS FORM SYSTEM, preferred by the authors, includes form panels that can be reused many times, depending on how they are handled.

Laying Out the Foundation Walls

We plot out the foundation walls the same way we did the footings. The goal is to pinpoint every corner and angle on the outside face of the foundation wall. Before we stripped the footing forms, we had scribed the corner points of the longest foundation wall on top in the concrete from points that had been marked on the forms. We double-check the distance between these points as well as the distances from the surveyor's stakes.

When we laid out the footings, we figured out all the diagonal measurements to find the location of the other corners and jogs in the foundation. Those same calculations are used again on top of the foot-ings for the foundation (see photo 1 on the facing page). When all our points have been established, we take diagonal measurements to be sure the layout is square (see photo 2 on the facing page). We then snap lines between the points that represent the outside face of the foundation walls to give us a guide to follow as we set the forms (see photo 3 on the facing page).

Assembling the Forms

As a couple of crew members work on the layout, the rest distribute forms around the perimeter of the hole, sliding them down along the sides of the hole in pairs. By the time the layout is done, enough

1 LOCATE THE FOUNDATION CORNERS. Working on the floor of the foundation hole or on top of the footings, you first have to find the outside point for every corner or jog in the foundation.

CHECK THE LAYOUT FOR SQUARE.
2 Diagonal measurements are then taken to check for square, and **3** chalklines are snapped for lining up the forms.

4 **FORMING STARTS IN A CORNER** that uses a right-angle form for the inside and special brackets for the outside.

forms are in the hole, and the layout crew can begin setting them up.

The forming starts in one corner. We use 90° forms for inside corners, but for outside corners we have special brackets that join two standard forms at a right angle (see photo 4 on the facing page). Once the corner forms are set up, we tweak them until they're exactly plumb, using shims if necessary. Plumbing each corner precisely simplifies the later job of squaring the top of the foundation.

When a corner has been set, crew members each take a direction and begin setting up the standard-size (2-ft.-wide) forms. To join our forms together, metal Ts are slipped through reinforced holes in the side rails of the form that is already set up. Then flat, slotted foundation rods are slipped over the ends of the Ts, locking the inside and outside panels at the specified width for the foundation wall, in this case 10 in. (see photo 5 at left). Foundation rods not only determine the width of the wall but also—along with the Ts—keep the forms from spreading during the pour.

The next panels, one inside and one out, are placed close enough to the previous ones to feed the ends of the Ts into the matching holes. Then the forms are pushed hard against each other, and a flat, tapered pin, or wedge, is slid into the slot on the end of the T (see photo 6 at left), locking the two panels together. At this point, the wedges are left loose in the slot until the walls have been squared and straightened.

⑤ **SLOTTED RODS THAT SLIP OVER Ts** hold the forms apart at the right wall width.

⑥ **TAPERED PINS, OR WEDGES,** through the Ts hold adjacent panels together.

⑦ **BRACING KEEPS THE WALLS** plumb during the setup and pour.

8 BEFORE THE CONCRETE TRUCKS ARRIVE, string lines are stretched as guides for straightening the walls.

Our forms come in 2-in.-wide increments from 2 in. to 24 in., so it's easy to anticipate what we'll need for each wall. A 30-ft. 2-in. wall will use thirty 24-in. panels plus a pair of 2-in. fillers. If a wall is 41 ft. long, we use forty 24-in. panels and a pair of 12-in. panels. If a wall length is specified to an odd inch or to a fraction (we just love those), we simply nail a spacer made of ¾-in.-thick furring or the appropriate-size plywood to the ends of an inside and an outside panel to make up the difference. The panels with spacers are then locked to neighboring panels with longer Ts.

Besides 90° corners, the most common angle we're asked to form is 45°. We have forms and brackets similar to our 90° system to create 45° walls. However, for other angles, we usually build forms on site.

The house featured here had sections offset from the main body of the house at 30° and 60°. We formed these angles by locking smaller-size panels together with perforated-steel strapping. The inside panels are connected to the outside panels with ¼-in. steel rod (called pencil rod). We bolt clamps onto the pencil rod to hold the panels at the 10-in. wall width. Voids between the forms are filled with rigid-foam insulation that we cut and insert.

9 THE TOP OF THE FOUNDATION is found with a transit, and 10 chalklines are snapped at that level.

11 BASEMENT WINDOW FRAMES ARE INSERTED and tacked to the forms, 12 and form-release oil is applied to the inside of the forms.

Grade nail

13

14

WHEN THE PREP WORK IS DONE, the forms are filled with concrete. 13 The backside of a shovel floats the top of the concrete until it's halfway through the grade nails. 14 The top is then screeded with a 2×4 to smooth it out.

TIP: If a wall length is specified to an odd inch or to a fraction, nail a spacer made of ¾-in.-thick furring or the appropriate-size plywood to the ends of an inside and an outside panel to make up the difference.

15 **ANCHOR BOLTS ARE INSERTED** while the concrete is still soft.

Straightening and Squaring the Walls

As the forms go up, we brace both the inside and outside sections with 2× bracing every 8 ft. to 10 ft. (see photo 7 on p. 79) to keep forms from racking and falling over. When all the panels are up and the job is closed in, we slip steel channel over the tops of the forms. The channel fits tightly, locking the panels into alignment with each other.

Next we string the whole job to straighten and square the foundation (see photo 8 on p. 80). Mason's twine is stretched from one corner to the other; the string line is kept lined up exactly with the face of the outside corner panels. Then a crew member walks along the top of the forms, telling two other crew members who are on the ground (one inside, one out) which way to adjust the 2× braces to straighten the wall. Braces are not nailed; instead, they are wedged under a horizontal member of the form.

The next job is squaring the foundation by measuring diagonally between the corners just as we did when laying out the foundation on the footings. If need be, we shift a corner or two until our diagonal measurements are equal. When the entire job is squared, we once more straighten the tops of the walls and tighten the bracing.

Next we check and tighten all the hardware, the easiest but probably most crucial job of the process. Each foundation rod is checked methodically inside and outside to make sure that it is properly engaged by a T. If a T misses the slot in the rod, it can cause the wall to blow out from the weight and pressure of wet concrete. As the rods are checked, each wedge is driven home to tighten the joints between the forms.

Final Prep before the Pour

We're now ready to shoot the grade, or the height of the foundation wall (see photo 9 on p. 81). Because we're on footings, we shouldn't have any high or low spots to factor in. Unless otherwise specified, the grade is established at 93 in. from the bottom of the form, and a 6d grade nail is driven at that elevation. (Our forms are 96 in. tall; our alignment channels are 2½ in. deep. A pour height of 93 in. keeps the concrete off the channel.) A yardstick is then placed on top of that grade, and the height is read through our transit.

The crew member with the yardstick works his or her way around the foundation, setting grade nails at each corner on the outside form at the height indicated by the crew member at the transit. If a wall is longer than 24 ft., we set a grade nail in the middle of the wall. Lines are snapped between the grade nails (see photo 10 on p. 81), and then extra nails are set in the snapped line about every 4 ft.

release agents. We use a handheld pump sprayer with a wand to apply a light coat on the panel faces.

Filling the Forms

Because concrete starts to cure within 2 hours, we begin the pour with the most time-consuming or hard-to-reach areas of the foundation and work our way around the foundation from there. This strategy keeps any of the walls from curing before the other walls can be poured.

During the pour, we keep a constant watch for blowouts or shifting panels. We stop the pour as needed to rebrace walls, keeping the forms aligned and plumb. When the concrete nears grade, we slow the pour rate a little and move the chutes to keep from overfilling the forms.

Once the walls are topped off, we check the string lines again to make sure the walls stayed straight, adjusting the forms if necessary. Our concrete mix is generally loose enough that we don't have a problem with voids from pockets of trapped air. But if a real stiff mix is specified for a job, we tap the forms with a rubber mallet, and in extreme cases we use a vibrator to remove trapped air from the mix.

With the forms filled, we grade the top surface by floating the backside of a shovel on the concrete and working it to level the surface (see photo 13 on p. 82). At this point, we also add or remove a touch of concrete until half of each grade nail is exposed.

A crew member then follows along, screeding the surface with a length of 2×4 (see photo 14 on p. 82). The edge of the 2×4 is pushed vigorously up and down, forward and back, to bring water up to the surface, making it smooth and level. The final step is inserting ½-in. anchor bolts into the top of the wet concrete (see photo 15 on p. 83). Some local codes may require that the bolts be in position before the concrete is poured to ensure proper aggregate consolidation around the bolts. But our building officials allow us to insert the bolts directly into wet concrete, moving them up and down slightly to make sure there is no trapped air around them. When we poured this job, CABO code required bolts every

Before the channel went on, we'd slipped the basement window frames down between the forms (see photo 11 on p. 81). At this point, the frames are brought up to the grade line and tacked to the inside of the forms. We also locate and nail in metal forms for the beam pockets. These forms leave a small shelf inside the wall to hold the end of the main beam. If the foundation requires a sewer chase or a chase for any other purpose, we slide a Styrofoam® block between the forms and secure it at the proper location with 16d duplex nails driven from the outside. These blocks are made on site to the required dimension and fit tightly between the forms.

The inside faces of the forms have to be coated with form-release oil to prevent the forms from sticking to the concrete as it cures. We usually apply the oil just before or as the trucks arrive (see photo 12 on p. 81). There are many types of form oil and release agents. Motor oil and diesel fuel used in the old days have been replaced with more environmentally friendly nontoxic mixtures. Many places require the use of these newer products, and we've had good luck with paraffin and vegetable-oil-based

16 FORMS ARE STRIPPED and carried to the truck. After the concrete has cured overnight, the crew strips off the forms and takes them to the truck to be stacked.

17 AS EACH FORM IS REMOVED, excess concrete along the top is scraped off.

18 THE ENDS OF THE FOUNDATION RODS are then broken off with a hammer.

6 ft. Here in Rhode Island, that requirement has since been upgraded to anchor bolts every 4 ft.

Stripping Forms: Setup in Reverse

The concrete is allowed to set up overnight, and the next morning, we're back at the site to strip the forms. Stripping is basically the setup process in reverse. First, we remove the string and the channel from the tops of the forms. Then the Ts, wedges, and any other removable hardware come off.

If the form oil has done its job, the panels should pop away from the walls easily (see photo 16 on p. 85). The excess concrete that built up at the grade line is scraped off the forms (see photo 17 on p. 85), which are brought to the truck.

After the forms have been stripped, we snap off the ends of all the foundation rods that held the forms together and that now project beyond the foundation (see photo 18 on p. 85). The rods are scored so that they break off safely below the surface of the foundation wall. We remove the rods to make the job site safer for the rest of the subcontractors and to allow the exterior of the foundation walls to be damp-proofed.

It's best to let the concrete cure before backfilling the foundation. Concrete doesn't reach its full compressive strength for 28 days or so, but 5 days to 7 days is usually sufficient curing time for the concrete walls to withstand backfill pressure. Still, it's always a good precaution to brace the inside of any green walls that are long and straight before backfilling against them.

Air-Sealed Mudsill Assembly

BY STEVE BACZEK

The mudsill is one of the most critical components of a successful Passive House. It involves a connection between dissimilar materials, and making such a connection airtight is a challenge. Even the best stemwall will have some imperfections. Also, the mudsill typically will be wet from its preservative treatment and from the lumberyard, and it will shrink as it dries. This means that there likely will be gaps between the wood and the concrete. Traditionally, this part of the building is sealed with a foam gasket. In a Passive House, however, even a minor gap is a major problem, so the assembly is a bit more complex.

This part of the build typically is done on the carpenters' first day, so it's often their first hands-on involvement with the extreme airtightness requirement of this kind of house. In most cases, the carpenters never will have built even close to a Passive House level of airtightness, so establishing a good mental standard for the job starts here.

The mudsill is a one-shot deal. This project relies on several blower-door tests to evaluate air leakage, but the first test won't happen until the walls and roof are in place and sheathed. By then, any air leakage at the mudsill is far more difficult to address. It needs to be right the first time; there is no second chance here.

Learning to Love Acoustical Sealant

There are various sealants, gaskets, self-adhering membranes, and building tapes for air-sealing mudsills. Although we used a gasket in one layer of the mudsill assembly on this house—a belt-and-suspenders approach—most of the airtightness hinges on the use of Tremco acoustical sealant. Sold in tubes at specialty retailers and online, the black sealant installs easily with a caulk gun. It's exceedingly sticky and highly elastic, and unlike construction adhesive, it never cures. While the gooey, get-everywhere sealant makes for an interesting job site (you'll want to keep a large bottle of Goof Off® or Goo Gone® on hand), it is the most effective air-sealing solution I have found.

One of the issues I have in sealing mudsills with a rubber gasket alone is the treatment of butt joints and changes in direction. A healthy bead of sealant eliminates any concern about gaps in these areas.

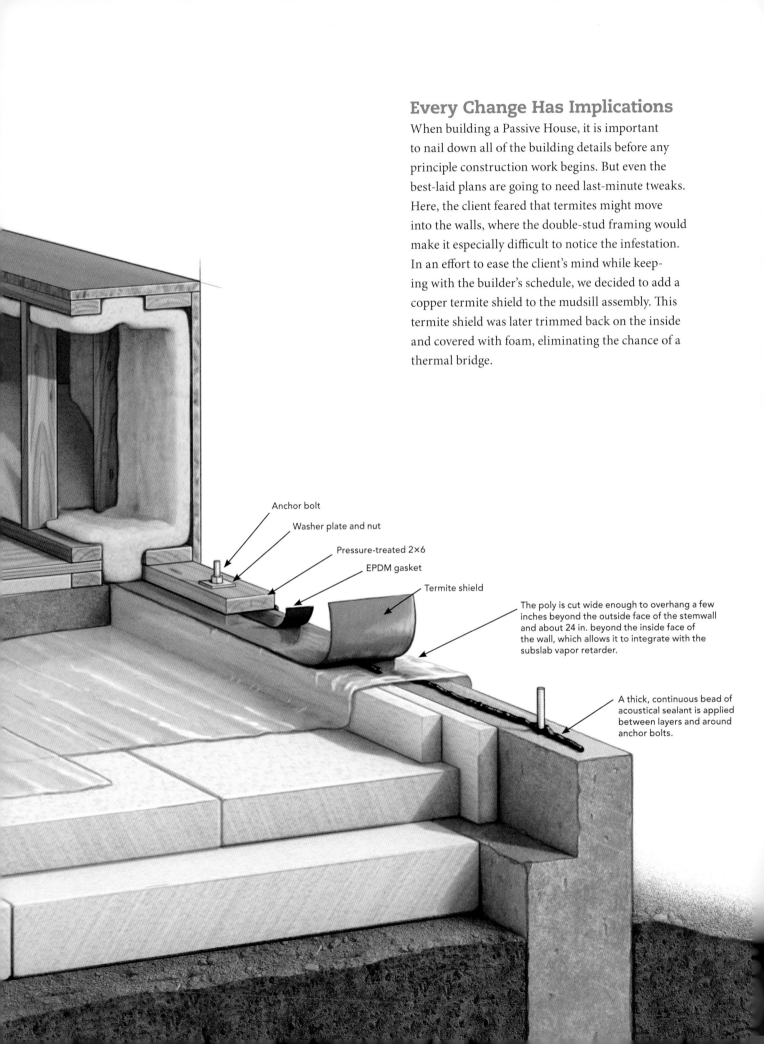

Every Change Has Implications

When building a Passive House, it is important to nail down all of the building details before any principle construction work begins. But even the best-laid plans are going to need last-minute tweaks. Here, the client feared that termites might move into the walls, where the double-stud framing would make it especially difficult to notice the infestation. In an effort to ease the client's mind while keeping with the builder's schedule, we decided to add a copper termite shield to the mudsill assembly. This termite shield was later trimmed back on the inside and covered with foam, eliminating the chance of a thermal bridge.

Anchor bolt

Washer plate and nut

Pressure-treated 2×6

EPDM gasket

Termite shield

The poly is cut wide enough to overhang a few inches beyond the outside face of the stemwall and about 24 in. beyond the inside face of the wall, which allows it to integrate with the subslab vapor retarder.

A thick, continuous bead of acoustical sealant is applied between layers and around anchor bolts.

PREP THE PLATE. To locate the bolts accurately, the mudsill is laid on edge across the top of the stemwall, and each bolt location is scribed onto the face of the 2×6.

NARROW WALLS REQUIRE OFFSET STRINGS. The tops of these stemwalls are only wide enough to carry the 2×6 walls, so the carpenters attach 2× spacer blocks to the stemwalls, and then they fasten an offset stringline to the blocks to use as a reference for measuring.

DRILL THE LAYERS AS A SANDWICH. Although they started out marking and boring through each layer separately, the carpenters quickly learned that it's faster to stack up the poly, termite shield, and 2×6 mudsill; clamp them together; and drill through everything at once.

THE GASKET IS TREATED SEPARATELY. The soft and stretchy EPDM gasket (see "Gaskets" on p. 91) tends to get snagged and wrapped up by a spinning drill bit, so after the other layers are drilled, the gasket is stapled to the underside of the mudsill and sliced with a utility knife at each bolt-hole location.

STACK THE LAYERS. The primary air-seal in this assembly is Tremco acoustical sealant. Highly elastic and sticky right out of the tube, this sealant won't harden over time like construction adhesives, so it creates a reliable air-seal at vulnerable joints.

PLASTIC COMES FIRST. After applying a thick, continuous bead of acoustical sealant to the top of the concrete, the carpenters lay the poly vapor retarder in place. They use hand pressure to push it firmly into the bead of sealant.

TERMITE SHIELD. Another bead of acoustical sealant is laid across the top of the poly before the termite shield, a copper-polymer composite membrane called YorkShield 106 TS™ (www.yorkmfg.com), is placed over it.

GASKETS

TRADITIONALLY, THE MUDSILL is laid atop a ¼-in.-thick polyethylene gasket. Although this sill sealer does help reduce air leakage between the sill and the concrete, it's far from airtight. On this house, the builders installed a soft rubber EPDM gasket (BG63) made by Conservation Technology (www.conservationtechnology.com). Unlike with poly gaskets, the manufacturer claims that its EPDM gaskets will stay flexible at extremely low temperatures and will respond well to shrinkage and swelling even after decades of compression.

POLYETHYLENE GASKET

EPDM GASKET

BUTTER THE BUTT JOINTS. Before placing the next 2×6 sill, a thick bead of sealant is applied to the edge of any adjoining sill. This is a commonly overlooked weak spot in an air-sealed assembly.

BELT AND SUSPENDERS. After all of the layers are in place and the foundation bolts have been fully tightened, another bead of sealant is applied to the exterior joint between mudsill and stemwall and at all butt joints.

An Energy-Smart Foundation in Two Days

BY TIM ROBINSON

We all know that time is money. That's why waiting for the footings and foundation to go in can be one of the most frustrating aspects of any home-building project. Trying to get a house out of the ground in the winter is even more challenging.

One time-saving solution I've come to like involves the installation of insulated, precast concrete panels to construct a building's foundation. I use a system from Superior Walls® (www.superiorwalls.com), but the same benefits are available from other companies in different parts of the country (see "Sources" on p. 98). In most cases, after a site is excavated, I can install the whole system in two days: one day for prep and one day to set walls. Because these panels sit on a compacted gravel footing, my crew can do the prep work.

Not only are the panels quick to install, but they're also insulated with 2½ in. of foam (R-12.5). The foam is visible on the inside surface of each panel; so are steel studs punched with holes for wiring and plumbing, making this type of foundation easy to finish inside. The outer concrete face is mixed at 5,000-psi, vs. the 2,500-psi concrete in standard poured walls, so the prefab walls are practically bulletproof and waterproof. (For the record, the manufacturer says these panels are "damp-proof"

and makes no claim about bullet resistance.) On this project, I elected to waterproof the foundation with a sprayed-on sealant and a dimple drain; the cost is minimal for the peace of mind gained.

Drainage Matters for All Foundations

Because no concrete footing is used, the code governing wood foundations applies (International Residential Code section R402), specifically, ½-in. compacted gravel. The depth of the stone (4 in., in this case) depends on soil type and the combined load per lineal foot (dead load + live load + wind/snow load = combined load; see p. 5 for more on building loads).

Drainage is important for all foundations, perimeter drains being the most common. Although code allows exceptions, Superior Walls does not. The perimeter drain's gravel must extend below the frost line, so if you have a wall with no backfill against it, you need to dig a trench and fill it with gravel to set the wall on (see the top left photo on p. 97). This trench requires its own drain. The width and depth of the trench vary depending on your location.

The overall excavation should be at least 2 ft. larger than the foundation on all sides so that there's ample room for the perimeter drain and room for

INSTALLING AN INSULATED, PREFABRICATED FOUNDATION costs about the same as installing and insulating a conventional foundation—but it takes a lot less time!

the installers to work. If you decide to waterproof (required in some areas), you'll need this room. It's also a safety issue (required by the Occupational Safety and Health Administration [OSHA]) to have at least 2 ft. of space from a foundation to the edge of the trench. On a simple rectangular foundation, we locate the two back corners first to ensure that we have this 2 ft. of working space behind the wall. Next, we pull the correct measurement perpendicular to this line and make a 3-ft. to 4-ft. arc in the gravel. After calculating the diagonal measurement of the building, I measure from the back pins to where that measurement intersects the arc to find the other two corners.

Spreading the Gravel

With the rental of a skid steer and a compactor, we can place and pack the gravel in less than a day. To keep the gravel bed even, I set up a builder's level in an out-of-the-way corner and measure off the level to set grade pegs throughout the footprint roughly 8 ft. to 10 ft. apart. Working from back to front, we fill in the gravel, raking it to the height of the grade stakes. Two carpenters easily can keep ahead of one skid steer, and working back to front like this, I never have to drive the skid steer on a finished area.

After the gravel is leveled, we tamp the entire area, reshoot grade, and fill in the low spots. The tolerances aren't exactly rocket science; the installation crew requires that the gravel be within only 1 in. of

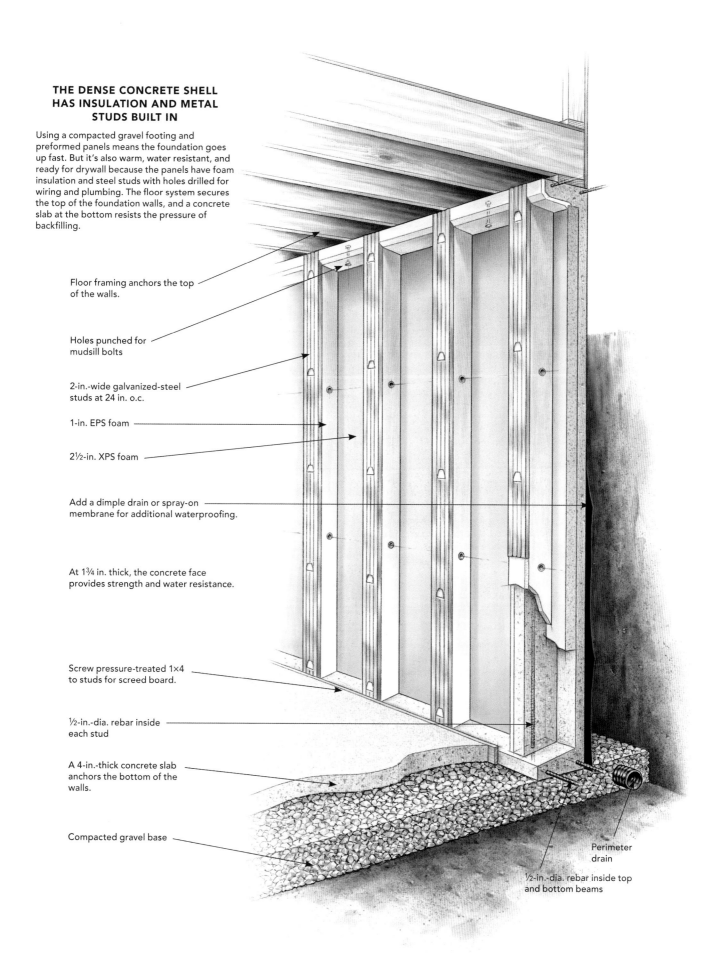

THE DENSE CONCRETE SHELL HAS INSULATION AND METAL STUDS BUILT IN

Using a compacted gravel footing and preformed panels means the foundation goes up fast. But it's also warm, water resistant, and ready for drywall because the panels have foam insulation and steel studs with holes drilled for wiring and plumbing. The floor system secures the top of the foundation walls, and a concrete slab at the bottom resists the pressure of backfilling.

Floor framing anchors the top of the walls.

Holes punched for mudsill bolts

2-in.-wide galvanized-steel studs at 24 in. o.c.

1-in. EPS foam

2½-in. XPS foam

Add a dimple drain or spray-on membrane for additional waterproofing.

At 1¾ in. thick, the concrete face provides strength and water resistance.

Screw pressure-treated 1×4 to studs for screed board.

½-in.-dia. rebar inside each stud

A 4-in.-thick concrete slab anchors the bottom of the walls.

Compacted gravel base

Perimeter drain

½-in.-dia. rebar inside top and bottom beams

level. They'll compact it and level it again before setting the walls.

Factory Crew Sets the Walls

The walls are trucked to the site in sections that fit together nicely. Stainless-steel bolts hold the panels together, and urethane sealant keeps the joints watertight. Because the walls are precast and square, the gravel base must be perfectly flat and level. That's why the installers reshoot grade, repack the gravel, and re-level it all. The project featured here is a cabin on top of a mountain accessed by narrow roads, so the walls had to be transferred from a semi-truck to a couple of smaller dump trucks that could navigate the hill.

Starting in a corner, a crane lifts the walls into place. The installers plumb and brace the wall; then

the rest of the panels slide into place quickly, with no additional bracing required. I hope that my block mason isn't reading this because I've never had a masonry wall turn out as well or as fast. At the end of the day, the diagonal measurement was within ¼ in. of square.

Reinforcing the Foundation

Because this foundation is composed of sections, it's possible that the joint between each panel could fold like a hinge under the pressure of backfilling, so the tops and bottoms of the walls need to be reinforced. A slab locks the bottom of the wall, and the floor framing secures the top (see the drawing on p. 95).

Blocking details in the floor framing resist inward force on walls parallel to the floor joists; they're explained and illustrated in the "Builder Guideline Booklet" from Superior Walls. Longer walls might require shear walls to provide extra bracing, depending on how tall the walls are and how much backfill will be placed against them.

Superior Walls panels come in three standard heights: 8 ft. 2 in., 9 ft., and 10 ft. You also can order custom heights; however, the cost advantage begins to diminish for crawlspace and irregular foundation details. For this project, the manufacturer needed 3 weeks to 4 weeks of lead time after the plans were finalized, but that can vary depending on complexity, location, and time of year. The blueprints must be accurate, showing all point loads, window and door positions, and partition walls. Although you can change the backing for interior partition walls pretty easily in the field, point loads must be engineered into the wall panels.

Precast foundation systems probably won't become my standard operating procedure anytime soon, but I use them whenever I can. The speed, quality, and price are hard to beat. Two days after the hole is dug, I'm framing a floor. To me, that's priceless.

PREFAB VS. POURED OR BLOCK FOUNDATION

THE PREFAB FOUNDATION for this project cost $12,400 in 2006. By comparison, the estimated cost for a block foundation framed with 2×4s was about $11,000. However, when you account for the cost of insulating a block foundation with 2½ in. of foam, the price difference is a wash.

But there's more: I saved about a week of work, and job site cleanup was nothing but a trash bag full of empty urethane-sealant caulk tubes; no piles of broken block, empty soda cans, candy wrappers, or leftover concrete block to deal with.

A prefab foundation is best used where there is a full basement with a consistent sill height. Different wall heights slow the process, minimizing the cost benefit. Although a prefab system might not be the best choice all of the time, it makes a lot of sense some of the time.

GRAVEL DEPTH VARIES DEPENDING ON SOIL TYPE. In this case, the gravel footing is 4 in. thick. A perimeter drain is buried in the footing to direct groundwater away from the foundation. The pipe extends to the steep drop-off at the right edge of the photo.

A GAS-POWERED COMPACTOR is used along the perimeter of the foundation line. Because the foundation crew does the fine-tuning, the gravel needs to be within only 1 in. of level.

STARTING IN A CORNER, the crew aligns the first panel with a string line and then braces it plumb. No additional braces are needed because the corners stabilize the walls. Additional panels are set to the string and bolted together top and bottom.

ALL JOINTS ARE SEALED WITH URETHANE. Corner panels are mitered; the others butt together. The crew used Bostik Chem-Calk® polyurethane sealant (www.bostik-us.com) on all panel joints before bolting them together.

SOURCES

CARBONCAST®
Available in North America
866-462-5887
www.altusprecast.com

SUPERIOR WALLS
Available in eastern part of United
States and in some western states
800-452-9255
www.superiorwalls.com

THERMAL-KRETE®
Available in New York and
Pennsylvania
585-762-8216
www.kistner.com

SO FAR, SO GOOD. After three corners are set, the crew checks the work. As it turned out, the dimensions of the house were within $\frac{1}{8}$ in.

A CONCRETE SLAB ANCHORS THE BOTTOM OF THE WALLS. To brace the walls before backfilling, a slab is poured inside the walls; the floor framing secures the top. A pressure-treated 1×4 fastened around the inside perimeter acts as a screed and keeps concrete out of the wall cavities.

Slab Foundation for Cold Climates

BY ANDY ENGEL

Every builder knows that conventional footings must be placed lower than the deepest expected frost depth. My area's 42-in. frost depth is one reason slab foundations are rare and basements are common here; if you're digging that far down anyway, a full basement doesn't cost that much more. The exception is garages. A slab on grade is about the only economical way to build a floor you can park a truck on. Here in Connecticut, garages are typically built by excavating perimeter trenches to below frost depth, pouring concrete footings, and building concrete or CMU-block stemwalls atop the footings. The stemwalls are backfilled, and the soil inside the garage is compacted (or not, often enough). A layer of gravel is placed, followed by a plastic vapor barrier, and then a 4-in.-thick concrete slab is poured within the stemwalls. Sometimes a layer of foam insulation is placed between the gravel and the plastic.

However, the deep trenches create a fair amount of soil to get rid of, and the stemwall uses a lot of concrete. When I thought about building a garage next to my house, all of this was on my mind. Because I planned to do the work myself, the prospect of laying a block stemwall while stooped over in a trench also affected my thinking. My back resented that

kind of abuse even before my hair turned gray. There had to be a better way.

Insulate the Ground

I found an intriguing technique in the IRC known as a frost-protected shallow foundation. The idea behind this technique is that insulating the ground around a building keeps the earth below from freezing and negates the need to build concrete footings below frost depth. How far the foam has to extend depends on the climate zone. For that detail, the IRC references American Society of Civil Engineers (ASCE) document 32-01: *Design and Construction of Frost-Protected Shallow Foundations*.

However, the IRC includes this detail only for heated buildings, where heat leaking from the building keeps the ground below from freezing. My garage would be heated only intermittently, so the code would view it as unheated. But ASCE 32-01 provides more details than the IRC, including a way to build frost-protected shallow foundations for unheated buildings. The main difference between the details for a heated building and those for an unheated building is that the latter requires insulation below the slab as well as extending out from the building. Heat rising from the earth's core keeps the ground below the foam from freezing. Because I had

planned to insulate below the slab anyway, the only extra thing I'd have to do would be to extend that 2-in. layer of insulation about 4 ft. beyond the footing area. That seemed like a no-brainer, but I had to get it approved.

Absence from the IRC doesn't forbid the use of a detail. It just means that the applicant has to satisfy the local building official that the detail complies with the intent of the code. I talked to my town's building inspector and provided him with a copy of ASCE 32-01 along with my permit application. Based on that, he approved my plans as an alternative to the IRC. In the end, the extra gravel and foam outside the building cost about $1,500, a few hundred bucks less than I would have spent on blocks and mortar for the below-grade stemwall I didn't want to build.

Planning the Excavation

The ASCE design is a haunched, monolithic slab, where the integral slab and footings are poured at once. The perimeter footings would be 12 in. deep and 12 in. wide, sloping up at 45° on the inside from the bottom of the footing to the bottom of the slab. I made my slab 5 in. thick instead of the minimum 4 in. because I planned to park a 7,000-lb. tractor on it—that's about twice the weight of a typical car. Slabs and footings work by spreading loads out. Designers size footings to spread out the loads so that they're less per square foot (or square inch—the unit of measure doesn't matter) than the maximum the underlying material can support.

All other things being equal, thicker concrete is stronger concrete because compression loads spread outward in a cone shape at about a 45° angle. Consequently, the thicker a slab or footing, the larger the area that the load spreads over. For example, a point load on a 4-in.-thick slab spreads over about 50 sq. in., whereas one on a 5-in.-thick slab spreads over about 78 sq. in. That's more than a 50% increase in bearing from 25% more concrete. Width factors in too, of course. Because of how the loads propagate out at 45°, footings are usually designed to be twice as wide as they are deep.

I had to include additional footings in three spots to support column loads from the second floor and in one spot to support a masonry chimney. Like the perimeter footings, these footings were also haunched, avoiding sharp corners that would be more likely to crack the slab. The slab and footings would rest on 2-in.-thick rigid foam. Below the foam would be 6 in. of ¾-in. clean gravel to promote drainage and to ease leveling.

To determine the depth of the excavation, I decided where I wanted the top of the slab to be in relation to the elevation of the driveway, then I used a backhoe to dig out the depth of the concrete (either 12 in. or 5 in. below the driveway top, depending on whether that spot was footing or slab), plus 2 in. for the foam and 6 in. for the gravel. The deepest dig was around the perimeter and was 20 in. lower than the driveway elevation. Starting at the same elevation as the perimeter footings, I dug a little more than 4 ft. beyond them to accommodate the exterior foam and gravel, sloping this area about ¼ in. per foot away from the building for drainage. The whole dig's center was left elevated, shaped like a low, truncated pyramid. Next, I dug for the column and chimney footings, and trenched for the underslab utilities. With the conduits and pipes laid and inspected, I backfilled and compacted those trenches, then compacted the entire excavated area.

Stone and Foam Keep the Ground Dry and Warm

After finishing the excavation, I laid 6-ft.-wide filter fabric around the edge, with about 3 ft. of the fabric inside the hole. On top of that at the outside of the excavation went 4-in. perforated pipe, which connects to solid pipe draining to daylight. Then I spread 6 in. of ¾-in. clean gravel in the excavation, rough-leveling it with the backhoe. I folded the exposed fabric over the edge of the gravel to keep dirt from washing in along the edge.

Because the gravel's top surface had to be flat to fully support the foam below the foundation, fine-tuning it there was fussy work. I used rakes, a builder's level, and my son Kevin. We checked the elevation within the building area every couple of feet.

Using batter boards and string to outline the perimeter of the foundation, I laid the foam out on the gravel, following the contours of the truncated pyramid. I made long cuts with a tablesaw and short ones with a handsaw. Spray foam sealed any big gaps, and rocks and lumber set on top of the foam kept the sheets from blowing away.

Poplar Makes Cheap Forms

For the forms, I bought green, roughsawn 5/4 by 12-in. poplar from a local sawmill for about half the cost of 2×12 boards. Some of it I ripped into 4-in. ribs to strengthen and straighten the forms. Forming was simple—I just outlined the slab perimeter with the poplar. Using strings to be sure the forms were straight, I braced them about every 4 ft. to stakes driven into the dirt at the edge of the excavation. This was overkill, but if you've ever heard the awful cracking sound a form filled with wet concrete makes when it lets go, you know overkill is the way to do it. Once the forms were up, I covered the foam with 6-mil plastic.

The ASCE document called for two rows of #4 rebar in the footings, and I added a rebar grid to reinforce the slab. I laid this out before the pour, then cut and bent the pieces as needed. I placed the pieces in the concrete as the pour progressed so there would be less to trip on as my helpers and I placed and screeded the concrete. Where two pieces of rebar meet, they should overlap by at least 16 bar diameters. The diameter of #4 rebar is ½ in., so I overlapped the pieces at least 8 in.

FOUNDATIONS HAVE LAYERS

The bottom layer is the ground, stripped of organic soil, shaped to mirror the bottom of the planned slab, then compacted. Next is a layer of ¾-in. gravel, which is followed by the extruded polystyrene (XPS) foam. Atop the foam is a 6-mil plastic sheet that serves as a vapor barrier.

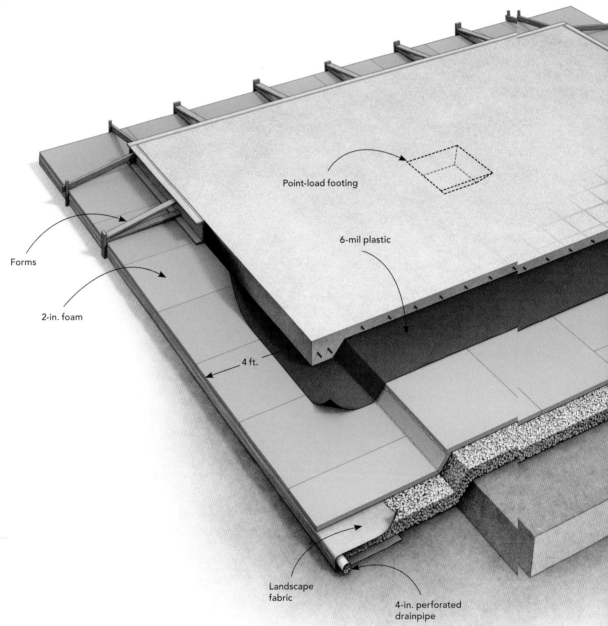

Point-load footing

6-mil plastic

Forms

2-in. foam

4 ft.

Landscape fabric

4-in. perforated drainpipe

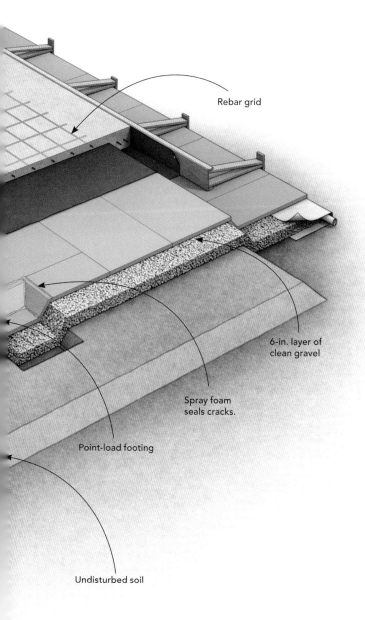

Rebar grid

6-in. layer of
clean gravel

Spray foam
seals cracks.

Point-load footing

Undisturbed soil

CALCULATING GRAVEL

GRAVEL IS USUALLY SOLD by the ton, and it weighs about 1.5 tons per yard. Simply calculate the cubic yards of gravel needed and multiply that by 1.5 to determine the tonnage. Gravel orders are approximate; expect to receive and to pay for a bit more than you order.

GRAVELED AND READY FOR FOAM. Strings between batter boards define the foundation perimeter. Conduit for electrical and phone lines is in the front, while stubs for plumbing stick up in the back. Perimeter drains are visible along the right.

No Different from Pouring Any Other Slab

Concrete is available in a variety of strengths, with 2,500 psi being the code minimum for residential footings. For a few dollars more per yard, I ordered 3,500 psi. Because the garage would be unheated much of the time, I also ordered air-entrainment, which introduces tiny air bubbles into the mix and reduces the chance of spalling caused by freeze/thaw cycles. That would be more important for a driveway than for an interior slab, but it cost only a buck a yard more.

I always schedule concrete for a slab for first thing in the morning. If it's cold, you have all day for it to set up. If it's hot, you do the hardest work in the coolest part of the day. After finishing the slab, I covered the new concrete with plastic. To develop concrete's full strength, it must be kept wet for as long as the chemical reaction between the portland cement and the water that causes it to cure continues. The curing slows as the reaction consumes the components, so the period soonest after the pour is the most important. If the slab dries out, the reaction stops permanently. Keeping it wet for even a day helps, and 28 days is ideal, if unrealistic in terms of construction schedules. I covered this slab for 2 weeks, flooding below the plastic with water each day.

Concrete always cracks. One solution is to cut it with a saw into sections about 10 ft. sq., with the kerf depth about one-quarter the thickness of the slab. These cuts weaken the slab so that it cracks along them and not randomly. Saw cuts look deliberate, and no one questions them. Cracks look like a defect, although they aren't necessarily a structural problem. Cracking can happen early in the cure as water evaporates and the slab shrinks, or as temperature swings cause movement. Also, uncured concrete is easier to cut than cured material. So the day after the pour, I made the cuts with a diamond blade in a circular saw. To keep dirt out of the kerfs, I sealed them with polyurethane caulk.

So that I could backfill against the garage high enough to slope the ground away for drainage and to cover the exterior foam with the required minimum of 10 in. of soil, I laid three courses of block atop the outside of the slab. To tie the block and the slab together, I had set L-shaped pieces of rebar every 6 ft. before the concrete set. I laid the blocks so that the rebar ran up through their cores. After grouting these cores, I set the foundation bolts in the grout. I installed 1-in. rigid foam outside this wall—extending to the bottom of the footings—and then covered it with expanded wire lath and two coats of portland-cement plaster.

Since pouring the slab, we've had several winters with below-zero temperatures (including one February when it got above freezing for only 8 hours). The framing has stayed plumb and level, and there are no cracks in the block walls or the slab. All told, the foundation is performing as expected. Plus, because I avoided laying block in a trench, I'm still able to walk upright.

LAYING DOWN FOAM IS DIRT SIMPLE. Make sure the foam fully contacts the gravel. Foam sheets don't need to fit tightly. Gaps can be filled with scrap pieces and spray foam.

CONCRETE DAY. Screed guides made from 2×s run the length of the foundation, breaking the 28-ft.-wide slab into narrower sections that can be screeded easily. The guides are pulled out as the pour progresses, and their trenches are shoveled full of concrete.

BUILD ON TOP OF FOAM? ARE YOU CRAZY?

THE COMPRESSIVE STRENGTH of the XPS foam I used is 25 psi. That works out to 3,600 lb. per sq. ft. (psf). The default bearing capacity of soil in the IRC, which I used to calculate footing sizes, is 1,500 psf. In essence, the foam has more than twice the assumed bearing capacity of the earth below. Foam comes in a variety of densities, so check with the manufacturer to be sure that what you use can handle the load. Calculating the amount of foam I needed was simple: length × width = sq. ft. of foam. Dividing that by 32 sq. ft. (the size of a 4×8 sheet of foam) gives the number of sheets.

CALCULATING CONCRETE

DETERMINING HOW MANY YARDS of concrete to order is usually a simple volume calculation, but the haunches added some complexity. I mentally broke the slab into pieces to figure the volume, then added an extra yard to be sure. Running short of concrete results in cold joints and finishing trouble. The $112 for that extra yard was cheap insurance.

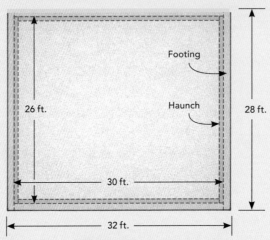

THE FOOTINGS
Figure the 12-in.-wide by 12-in.-deep footing section. Its combined length is 116 ft.
1 ft. × 1 ft. × 116 ft. = **116 cu. ft.**

THE SLAB
The slab measures 26 ft. × 30 ft. × 5 in.
26 ft. × 30 ft. × $^5/_{12}$ ft. = **325 cu. ft.**

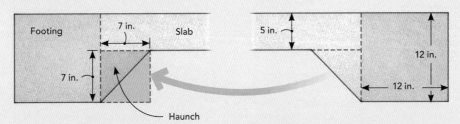

THE HAUNCHES
The haunches measure 7 in. on each leg and are about 112 ft. long. Rather than figure the volume of a triangle, combine the two triangles into a rectangular section that's half the total length.
$^7/_{12}$ ft. × $^7/_{12}$ ft. × 56 ft. = **19 cu. ft.**

THE TOTAL CUBIC YARDAGE*
116 cu. ft. + 325 cu. ft. + 19 cu. ft. = 460 cu. ft. To find cubic yards, divide cubic feet by 27.
460 ÷ 27 = **about 17 cu. yd.**

*The point-load footings used in this project are not typical and so are not included here.

Superinsulated Slab

BY STEVE BACZEK

When you're dealing with a Passive House design, the insulation levels must be proportionate. It doesn't make sense to invest in heavy insulation for the walls and the attic if you aren't going to insulate the floor to the same level. The performance of critical components—thermal insulation, air-sealing materials, mechanicals, and windows and doors—should improve as a group, not just individually.

Given the location of this project (Falmouth, Massachusetts) and the amount of insulation we chose for the rest of the structure, the energy modeling done during the design stage told us that we needed about R-50 worth of insulation in the floor system. Although that may seem like a lot, it's in harmony with the rest of the house: It's just over 50% of the R-value in the walls and 30% of the R-value in the attic.

Because this house was built on a slab, I relied on layers of rigid foam set below the concrete to reach my required level of insulation. Of the three commonly available types of rigid insulation—polyisocyanurate (polyiso), extruded polystyrene (XPS), and expanded polystyrene (EPS), I chose EPS for its reliability below grade and its low environmental impact.

Although the plans showed this subslab insulation built up in 2-in. layers, the builder was able to source thicker 4-in. and 6-in. panels, which sped up the installation. When it comes to the foam under the slab, you don't need to worry as much about air movement complicating the issue. In this case, the concrete is the air barrier, so R-value is R-value, and whether you achieve the desired number by stacking five layers of 2-in. foam or using a layer of 6-in. foam followed by a layer of 4-in. foam as was done here, the result is the same.

Limit the Chinks in Your Thermal and Air-Sealing Armor

With any building project that sets a high bar for energy efficiency, the air-sealing and thermal barriers should be continuous. That means you should be able to look at the building plans and trace the barrier continuously around the entire structure from footings to attic. In doing so, you can highlight weak spots in a structure's outer shell.

One spot that is typically overlooked is the edge of the slab. On this project, rather than just insulating under the slab, I designed the foundation so that the subslab insulation wraps around the edges and then is connected to the spray-foam wall insulation. This seamless transition of insulation materials allows for total thermal isolation of the interior of the house.

Likewise, to minimize the potential for short circuits in the underslab airtightness and thermal performance, the plumbing and electrical systems were laid out so that only the necessary pipes and conduits run under the floor. The electricians and plumbers responsible for these installations gave prior approval to the plan, including carefully planned entrances into and exits from the house, all of which were strictly enforced.

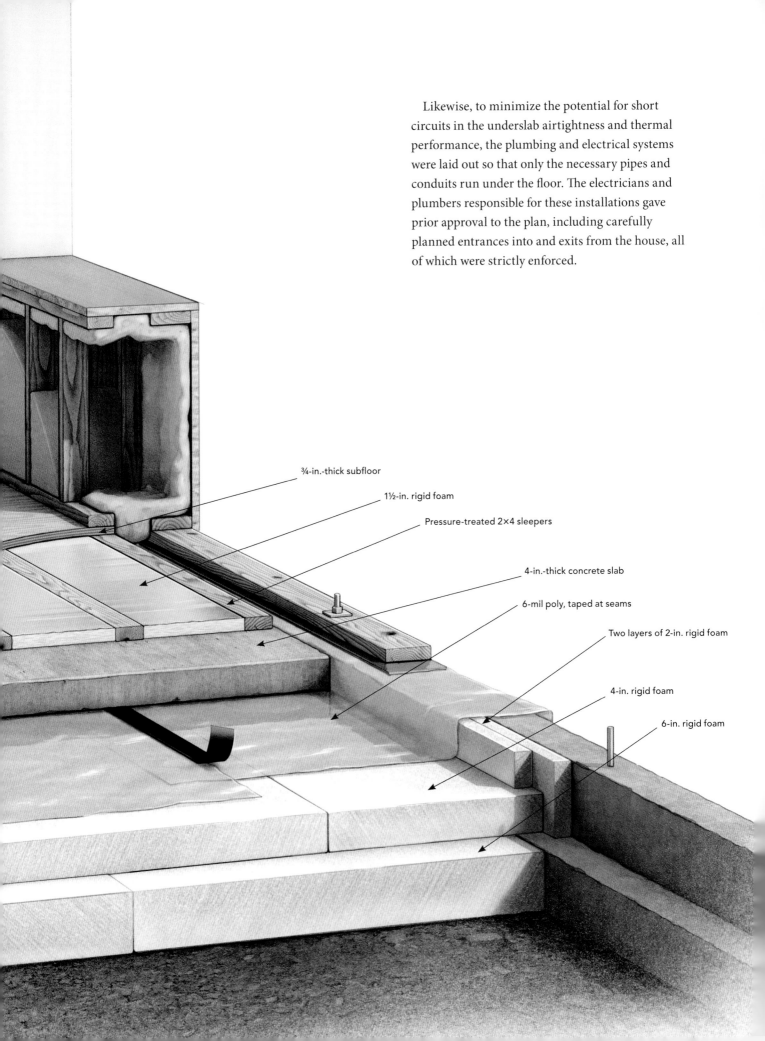

¾-in.-thick subfloor

1½-in. rigid foam

Pressure-treated 2×4 sleepers

4-in.-thick concrete slab

6-mil poly, taped at seams

Two layers of 2-in. rigid foam

4-in. rigid foam

6-in. rigid foam

THICK FOAM MEANS NEW TECHNIQUES. Because the dense foam panels are too thick to be cut with a tablesaw or circular saw, the builders rely on a reciprocating saw with a 12-in. coarse-tooth blade for making crosscuts, rip cuts, and notches.

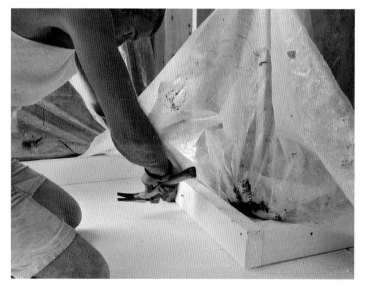

DRILL FROM BOTH SIDES. When you need to drill holes for pipes and other penetrations in the thick foam, a standard spade bit or hole saw won't be long enough. Instead, use a long bellhanger-style drill bit to bore a pilot hole all the way through the foam. Then, using a standard spade bit, widen the pilot hole from both sides of the panel. For holes of a larger diameter, skip the drill bits and go right for the reciprocating saw.

TACK ON THE EDGE. The innermost pieces of perimeter foam come last and act as the screed level for the concrete slab. After applying a bead of spray foam to the outer perimeter foam, a worker tacks the inside pieces to that first layer of foam with nails every few feet to keep them from shifting until the spray foam sets up.

DETAILING PIPES AND PERS. Roughing in mechanicals 14 in. below the level of the mudsill, especially with the pitches of drains and the sweeping curves of continuous runs of PEX tubing, can be challenging. The builders are left with a few drainpipes peeking above grade and some supply lines that angle up and through both layers of foam. To lay the foam over the pipes, they use a reciprocating saw to cut a V-notch in the underside of some panels. For the sweeping supply lines, they make oversize cutouts to slide the panels into place. Expanding foam seals up the remaining voids.

ABOVE: TAPE TO AVOID ICEBERGS. After laying out the poly vapor retarder over the foam base, the inner flap of the poly that was installed as part of the mudsill assembly is folded down and taped along all edges. This taped seam prevents concrete from getting under the foam panels and causing them to float—a hard-learned lesson from one of the architect's previous projects.

GRADE DOWN FROM ABOVE. As the pour progresses, the concrete crew uses a reference stick placed against the ceiling joists to establish the surface of the slab. Working in a small area, the crew adds or removes concrete until the stick just brushes the surface. The area is then marked with an X and used as a reference when screeding the slab surrounding it.

INSULATED SUBFLOOR. Using powder-actuated nails, the builders fasten pressure-treated 2×4 sleepers to the slab at 16 in. on center. To increase the overall R-value of the floor system, they fit pieces of rigid foam between the sleepers and fill remaining gaps with expanding foam. Finally, they fasten the ¾-in. subfloor.

It's Time to Consider Helical-Pile Footings

BY JEREMY HESS

After almost 20 years in construction, I became a dealer for Techno Metal Post™ (TMP), a helical-pile manufacturer. Helical piles can be driven almost anywhere, install in minutes, don't make a mess, and come in sizes that can support an enormous variety of structures. Since becoming a dealer, I've installed piles to support decks, porches, boardwalks across wetlands, industrial equipment, and business signs; to shore up failing house footings; and to underpin concrete slabs that were settling. Some of the machines used to drive the piles are small enough to be used inside a house—for example, to add a footing to a basement. It is not uncommon for my helper and me to pull up to a job site first thing in the morning, install 10 or 12 piles for a large deck, and leave by mid-afternoon with no evidence of our having been there besides the piles themselves.

Helical piles are essentially large steel screws that thread into the ground to serve as footings, and they have been in use since the early 1830s. The machines used to drive the modern versions come in many sizes, from the walk-behind machine I use to versions that are mounted on excavators. All of them work pretty much the same way. A gas or diesel engine drives a hydraulic pump that provides the power to spin the pile into the ground.

The first project I ever did—a 30-ft. by 80-ft. deck for a winery—exemplifies some advantages of helical piles. The original design called for concrete footings. However, because the deck was to be built over uncompacted fill, those footings needed to be 14 ft. deep to reach bearing soil. The owner almost abandoned the project after finding that concrete footings would cost $20,000. I was able to save him $8,000 with helical piles. And even on the steep slope of that site, the installation took a couple of days instead of a week.

When you account for all the costs of conventional footings, helical piles are surprisingly affordable. Consider these costs: renting an auger or hiring an excavator (or the time it takes to dig by hand), removing spoils from the excavation, and repairing site damage from heavy equipment. If the concrete will come from a truck, how will it be moved to the hole? How do you know that the soil will support the structure? And what about weather issues? Helical piles overcome all of these concerns. Although pricing for piles can vary widely based on availability, contractor, and location, my company can install four piles for a typical residential deck for $600 to $900.

Although there are other helical-pile installers, most don't focus on residential work like TMP does. That said, you may have a local contractor who

KEEP IT PLUMB. Because of soil obstructions and the way the machine's geometry changes as the boom lowers, the operator needs to make regular adjustments to plumb the pile.

does residential work using other manufacturers' products. Many of the advantages I discuss here are common among manufacturers.

What Are Helical Piles?

A helical pile consists of three main parts. The shaft is either a hollow square bar, a solid square bar, or a hollow pipe. The helix is a deformed round plate resembling a section of screw thread that is welded to the bottom of the shaft. Once the pile is installed, a cap attached to the top of the shaft connects the structure to the pile.

The first section of shaft with the helix is referred to as the lead section. The length of the lead section varies by manufacturer and application, but it's typically between 5 ft. and 7 ft. For greater depths, extensions are added as necessary. Extensions are just shafts without a helix that are welded or bolted to the installed pile. In poor soils, additional lead sections with their helices sometimes are added to improve bearing.

The size of the helix used is determined by a number of factors, but the load to be carried and the soil type are the main considerations. In soft soils, a larger helix is needed to spread the load over a wider area. In rocky or very dense soils, a smaller helix is typically used. Most helical-pile manufacturers offer helix sizes ranging from 6 in. dia. to 24 in. dia. The helix sizes my company uses in residential work range from 6 in. to 12 in., but we've used helices as large as 18 in. when working in very soft ground. Larger sizes are available but are used typically in heavy commercial or industrial applications.

Every helical-pile manufacturer has its own selection of pile caps for attaching to wood, concrete, and steel. Typical pile-to-wood connections are made through U-brackets or flat plates. Usually called heads, they either are fixed, meaning there is no adjustment after installation, or are adjustable by means of a threaded stalk so that the elevation may be fine-tuned. Heads used to support slabs and grade beams are flat plates with short pieces of rebar attached. Custom heads can be made for attaching almost anything imaginable.

NO MESS

THE HELIX SIMPLY THREADS into the ground, leaving virtually no surface disturbance.

Piles Can Last a Lifetime or Longer

Helical piles are made of either black steel or hot-dipped galvanized steel. Used properly, both should last several lifetimes. I generally install galvanized piles for decks, boardwalks, light posts, or other applications where the shaft is exposed. (People don't like to see rust.) For grade beams, foundation repairs, and other applications where the pile will be encased in concrete or buried deeply, I typically use black steel. When the piles are buried or encased in concrete, air can't get to them as easily, so corrosion isn't as much of a concern. However, some local codes require all steel in the ground to be galvanized.

Additional corrosion-protection systems can be used if clients request it. In places where piles are to support a whole building, the extra peace of mind from the corrosion protection can be considered cheap. There are both passive and active systems. Passive systems use magnesium anodes that attach to the piles and work the same way a sacrificial anode does on a boat or buried propane tank—that is, the anode corrodes first, leaving the steel intact. Eventually, though, oxidation will consume a sacrificial anode. An active kind of corrosion-protection system known as an impressed-current system works by connecting all the piles in a foundation and passing a small electrical current through them to prevent corrosion.

Verifiable Bearing Capacity

The capacity of an installed pile depends on its size and on the soil. Dense, gravely soils generally have a much higher bearing capacity than clay or sand. To carry greater loads, piles may need to have additional lengths of shaft so that they can be driven deeper to reach better soils. Helical piles have excellent uplift resistance because the soil above the helix is not disturbed. As a rule of thumb, uplift resistance is one half of compression resistance.

One of the chief benefits of helical piles is that the installer can verify the capacity of the installed pile. Building codes cover helical piles, but most inspec-tors haven't dealt with them in person. Inspectors may be skeptical, but once they learn about the product and see engineer-stamped documentation of the bearing capacity, they become receptive. When a building department requires an installation report, I submit a sketch of the footprint of the structure, the pile layout, and the installation data for each pile to our engineer. He reviews the building loads and the pile data to verify that the pile will support the design weight. He then stamps and signs this report and submits it to the building department.

Accurate Placement

Rocks did not prevent the installation of any of the hundreds of piles my company set last year, although they made a few jobs difficult. Except for in very rocky soils, a pile can be installed within ¼ in. of its designed location and made plumb in all directions. A skilled installer can manipulate the pile around rocks the size of a basketball. Smaller rocks are no more than an inconvenience.

In soils with larger rocks, helical piles are a little more challenging to place accurately. A boulder may have to be removed with a backhoe, or the pile may need to be relocated. Sometimes, though, I've been able to attach a cable winch between the boom of the pile machine and a stationary object to steer a pile through very rocky soils.

If a pile lands on ledge or on a large rock that is below the frost line, and if lateral stability is achieved through the framing of the structure and not the soil's resistance to pile movement, it may be fine to rest the pile on top of the rock. This situation requires hammer testing the pile to be sure it won't sink once the structure is built and is generally an option only for light structures such as decks and sunrooms.

Winter doesn't have to halt construction. Helical piles can be installed in frozen ground. To do that, I drill a hole through the frost with an electric demolition hammer. Then I insert a 3,000w electric heater into the hole. It takes 10 minutes to 15 minutes to thaw enough ground to install a pile.

LEFT: VERIFYING A PILE'S BEARING CAPACITY. There are two ways to verify bearing: a high-tech approach based on hydraulic pressure and a low-tech approach that involves whacking the pile with a sledgehammer. Hydraulic pressure equates to torque and bearing capacity. The more torque needed to drive a pile, the greater its bearing capacity. Think of a wood screw. The harder it is to spin the screw into the wood, the harder it will be to pry the screw out or to hammer it farther in.

BELOW LEFT: THE LOW-TECH APPROACH. An alternative test measures how far the pile sinks under impact loads. Slick soils such as wet clay don't require much torque to drive a pile, and when the pile is stopped by ledge rock, torque ceases to be a factor. In those cases, a benchmark is made on the shaft using a laser level and a permanent marker.

BELOW RIGHT: SWING LIKE JOHN HENRY. A steel bumper placed in the shaft is hit hard with a sledge, and the benchmark is checked against the level to see if the pile went down. Depending on how far it sinks, up to 5,000 lb. of bearing can be assumed.

GO-ANYWHERE MACHINES

HELICAL PILES ARE VERSATILE, and the smaller machines can even retrofit footings inside an existing house.

JACKING UP A HOUSE

OVER A BANK

IN A KITCHEN

ON LAKE ICE

STABILIZING HOUSE FOOTINGS

IN WETLANDS

SOURCES

Most helical-pile installers are regional, but you can find links to multiple contractors at these websites.
www.helicalpileworld.com
www.myfoundationsolutions.com

WHERE THE METAL HITS THE WOOD. Providing bearing and uplift resistance is only half the battle. You also need to attach the helical pile to the structure, and that requires some kind of cap. A welded connection between the head and the pile transfers lateral and uplift loads from the structure to the pile.

SADDLE UP. This U-shaped bracket makes a stout attachment for a deck beam.

ADJUSTABLE HEIGHT. In some jurisdictions, a threaded stalk can be used to fine-tune the height of column bases.

HOLD THE HOUSE DOWN. Steel plates are lined up and welded to the piles. The vertical legs provide attachment for perimeter beams.

Waterproofing

Keep Your Basement Dry with a Curtain Drain

BY ERIC NELSON

When it comes to unwanted moisture in the basement, an ounce of prevention is worth many gallons of cure. That's why I start solving basement water problems by looking at grade, gutters, and foundation cracks. Grade should be pitched away from the house. Gutters should be clean and should channel water away from the house. Foundation cracks should be repaired with mortar or masonry sealant. If you still have water problems, think about where the water is coming from: groundwater seeping up or surface water seeping down. For high water tables, an internal drain with a sump pump could be the answer. For runoff, a curtain drain is a great low-tech solution.

A curtain drain is a trench filled with gravel and a perforated pipe to channel water away from the house; line the ditch with filter fabric to increase its longevity. I avoid generic landscape weed-blocking fabrics, opting instead for a high-quality product such as Typar® landscape fabric (www.typargeo synthetics.com). Don't overlap the ends of the fabric close to the pipe. Instead, line the ditch sides with fabric, then fold the fabric over the gravel a few inches below the surface. Fine aggregate, such as silt, will be prevented from sifting down deep into the curtain drain and eventually clogging the pipe.

As long as you're digging up the yard, consider laying gutter drains in the same ditch, but don't connect gutter drains to the perforated pipe. Instead, run gutter pipe alongside the curtain drain. And don't gamble with your safety; call 811 (www.call811.com) before you dig to find out where utilities lines are buried.

It's Like a Gutter for the Foundation

When installed correctly, a curtain drain can intercept surface runoff and groundwater before it gets to the foundation. The water flows into a gravel-filled ditch that contains a perforated pipe pitched to promote good drainage. The ditch should be 18 in. to 24 in. deep and slope downhill. Terminate the drain in an area where flowing water won't create problems. Lining the ditch with filter fabric helps keep the pipe clean so that the drain works maintenance free for a long time.

Rigid 4-in. PVC perforated pipe is available in 10-ft. lengths; the straight and bell ends are glued together with PVC primer and cement, and laid with the bell end facing uphill. The 3,000-lb. crush strength meets almost all needs. For under-road or under-driveway applications, use SDR-35 sewer pipe.

Flexible black plastic is less expensive than rigid PVC. Available in rolls with specialized fittings, flexible pipe is easy to work with, but not as tough as PVC. Be careful not to crush the pipe with rocks while backfilling. If you use flexible black-plastic pipe, don't clear clogs with a power snake or you could destroy the pipe.

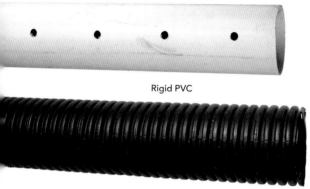

Rigid PVC

Flexible black plastic

CLEANOUTS CAN PREVENT A BIG HEADACHE

IT'S A GOOD IDEA TO THINK AHEAD to the day when the drainpipe becomes clogged with some type of debris. If you use sanitary tees in the corners and add wye fittings in long runs (and mark them or photograph them), you'll be able to blast the system out with a power snake, which saves a lot of digging and pipe replacement.

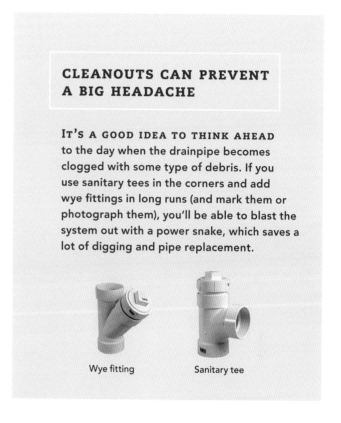

Wye fitting

Sanitary tee

USE A LEVEL TO MAKE SURE THE TRENCH ISN'T. The trench should slope away from the center point to prevent puddling. Don't overdig because backfilling with uncompacted soil causes settling and low spots.

SET THE PIPE IN A BED OF GRAVEL. Filter fabric lines the trench to keep silty sediment from clogging the pipe. You can adjust the pitch of the ditch before laying the pipe by varying the thickness of the gravel layer.

KEEP THE FABRIC NEAR THE SURFACE. The top layer of filter fabric eventually clogs. If that top layer is close to the pipe, you'll have to do a lot of digging to fix the problem. By folding the fabric over the gravel a few inches below the surface, you leave it accessible.

TOP THE TRENCH WITH GRAVEL. For a better look, you can buy decorative gravel that matches the landscape for the top layer. Where the underlying pipe is nonperforated (beyond the curtain drain and into the bulk-water removal), you can skip the top layer of gravel and plant grass.

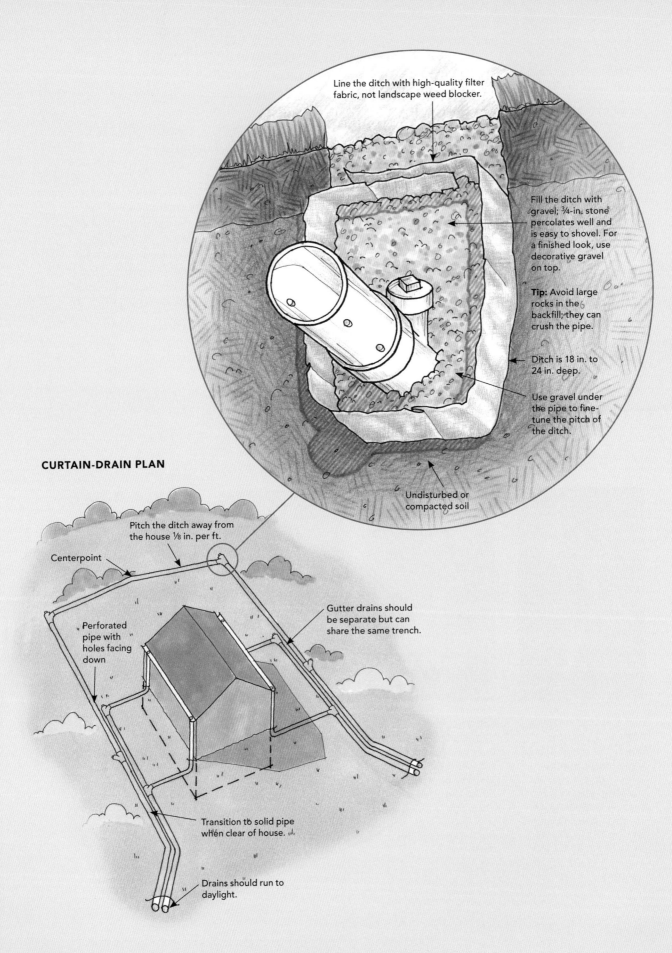

Line the ditch with high-quality filter fabric, not landscape weed blocker.

Fill the ditch with gravel; ¾-in. stone percolates well and is easy to shovel. For a finished look, use decorative gravel on top.

Tip: Avoid large rocks in the backfill; they can crush the pipe.

Ditch is 18 in. to 24 in. deep.

Use gravel under the pipe to fine-tune the pitch of the ditch.

Undisturbed or compacted soil

CURTAIN-DRAIN PLAN

Pitch the ditch away from the house ⅛ in. per ft.

Centerpoint

Perforated pipe with holes facing down

Gutter drains should be separate but can share the same trench.

Transition to solid pipe when clear of house.

Drains should run to daylight.

Details for a Dry Foundation

BY WILLIAM B. ROSE

As a research architect at the Building Research Council of the University of Illinois, I am paid to solve some of the more nagging problems that houses have. Frequently, I visit troubled houses, and the most common problem I encounter is poor drainage away from the foundation. This problem became worse as wetlands were developed; I know what to expect when the name of the development is Frog Hollow.

I was once asked to look at a house that had settling problems. An addition, built over a crawlspace, was moving down relative to the main house. The dirt floor of the crawlspace was even with the bottom of the footing. The soil along the edge of the footing was in small clumps, unlike the grainy, gritty surface of the rest of the floor. I dug away at the clumps, and my fingers hit air. I dug a little more and found a space that reminded me of a prison escape tunnel. In all, 10 ft. of the footing was undermined.

Water from a downspout draining too near the corner of the house and the addition was the culprit. The water was taking the path of least resistance to the footing drain and sump pump in the basement of the main part of the house. That path happened to be under the addition's footing. By following that path, the runoff had washed away the ground under the footing and caused the addition to settle.

Bad Drainage Can Cause a Raft of Problems

I call my studies of the zone where the house meets the ground *building periodontics*. Proper preventative care of this area can avoid a variety of problems, some less obvious and a lot more serious than a damp cellar.

For example, a common problem in basements, particularly those with block walls, is inward buckling. This usually shows up as a horizontal crack one or two blocks below grade, or at windowsills, stepping up or down at the corners. A study I did with the Illinois State Geological Survey revealed the cause. Clay soils shrink during dry spells, forming a crevice between the soil and the foundation wall. Wind and light rains carry dirt into this crevice. Then, when seasonal rains come, the soil swells back to its original dimension, plus the increment of added soil. Over time, the wall is ratcheted inward and eventually buckles. You avoid this problem by keeping the soil next to the foundation dry.

Slabs suffer from water problems, too. Garage floors, for example, commonly crack at outside corners near where gutters drain. This cracking may be due to upward expansion of water directly below the corner. It can also be due to adhesion lifting of the perimeter wall, a situation occurring when saturated

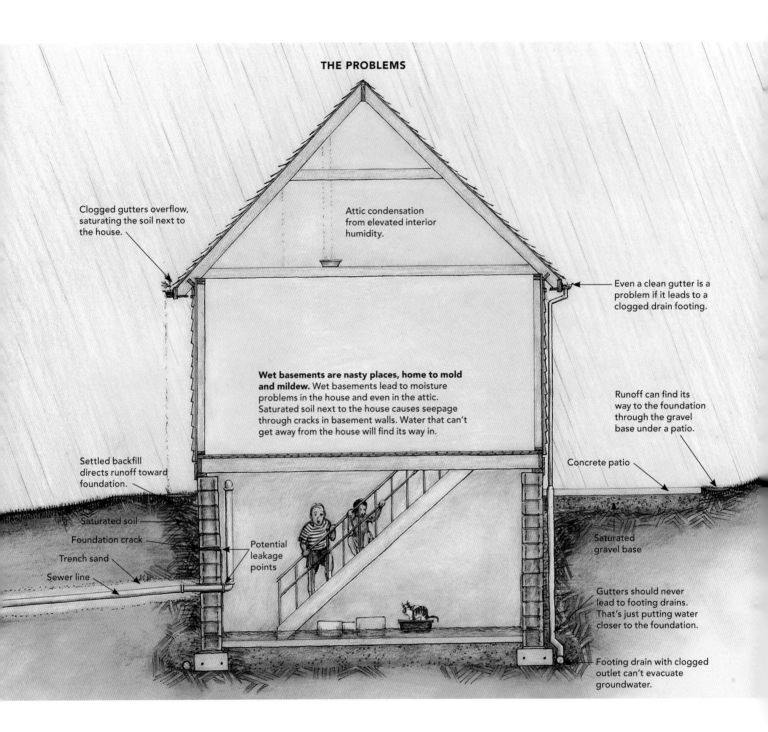

Clogged gutters overflow, saturating the soil next to the house.

Attic condensation from elevated interior humidity.

Even a clean gutter is a problem if it leads to a clogged drain footing.

Wet basements are nasty places, home to mold and mildew. Wet basements lead to moisture problems in the house and even in the attic. Saturated soil next to the house causes seepage through cracks in basement walls. Water that can't get away from the house will find its way in.

Runoff can find its way to the foundation through the gravel base under a patio.

Settled backfill directs runoff toward foundation.

Concrete patio

Saturated soil

Foundation crack

Trench sand

Sewer line

Potential leakage points

Saturated gravel base

Gutters should never lead to footing drains. That's just putting water closer to the foundation.

Footing drain with clogged outlet can't evacuate groundwater.

soil freezes fast to the foundation wall (see "Saturated Soil Leads to Frost Heaving" on p. 129). The soil nearest the surface is the first to freeze, and as the cold weather continues, deeper soil freezes. This saturated soil expands by 8% as it freezes, exerting a tremendous force that lifts the soil frozen to the wall above. The wall lifts and cracks the slab.

Moisture damage around foundations isn't limited to masonry problems. In 1947, Ralph Britton, the government researcher whose work led to the current attic-ventilation standards, showed that water vapor traveling upward from damp foundations caused most attic moisture problems. He concluded that if attics were isolated from wet

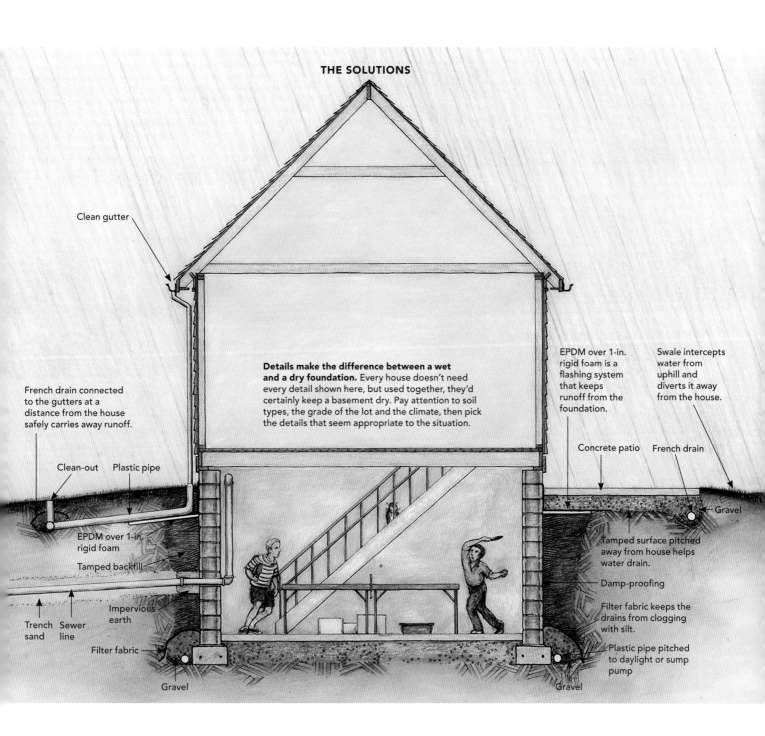

Clean gutter

French drain connected to the gutters at a distance from the house safely carries away runoff.

Clean-out Plastic pipe

EPDM over 1-in. rigid foam

Tamped backfill

Impervious earth

Trench Sewer
sand line

Filter fabric

Gravel

Details make the difference between a wet and a dry foundation. Every house doesn't need every detail shown here, but used together, they'd certainly keep a basement dry. Pay attention to soil types, the grade of the lot and the climate, then pick the details that seem appropriate to the situation.

EPDM over 1-in. rigid foam is a flashing system that keeps runoff from the foundation.

Swale intercepts water from uphill and diverts it away from the house.

Concrete patio French drain

Gravel

Tamped surface pitched away from house helps water drain.

Damp-proofing

Filter fabric keeps the drains from clogging with silt.

Plastic pipe pitched to daylight or sump pump

Gravel

foundations, the standard 1:300 venting ratio could be reduced to 1:3,000.

First, Pinpoint the Trouble Spots

Let's take a walk around an imaginary house and study the sources of its foundation water problems (see "The Problems" on the facing page). We easily spot the first one: The front gutters are clogged. Been clogged for so long, in fact, that saplings are sprouting in the composted leaves. Rainwater overflows these gutters, causing the ground below to settle. A small crater has developed, and its contents have nowhere to drain but down and into the cellar.

The gutters at the back of the house, however, are clean. The leader feeds into an underground drain that goes . . . where? Walking downhill, we find an outlet pipe at about the right elevation to be a footing drain. Composting leaves and granules from asphalt shingles clog the corrugated pipe. Might the water that should flow from this pipe be ending up in the basement?

A concrete patio, probably poured on a sand or gravel base, extends off the back of the house. A shallow depression next to the patio's edge collects a pool of runoff. This collected water will drain down the path of least resistance—through the gravel, under the patio and down the foundation wall.

Going into the basement, we find leaks in places that confirm our observations. There is also a leak where the sewer line exits the house, indicating that water is flowing into the house through the sand in which the sewer line is laid.

Timing can provide clues to the source of leaks. If they occur in a matter of hours after a rain, the problem is surface water. If leaks follow a day or so after a rain, a rising water table is likely the cause.

Know Your Soil

As I write this, I am sitting in the middle of the Midwest. The soil here is Drummer silty clay loam, great for agriculture, murder on construction. The available water capacity is about 20%. This means that if I had 5 cu. in. of dry soil, adding 1 cu. in. of water would saturate it. Being clay, the soil will swell as I add water. The permeability is about 1 in./hour. This means that any layer of rain will need an hour to get through a horizontal layer of soil 1 in. thick. That's really slow. From these numbers, I can estimate that a 1-in. rain will saturate 5 in. of soil and take 5 hours for full penetration.

That's useful information. It is from the U. S. Department of Agriculture's county soil survey, available from your county cooperative extension service agent. It allows a builder to estimate how much vertical water penetration there will be and how much of the rain runoff must be treated as sheet flow on the surface. This information matters a lot more on flat lots than on sloped ones, but it can still be important on the uphill side of sloping sites.

The perc test for septic systems is also a good predictor of how well the soil drains. If your soils have a good percolation rate, say, 10 in./hour to 15 in./hour, to below the bottom of your footings, you may not have to do much to ensure a dry foundation. Install gutters and downspouts and make sure the first 10 ft. of ground around your house slopes away at something like 1 ft. in 10.

First Lines of Defense

What if your percolation rate is considerably less than 10 in./hour? First, don't build on the lowest part of the lot, because that is where the water will go. Gutters and downspouts are at the heart of rainwater management, the heart of moisture control in buildings. Deposit rainwater from gutters onto splash blocks and onto undisturbed soil so that the water runs away from the house.

Most modern houses are damp-proofed; that is, the exterior of the basement wall receives a bitumen coating. This provides a considerable amount of water protection. But water can enter through cracks resulting from utility penetrations, concrete curing, settlement, swelling soils, seismic activity or other causes. Think of damp-proofing as a secondary defense against water.

Dealing with a Rising Water Table

Footing drains have been used for decades to intercept rising groundwater. Rising groundwater usually isn't the major problem for foundations. Surface water is much more likely to cause trouble if it isn't led away from the foundation. Still, footing drains should be installed. They don't cost much when you're excavating, anyway, and they're the devil to retrofit if you find later that you have a high water table.

Footing drains should consist of a foot or so of gravel around the outside of the foundation. Use a filter fabric over the gravel to keep it from clogging

SATURATED SOIL LEADS TO FROST HEAVING

In a common scenario, water from downspouts has nowhere to go but next to the foundation. This results in damage to a garage slab from soil freezing.

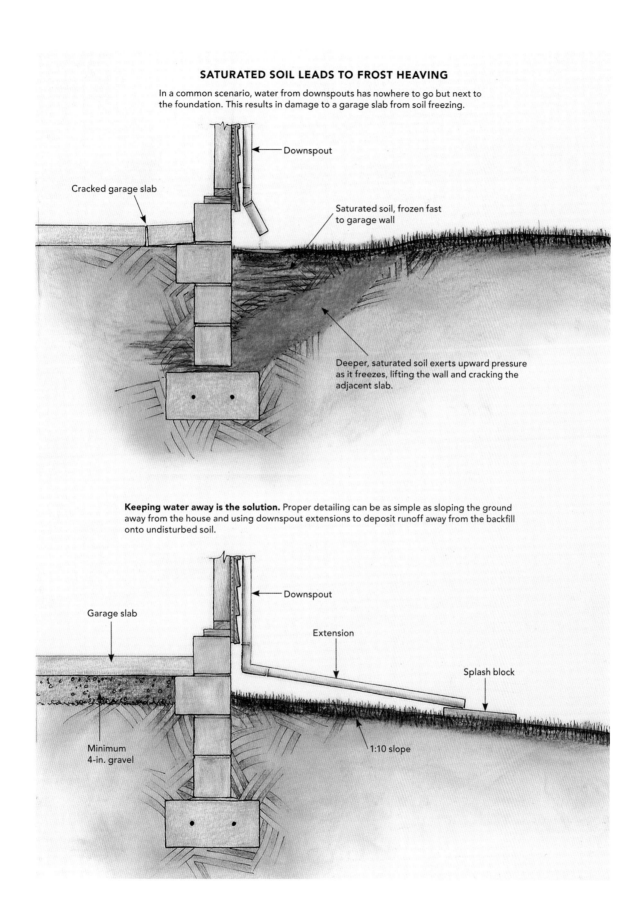

Downspout

Cracked garage slab

Saturated soil, frozen fast to garage wall

Deeper, saturated soil exerts upward pressure as it freezes, lifting the wall and cracking the adjacent slab.

Keeping water away is the solution. Proper detailing can be as simple as sloping the ground away from the house and using downspout extensions to deposit runoff away from the backfill onto undisturbed soil.

Garage slab

Downspout

Extension

Splash block

Minimum 4-in. gravel

1:10 slope

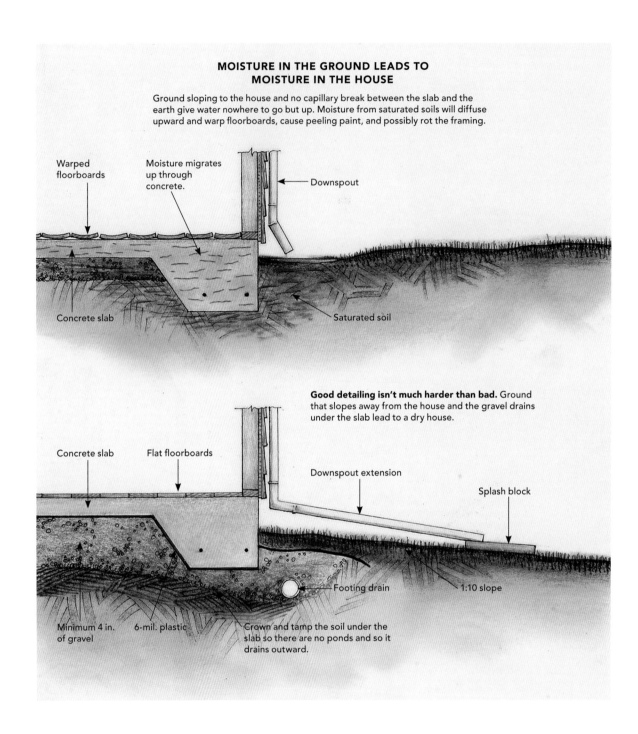

MOISTURE IN THE GROUND LEADS TO MOISTURE IN THE HOUSE

Ground sloping to the house and no capillary break between the slab and the earth give water nowhere to go but up. Moisture from saturated soils will diffuse upward and warp floorboards, cause peeling paint, and possibly rot the framing.

Warped floorboards

Moisture migrates up through concrete.

Downspout

Concrete slab

Saturated soil

Good detailing isn't much harder than bad. Ground that slopes away from the house and the gravel drains under the slab lead to a dry house.

Concrete slab

Flat floorboards

Downspout extension

Splash block

Footing drain

1:10 slope

Minimum 4 in. of gravel

6-mil. plastic

Crown and tamp the soil under the slab so there are no ponds and so it drains outward.

with silt. Filter fabric comes in several weights; the lightest is just fine for residential use. Footing drains can have 4-in. perforated plastic pipe with the holes pointing down. They must lead to a sump pump or a gravity drain consisting of solid pipe leading to daylight. If you use pipe (as opposed to just gravel) in a footing drain, it should be slightly pitched toward the outlet, or at least not pitched backward. It should have surface clean-outs every 50 ft. Discharge by gravity flow is preferable to a sump pump. Sump pumps are a weak link, likely to fail when most needed, but a gravity drain may not be possible if the footing drains are deeper than any possible discharge point.

> Gutters and downspouts are at the heart of rain-water management, the heart of moisture control in buildings.

Gravel alone is probably just as good as gravel with pipes in it. A continuous gravel base that leads to a sump pump or to a daylight drain of solid 4-in. plastic pipe will handle most rising groundwater. The gravel is the main water route, so pipe used as a collector is not critical. In fact, I believe that most pipe is placed by people who don't really know what water is supposed to go where. Drainpipe here symbolizes good practice while making a doubtful contribution.

Never connect the downspouts to the footing drains, even if the drains run to daylight and not to a sump pump. Putting that volume of water closer to the footings makes no sense at all in light of my opening story. I'm trying to solve problems here, not create them.

Good Backfilling and Grading Are Crucial

Proper backfill procedures go a long way toward eliminating water problems. At the risk of sounding simplistic, be sure the ground slopes away from the house. You'd be amazed how many builders get this wrong. I recommend a slope of 12 in. in the first 10 ft. as a minimum (see "Moisture in the Ground Leads to Moisture in the House" on the facing page). Builders commonly don't allow enough extra soil for settling, and they almost never compact the backfill. Lightly compacted backfill may settle 5% of its height or more, often resulting in a situation in which the grade pitches toward the house. When backfilling, include a correction for settlement. There really aren't any hard-and-fast rules. Deep, lightly compacted backfill needs a big correction. Shallow, well-compacted fill might require none.

SLABS NEED GOOD DETAILING

GETTING WATER AWAY FROM SLAB FOUNDATIONS is just as critical as with basements or crawlspaces. Remember, there are retrofit draining and venting options that can, to a degree, rescue a damp basement or crawlspace. There is none that works on slabs.

Good preparation of the ground surface is critical before slab placement. Level the center, slope down to the excavation for the thickened edge of the slab, and compact the soil well. Pour the slab on 6-mil polyethylene over at least a 4-in. tamped gravel base. This base serves as a capillary break between the soil and the underside of the slab. Extend the gravel base to a footing drain to carry water away. It is important to remember that a capillary break works only as long as it remains unflooded.

Remember, too much slope near the house doesn't create water problems; too little does.

Compact the backfill as tightly as possible without damaging the foundation walls. Brace them well, using trusslike assemblies of heavy framing lumber spanning from wall to wall. Have the first-floor deck on, and fill all sides evenly. Block walls require more caution than poured concrete. Compact the backfill in 1-ft. lifts using a hand compactor, commonly called a jitterbug, or careful pressure from a backhoe. Because intersecting walls brace each other, the soil at outside corners can be compacted with less risk than in the middle of a long wall. For a minimum, compact these corners well, and be sure that all the downspouts drain near them.

Utility lines are frequently laid in sand that provides a direct path for water to reach the foundation.

Take special care where utility lines enter the house. They are frequently laid in sand that provides a direct path for water to reach the foundation. Be sure the soil under the utilities is well compacted, and cement and damp-proof the utility penetrations. Then use an impervious earth such as clay soil, or mix a bag of portland cement with the soil you have, to fill around the utility penetration. Tamp well.

Swales and French Drains

Other means of transporting water away from the house besides sheet flow (when the surface is effectively running water) are the swale and the French drain. A swale is a small valley formed by two sloped soil surfaces. Swales must be pitched, or they become ponds. A swale should be located away from the building, and it is often used to divert sheet flow coming from uphill (see "The Solutions" on p. 127).

A French drain is a trench filled with rock or gravel that collects water and transports it laterally (see "French Drains Collect and Transport Water" on the facing page). I prepare the bottom of the trench so that it is smooth and carefully pitched toward the outlet. Mix dry cement with the soil in the bottom of the trench to make it less permeable, and fill the trench with whatever clean gravel is locally available. I hesitate to use road stone, a blend of gravel and stone dust, because water passes through it slowly. If the gravel is to be exposed, I try to cap it with an attractive rounded stone. If the drain is to be covered, I provide graduated layers of smaller stone toward the surface, then perhaps filter fabric before the sod covering.

I sometimes use 4-in. smooth-wall perforated plastic pipe in a French drain, particularly if I expect it to carry a big volume of water, say runoff from the gutters. There are fittings that connect downspouts directly into this pipe. If you do this, install clean-outs at least every 50 ft. and keep the gutters clean. Otherwise, the pipe can become clogged with leaves. I don't use corrugated pipe for drainage because it is more difficult to ensure smooth, straight runs. It clogs more easily and is more difficult to clean out.

Concrete patios, stoops, driveways, and sidewalks abutting the foundation present problems. It is important to design them so that the gravel base beneath drains outward, a perfect use for a French drain. You may find that the driveway is one of the most convenient sites for a French drain. Driveways usually pitch away from the house, and a French drain can be integrated with the driveway so that it will not call attention to itself.

Where Should the Water Go?

To my knowledge, municipalities no longer provide storm-sewer service for new residential runoff. In my area, they do not receive the output from sump pumps. They receive and treat storm water to keep streets open, and that's about it.

If there isn't enough elevation difference between the house and a point on the lot where a pitched drain can come to daylight, then another solution is needed. Theoretically, if the pipe never pitches back, you don't need more than the diameter of the pipe in elevation difference. Practically, more is better, and ¼ in. per foot is a good number to shoot for.

But say you don't have even that much pitch. For hundreds of years, cisterns and dry wells collected water below grade. Often, there was an overflow toward a leach field. Such design is still feasible, and indeed it is useful for garden irrigation where fresh water is scarce. Some municipalities require new subdivisions to handle runoff with on-site dry wells, rather than feeding it to a common detention basin. Usually a 1,000-gal. precast-concrete dry well (see "Dry Wells Avoid Draining Runoff on the Surface" on the facing page) or commercially available plastic drainage structures are buried somewhere on site.

FRENCH DRAINS COLLECT AND TRANSPORT WATER

A French drain can play an important role in draining slabs, gutters, and ground-roof systems of water.

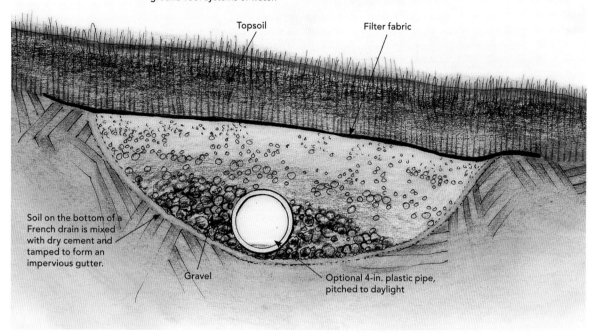

Topsoil

Filter fabric

Soil on the bottom of a French drain is mixed with dry cement and tamped to form an impervious gutter.

Gravel

Optional 4-in. plastic pipe, pitched to daylight

DRY WELLS AVOID DRAINING RUNOFF ON THE SURFACE

Required in some municipalities, dry wells give runoff time to soak into the ground. Their success depends highly on how well the surrounding soil drains.

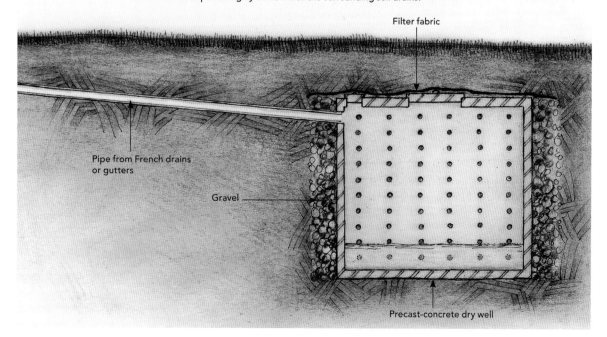

Filter fabric

Pipe from French drains or gutters

Gravel

Precast-concrete dry well

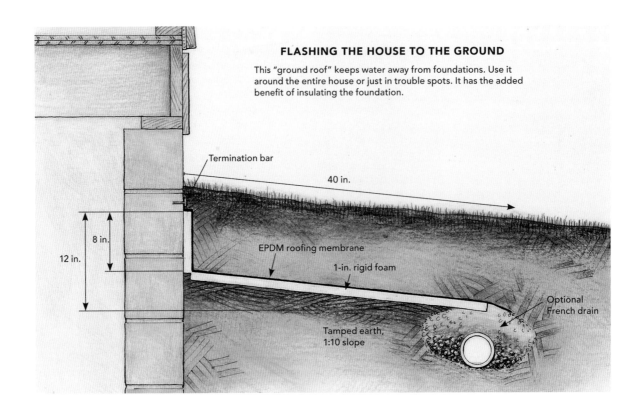

FLASHING THE HOUSE TO THE GROUND

This "ground roof" keeps water away from foundations. Use it around the entire house or just in trouble spots. It has the added benefit of insulating the foundation.

Termination bar

40 in.

8 in.

12 in.

EPDM roofing membrane

1-in. rigid foam

Optional French drain

Tamped earth, 1:10 slope

Water from the gutters is piped in and stored until it can soak into the surrounding soil. The likelihood of success with either one of these systems depends on the perc rate of the soil and sufficient storage capacity to handle the maximum likely runoff. It also depends on how big the design rainfall is.

If you are not required to treat runoff in a specific manner, then take advantage of natural drainage courses on your lot. Get the water away from the house responsibly. If several downspouts connect to a French drain, enough water may flow from it to cause erosion problems. Place rocks under the end of the pipe and in the outwash area to spread the flow out and reduce erosion. Don't flood the neighbors' basements to spare your own.

Flashing the Intersection of the Ground and the Foundation

I call that zone where the house meets the soil the *ground roof* because the soil surface must shed rainwater away from the foundation and the soil below.

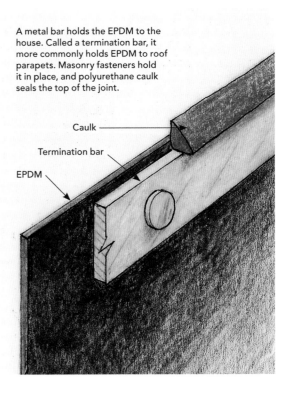

A metal bar holds the EPDM to the house. Called a termination bar, it more commonly holds EPDM to roof parapets. Masonry fasteners hold it in place, and polyurethane caulk seals the top of the joint.

Caulk

Termination bar

EPDM

During dry spells, I commonly see a ½-in. crevice between the soil and the foundation. If that gap appeared on a roof, wouldn't we flash it? In severe cases or in old houses with hopelessly porous foundations, I have flashed this gap in the ground roof with EPDM roofing membrane (see "Flashing the House to the Ground" on the facing page). Polyethylene sheets and bitumen membranes would work, but they degrade more easily when backfilled.

Ideally, I would flash a house as it was being built. In reality, I've done it only as a retrofit. A frost-protected shallow footing would lend itself well to a ground-flashing system. I dig down 8 in. at the foundation wall and extend outward 40 in., sloping the excavation 1 in. in 10. The hard work is the digging. Having done it, I should get as much benefit as possible, so I take this opportunity to insulate the foundation. Slice through one side of a 4×8 sheet of 1-in. rigid foam, 8 in. from the edge, and fold along the cut. The resulting piece fits neatly into the 8-in. by 40-in. excavation. In the South I suggest high-density mineral wool because it is less hospitable than foam to termites. In new construction, compact the backfill under the flashing well. Otherwise, settling could tear the EPDM from the wall or cause it to pitch toward the house.

After placing the insulation, I roll out the EPDM, letting it hang over the end of the foam. A metal strip called a termination bar, more commonly used to attach EPDM to roof parapets, clamps the membrane to the foundation at grade level. I attach the termination bar to the foundation with expanding nail-in fasteners: alloy or plastic sleeves that slide into holes drilled into the foundation and then expand as a nail is driven in. I run a bead of cutoff mastic, a high-quality polyurethane caulk used for waterproofing termination bars on roofs, on this joint and backfill.

The flashing could extend farther outward from the building at the downspout locations. In existing buildings, you can often get away with flashing only the trouble spots, usually inside corners with down-

CONSIDER YOUR SITE AND PLAN ACCORDINGLY

THERE ARE SO MANY SOIL classifications, foundation types, and climate variables that assembling general rules is challenging. If there is a general rule, it is this one: Design the soil surface that goes around the building to act as a roof. The overall aim is preventing the soil that is in contact with the building from being saturated with water. This *ground roof* should ensure that rainwater moves quickly and effectively away from the building. Downspout discharge, grading, flashing, drains, and soil treatment at the surface all play major roles in keeping the ground in contact with the building dry.

Basements, crawlspaces, and slabs all have their own peculiarities. With thoughtful design of the area where the house and the ground intersect, any foundation can be dry. Well, maybe any foundation that doesn't have provisions for boat docking.

spouts. The ground roof need not be as watertight as a house roof. After all, moisture control in soils is always a matter of playing the percentages.

In soils with an average percolation rate, flashing by itself is enough to keep the water away from the foundation. If your perc rate is slow, install a French drain near the outboard edge of the flashing. Shallow plantings can go right on top of the EPDM.

Keeping a Basement Dry

BY LARRY JANESKY

I was standing in water a quarter inch deep that covered an entire basement floor. The homeowner asked me in a surprisingly calm voice, "Is there any reason the basement of a brand-new million-dollar home should leak?" "Even if your house cost $100,000, it still shouldn't leak," I answered. I also told her that she had lots of company in her misery: A recent survey of 33,000 new-home owners revealed that 44% had leaky, wet basements. It was my guess that most of the basement problems were the result of a builder's neglect or efforts to cut costs.

As a basement-waterproofing contractor, I fix the mistakes of others. Having been a builder myself, I can empathize with the emotional struggle to "spend more and be safe" vs. "spend less, make a profit, we should be okay." However, no matter how much you spend, you shouldn't end up with a basement that seeps water like a cave; it's not good for the house or its occupants. Remember that it's much easier (and cheaper) to build it right the first time than to dig it up later with a jackhammer. To that end, I like to seal foundation walls, drain water away from the foundation's exterior, and expel the water that does manage to leak into a house's basement.

Sealing Foundation Walls

When water saturates the soil surrounding a foundation, it essentially creates a column of water whose cumulative weight increases as it rises in the backfill. This force pressing down is known as *hydrostatic pressure*; it drives water through joints, cracks, form ties, and other foundation imperfections. The first line of defense is some sort of exterior coating on the foundation walls.

These sealants are categorized into two groups: dampproof and waterproof coatings. Dampproof coatings are typically thin asphalt-based solutions that are sprayed or painted onto the foundation's exterior. The asphalt reduces the porosity of the concrete, but over time, it emulsifies in water and won't seal cracks. Some contractors mix fiberglass fibers with the asphalt to strengthen the mix but still offer only a one-year warranty. The low cost of dampproofing makes it attractive to many builders, but the brief or nonexistent warranties (usually only a year) should make consumers wary.

Waterproof coatings, on the other hand, are a mixture of rubber and asphalt or all rubber (sometimes called *elastomeric*) and can cost three times as much. Like dampproof coatings, waterproof coatings are sprayed onto the foundation (see the top photo on the facing page), but the material must

WATERPROOFING, NOT DAMPPROOF- ING, seals the foundation walls. More expensive than asphalt-based mixtures, a rubber-based membrane sprayed onto foundation walls remains flexible and waterproof.

RIGID-FOAM PROTECTION BOARD shields the membrane from backfill damage. Applied while the waterproof- ing is still tacky, the ¼-in. foam panels also provide a thermal break between the foundation and the backfill.

MAKING THE FOUNDATION'S EXTERIOR IMPERVIOUS TO WATER

Because most water problems come from saturated backfill, it's important to seal foundation walls. An elastic rubber membrane sprayed onto the concrete seals small cracks, holes, and other imperfections. A PVC drain laid along the footing carries excess water away from the house. A multistage filter of stone, filter fabric, and coarse sand keeps the drain from clogging with silt.

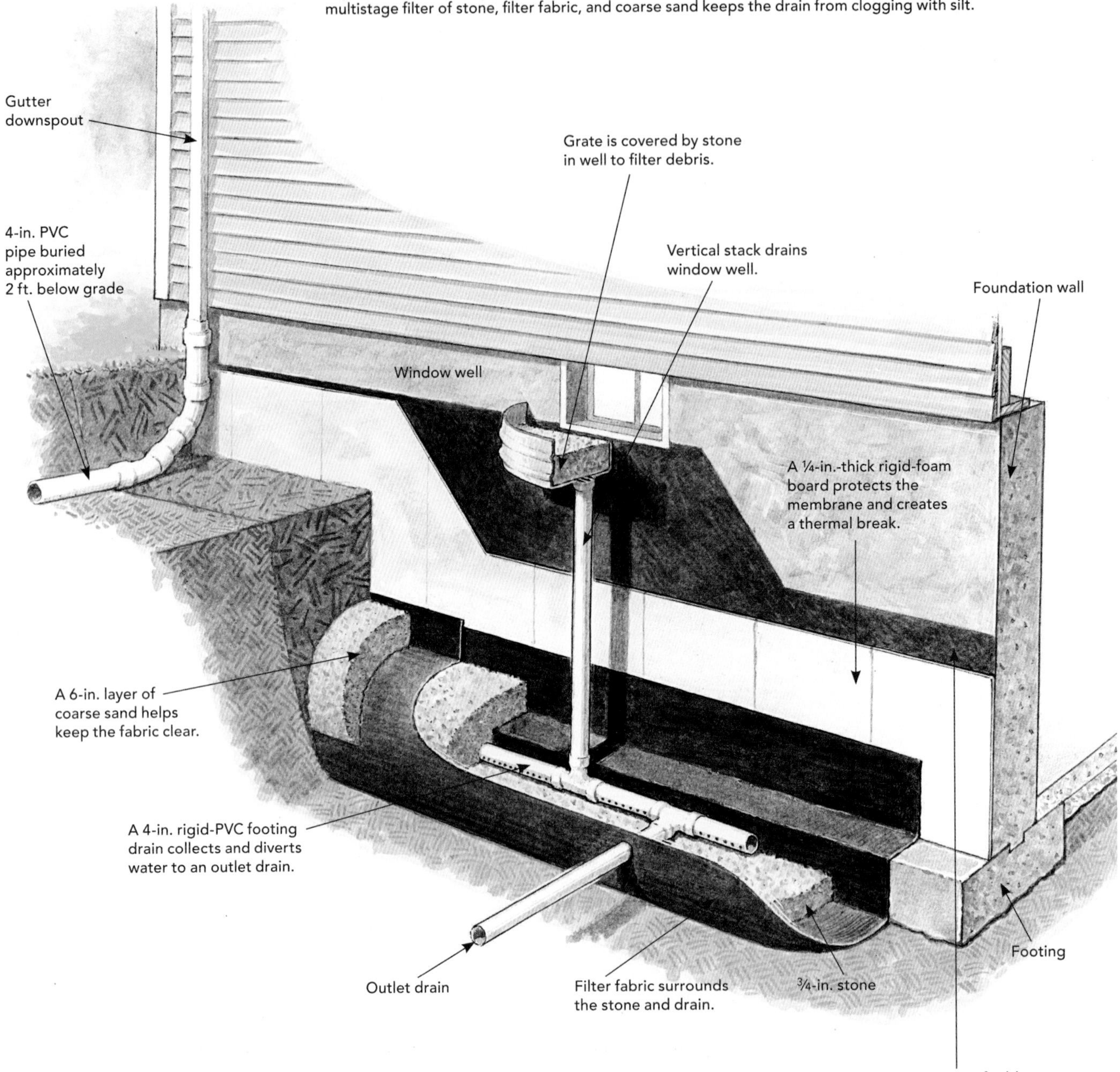

Gutter downspout

4-in. PVC pipe buried approximately 2 ft. below grade

Grate is covered by stone in well to filter debris.

Vertical stack drains window well.

Foundation wall

Window well

A ¼-in.-thick rigid-foam board protects the membrane and creates a thermal break.

A 6-in. layer of coarse sand helps keep the fabric clear.

A 4-in. rigid-PVC footing drain collects and diverts water to an outlet drain.

Outlet drain

Filter fabric surrounds the stone and drain.

¾-in. stone

Footing

Waterproof rubber membrane

Draining downspouts and window wells

If left unattended, rainwater that drains off the roof will end up in the basement. Gutter downspouts can be connected to 4-in. drain lines that run to daylight, away from the house. To keep window wells from leaking into the basement, a 4-in. vertical pipe run from a tee in the footing drain can divert any water that collects there.

CLOGGED FOOTING DRAINS CAN'T DO THE JOB. Water draining into the pipe carries silt that eventually fills the pipe. To avoid replacing a clogged footing drain, the author surrounds the pipe with a layered filter that stops sediment.

TIP: The black coiled, slotted pipe often used as a foundation's drainage system can be difficult to keep straight. Any dips in the pipe cause poor flow and clogs. Try 4-in.-dia. rigid PVC pipe instead.

be heated before application; it's also applied in a thicker coat and is elastic enough to bridge $\frac{1}{16}$-in.-wide cracks and small holes. The key to the waterproofing's performance is the amount of rubber in the mixture; more rubber means better performance and higher costs.

To protect any coating's integrity when the foundation is backfilled, many contractors cover the sealed concrete with what is known as protection board: sheets of fiberglass, rock wool, or extruded polystyrene foam. I use a $\frac{1}{4}$-in.-thick foam board that adheres to the fresh layer of waterproofing (see bottom photo on p. 137); at the very least, it provides a thermal break between the backfill and the foundation. A number of waterproofing manufacturers such as Rub-R-Wall® (770-410-1545; www.rpcinfo.com) and ElastiKote® (800-457-4056; elastikote.com) produce an extremely resilient coating that doesn't need protection board. But I still like to have the extra insulation provided by the foam.

When applying waterproofing, I make sure the joint between the footing and the wall is sealed. This means the top of the footing has to be clean before the wall is sprayed. Form ties should be knocked off both inside and out before spraying. It's also a good idea to determine the finish-grade height and spray

to that line. If this elevation is miscalculated, 6 in. or more of untreated wall can end up beneath the backfill, causing leaks when the inevitable shrinkage cracks begin to appear in the foundation.

A popular alternative to waterproofing is waterproof drainage mats. The dimpled polyethylene sheets are unrolled and nailed onto the foundation wall, caulked at the top and left open at the bottom. The mat's dimpled shape creates an airspace between the wall and the soil, so if water does leak in at the top or through a joint, it can drain to the bottom.

The problem with these drainage mats is that they must have an open footing drain below. If (or when) the footing drain clogs, hydrostatic pressure forces water up between the matting and the wall. Because the wall was never waterproofed, every crack and form-tie hole is vulnerable to easy water entry. In contrast, if a footing drain fails along a wall that was waterproofed, the form ties, wall cracks, and footing/wall joint are sealed and protected. However, even the best waterproofing guarantees only that water won't penetrate walls and doesn't prevent water from coming up around the footings and floor.

Keeping Footing Drains Clear

To keep a basement dry, you need to channel water away from the house with footing drains. Although most building codes say that foundations must have a drainage system of drainage tile, gravel, or perforated pipe, I always use 4-in.-dia. rigid PVC pipe. (I've found that the black coiled, slotted pipe often used is difficult to keep straight; any dips in the pipe cause poor flow and clogs.) Two rows of

INTERIOR PERIMETER DRAINS ARE GOOD INSURANCE in new construction or retrofits. Plastic drains on top of the footing collect water that leaks in through the walls and channel it to the sump pump. The entire drain is to be covered with concrete, except the opening facing the wall.

As long as the lot's grade allows it, the exterior footing drains should always be run to daylight, pitched at ¼ in. per ft. or more, if possible.

½-in. holes drilled at the 4 and 8 o'clock positions keep the pipe's sediment intake to a minimum; slots will clog much faster than holes in most soil conditions. To make sure the pipe doesn't become clogged (see the photo on p. 139), I wrap the pipe with a succession of filters that resembles a giant burrito.

I start by cleaning the excavation to the bottom of the footing, usually with a shovel; a half-buried footing causes poor drainage. Next I unroll 6-ft.-wide filter fabric along the footing, spreading excess on the ground away from the foundation and up the sidewalls of the excavation (see "Making the Foundation's Exterior Impervious to Water" on p. 138). I then dump 3 in. of ¾-in. stone on top of the fabric, level it off by hand, then set the PVC pipe so that at worst, it's level around the entire foundation. Because the footings are mostly level, I'm happy if I can gain a few inches of pitch to the outlet. During this stage of the project, it's convenient to tie the drains below each window well to the footing drains. Vertical risers made of solid 4-in.-dia. pipe run up from the footing drains under the window wells and terminate with a grate about 4 in. below the windowsill. The well can be filled later with stone so that leaves won't clog the grate.

I backfill over the footing pipe with more ¾-in. stone to an elevation of 8 in. above the top of the footing. As a rule of thumb, 1 yd. of aggregate will cover 12 lin. ft. of exterior footing drain; therefore, a house with 150 ft. of foundation will require a little more than 12.5 yd. of aggregate. I pull the filter fabric up over the top of the stone and against the wall, using shovelfuls of sand or stones to hold it in place. If the fabric is not long enough to reach the wall, I add another course, overlapping by at least 12 in. Now the burrito is nearly complete. Because the filter fabric will eventually clog, I put about 6 in. of coarse sand on top of it. This progression of materials will keep the drain clear longer than any other practical way I know. The fabric protects the stone, the sand protects the fabric, and the soil won't wash into the sand.

As long as the lot's grade allows it, the exterior footing drains should always be run to daylight, pitched at ¼ in. per ft. or more, if possible. If the drains are servicing more than 200 lin. ft. of foundation, you might want to consider added measures. For example, you could put two outlets to daylight or increase the diameter of the outlet pipe from 4 in. to 6 in.

If there isn't considerable pitch on the lot or a handy storm sewer, the footing drains must run inside to a sump pump. A single 6-in. pipe that connects the exterior drain to the pump should be cast through the footing at the sump location and should give the drain as short a run as possible.

SUMP PUMPS FOR INTERIOR DRAINAGE

ANY DRAINAGE TECHNIQUE is dependent on one thing: a good sump pump. After installing more than 10,000 pumps myself, I have some criteria for choosing a pump. First, it should have a cast-iron body; second, it should be able to pump ½-in.-dia. solids; and third, it should have a mechanical float switch (a float riding up and down on a rod), not a pressure switch or a "ball on a wire" design that often hangs up. A Zoeller M-53 (Zoeller® Company; 800-928-7867; www.zoeller.com) fits the bill perfectly and pumps 2,600 gal. per hour.

The pump sits inside a plastic bucket called a liner that collects water and separates it from the surrounding dirt so that the pump can push it out. The liner should be perforated and set in a bed of aggregate. Any drainage system that feeds water to the sump should have a pipe cut through the sidewall of the liner. The liner should have an airtight lid that will keep moisture from evaporating into the basement; it also keeps objects from falling into the sump hole that could interfere with the switch operation.

Relying on a lone sump pump to keep the basement dry is risky. It's all too common for a storm to knock out the power and flood the basement all in one night. A battery-operated backup pump provides insurance and often is equipped with an alarm that announces a pump failure. The backup can usually be installed in the same sump hole as the primary pump and use the same discharge line. The best backup systems use pumps that sit up off the sump floor, have float switches and use matched chargers and batteries made specifically for long-term standby use. This last item is critical. Many backup units don't provide a battery; if the battery and charger aren't matched, the system won't charge properly.

Discharge from the sump pump should be piped to a storm drain if one is available or to the exterior, where it will flow away. The discharge line should be installed so that it doesn't freeze during the winter.

KEEPING THE INTERIOR DRY WITH A SYSTEM OF DRAINS AND PUMPS

To handle any leakage through foundation walls and to ensure a dry floor, an interior perimeter drain collects water from the walls and channels it to the sump pump. On sites where exterior drainage is poor, the pump can also be connected to the exterior footing drains.

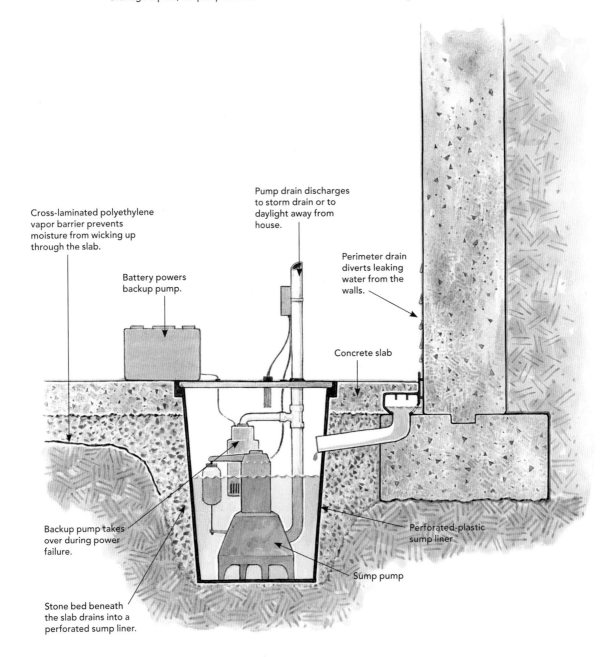

Cross-laminated polyethylene vapor barrier prevents moisture from wicking up through the slab.

Battery powers backup pump.

Pump drain discharges to storm drain or to daylight away from house.

Perimeter drain diverts leaking water from the walls.

Concrete slab

Backup pump takes over during power failure.

Stone bed beneath the slab drains into a perforated sump liner.

Perforated-plastic sump liner

Sump pump

It's worth mentioning that it's never a good idea to connect an interior footing drain with a cross-over pipe in the footing to an exterior footing drain that drains outside the house. The probability of failure on an exterior component of the system is high, while the probability of a failure to the interior system is low. If and when the exterior footing drain fails, the water will back up into the interior footing drain and flood the basement.

Drain the Gutters Far Away from the House

It may seem obvious, but many houses don't have adequate drainage for gutters and downspouts. Rather than carry water away with splash blocks, it's more efficient to connect the downspouts to a 4-in.-dia. PVC pipe (see "Making the Foundation's

A TOUGH VAPOR BARRIER KEEPS THE BASEMENT SLAB DRY. Made of 2-ply high-density polyethylene, the vapor barrier can be installed under or over the gravel base and keeps moisture from wicking up through the slab.

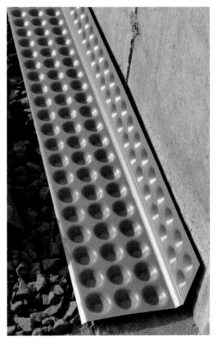

DRAINAGE FLASHING IS A SIMPLER, LESS-EXPENSIVE INTERIOR DRAIN. Installed at the junction of wall and footing, this flashing has a dimpled profile that allows any water from the walls to flow beneath the slab and into the sump pump. Obviously, it's important to keep the top of the flashing clear when pouring the slab (left).

Exterior Impervious to Water" on p. 138). Starting at about a 2-ft. depth at the house, the pipe should be pitched toward daylight as steeply as possible so that it can flush out the dead leaves and sticks that always accumulate.

Because gutters collect debris, it's a good idea to enlarge the downspouts to 3 in. by 4 in. instead of the usual 2 in. by 3 in.; this will also drain the gutter twice as fast in a heavy rain. The underground drain itself can be enlarged to a 6-in. dia. if necessary. In

the drain, it's best to avoid 90° bends, which trap leaves and gunk, and use 45° bends instead. If there's a long run of gutter, give it two outlets. Finally, never connect the gutter drains to the footing drains, no matter how far downstream. Gutter drains are always voted "most likely to clog" and will back up the footing drains, too.

INTERIOR VS. EXTERIOR FOUNDATION DRAINS

When an existing home has a wet basement, there are two basic approaches to solving the problem: an interior or an exterior drainage system. Several things should be addressed, however, before any system is installed. First, make sure the grade is pitched away from the house to drain away surface water effectively. The grade should not be any closer to the siding than 6 in. because of rot and termite concerns. Next, extend the outlets of the downspouts away from the house, and keep gutters free of debris to help keep water away from the foundation. Although these two steps nearly always help, they rarely keep a wet basement completely dry, and a drainage system should be considered.

EXTERIOR DRAINAGE SYSTEMS

The installation of an exterior system requires the excavation of soil around the entire house down to the bottom of the foundation footing. This process can be disruptive because landscaping, driveways, sidewalks, porches, decks, and so on, have to be removed and replaced. In addition, the soil taken out of the hole has to be stored in the yard temporarily, which is usually a huge mess. Once excavation is done, the footing drain can be installed. The system then has to drain to a sump pump inside the house or by gravity to daylight if the grade permits, which would require an additional trench.

Exterior drainage systems are not easily serviced. If something goes wrong, it's tough to find and fix the problem easily. Last but not least, the cost of an exterior system can be many times greater than that of an interior system. For all these reasons—cost, mess, difficulty in servicing—I do not recommend exterior drainage systems on existing houses, except in extreme cases.

INTERIOR DRAINAGE SYSTEMS

Interior footing drains are the best solution for most wet basements. With this type of system, the edges of the slab are removed. Next, a trench is dug around the perimeter of the foundation. Perforated pipe (usually 4 in. dia.) is placed in the trench and covered with crushed stone. Then concrete is poured over the trench.

Usually, interior systems drain to a sump pump, but in rare cases, they can be run to daylight. Sump pumps have come a long way. Some super systems feature sealed lids with built-in floor drains, alarm systems, and a host of other features. I also recommend a battery backup to keep the system working should the power fail.

Other hybrid interior systems that I recommend are less prone to clogging and are less disruptive than a round-pipe system. These systems also take water from along the walls, which can be crucial if a wall cracks, a pipe penetration leaks, or a window well floods unexpectedly. Whatever system you choose, put drainage around the entire basement, even if only part of the basement seems to be leaking. If fixing your basement isn't a project that you're comfortable doing, call a basement-waterproofing professional.

Getting Rid of Water in Basements

Although installing interior basement drains in new construction is a good idea, they're usually installed to fix problems in existing construction. Typical strategies include the use of interior perimeter drains that collect water from foundation walls, a vapor barrier below the slab that prevents water and vapor from wicking up through the concrete, and a good sump pump that will eject any water that collects in the drains and under the slab. In new construction, these methods all start with a new basement floor.

Under the slab, I like to lay 8 in. to 10 in. of clean ½-in. to ¾-in. stone. This stone allows the entire subslab area to drain and makes a good base for the slab. Once the gravel is laid, I always like to install a puncture-resistant vapor barrier (see the photos on p. 143). The strongest material is a 4-mil cross-laminated high-density polyethylene such as Tu-Tuf (Sto-Cote Products; 888-642-3746). It comes in 20-ft. by 100-ft. rolls. I overlap adjoining pieces at least 18 in. and seal the lap with housewrap tape. The concrete guys aren't crazy about the barrier because it doesn't allow the water in the mix to settle out, making the finishing process longer, but a 3-in. bed of sand laid over the barrier will alleviate the problem. (You can also lay down the barrier before the gravel is brought in.) Either way, the long-term benefits of an unbroken barrier under the floor are well worth the temporary inconvenience of installation.

Because water usually comes into the basement through the walls and the footing/wall joint, the best place to capture and channel the water is at the junction of the floor and wall (see "Keeping the Interior Dry with a System of Drains and Pumps" on p. 142). The most efficient method is to install a plastic perimeter drain that sits on top of the footing and below the slab (see the photo on p. 140); this perimeter drain collects any water that seeps in through the walls. In retrofit jobs, the first 6 in. of slab perimeter is cut away to expose the footing; once the drain is installed, the slab is patched. There are many manufacturers' variations on this theme; I use a drain that I designed and now manufacture. Rectangular in cross section, it has a slotted opening facing the wall that channels water down and out toward the pump. The interior footing drain costs $30 to $40 per ft. in a retrofit. A less-expensive version of this system for new construction is known generically as a draining floor edging (see the photos on p. 144). It's a 6-in. by 4-in. L-shaped plastic flashing with a dimpled design. The dimples are laid against the wall and footing side and allow water to pass into the gravel below the slab, where it can be pumped out. You can find versions of these products through your local waterproofing contractor, or you can contact my company, Basement Systems®, at (800) 638-7048; www.basementsystems.com.

Sealing a Crawlspace

BY LARRY JANESKY

Dirt crawlspaces are never-ending sources of moisture. Even if the dirt's surface is dry, digging down a little bit reveals moist earth. Moisture ruins houses by providing a hospitable environment for the fungi, mold, and insects that destroy wood framing. Moisture in a crawlspace affects not only the floor system directly above it but also the entire house. Warm air in a heated building rises. As it rises, replacement air is sucked from the lowest part of a house. This natural air movement, called the stack effect, is how chimneys work. Consequently, whatever is in the air at the lowest point eventually flows through the upper sections of living space (see the left drawing on p. 149). If mold spores and radon are present in the crawlspace, you can bet they're in the living space as well.

Separate the House from the Earth

With little headroom, light, and habitability, the crawlspace may not seem to be an important part of the house. In fact, it's very important. Moist crawlspaces may be a bigger problem than wet basements (see "Keeping a Basement Dry" on p. 136) because they can produce an unseen moisture stream through the building envelope.

To avoid moisture's negative effects, a crawlspace should be fully sealed and isolated from the ground and the outside. Part of my technique involves placing a 20-mil, 7-ply sandwich of high- and low-density polyethylene with polyester-cord reinforcement on the dirt floor and up the walls. I have this pool-liner-like sheeting made specially for my system (www.basementsystems.com; 800-638-7048). It is easily strong enough to crawl on and to store materials on. Its bright white color makes the crawlspace a light, relatively pleasant place to be (see the top photo on p. 148). A vapor barrier such as Tu-Tuf (Sto-Cote Products; 888-642-3746) also could be used, but it offers less durability, UV resistance, and fire resistance. Some contractors solve the problem of moist crawlspaces by pumping in concrete. But for this method to work, the concrete needs a vapor barrier. Even with a vapor barrier, this alternative doesn't address water-vapor diffusion through the walls. If the vapor barrier is doing all the work, then why use expensive concrete?

Despite what the building code says, many colleagues and I believe that venting crawlspaces is a bad idea. Code requires 1 sq. ft. of ventilation for every 150 sq. ft. of dirt floor. Using a vapor barrier over the dirt floor reduces the ventilation require-

Close the vents and
let a heavy-duty vapor
barrier keep moisture,
mold, and radon out of
the living space.

DRAMATIC TRANSFORMATION. Proper detailing
changed this crawlspace from a spelunker's nightmare
(bottom photo) into a bright, clean, dry storage space
(top photo).

IF IT'S IN YOUR CRAWLSPACE, IT'S IN YOUR HOUSE

AS WARM AIR RISES INSIDE THE HOUSE, replacement air enters from the lowest part, often the crawlspace. Properly sealing the crawlspace and channeling rainwater away from the house can provide mold-free and radon-free living spaces.

PROBLEMS

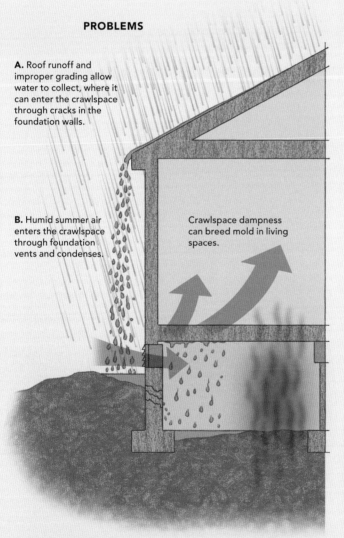

A. Roof runoff and improper grading allow water to collect, where it can enter the crawlspace through cracks in the foundation walls.

B. Humid summer air enters the crawlspace through foundation vents and condenses.

Crawlspace dampness can breed mold in living spaces.

C. Radon rises through the soil, into the crawlspace, and ultimately into the living space.

SOLUTIONS

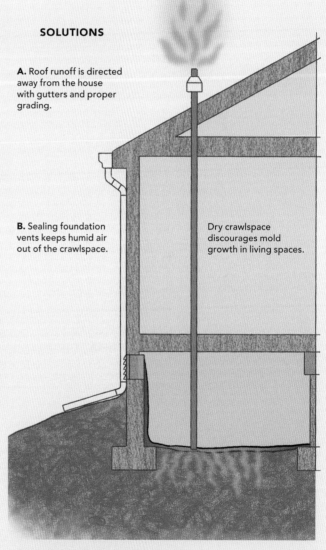

A. Roof runoff is directed away from the house with gutters and proper grading.

B. Sealing foundation vents keeps humid air out of the crawlspace.

Dry crawlspace discourages mold growth in living spaces.

C. A sealed crawlspace keeps moisture from the ground out and passively mitigates radon. In tough cases, a PVC pipe and inline fan exhaust radon outside.

ment to 1 ft. per 1,500 sq. ft. of floor space. The intent is to vent out the humidity that the exposed earth lets in.

But venting creates its own problems. In winter, there's an energy penalty: cold floors and higher heating costs. In summer, vents actually admit moisture in the form of warm, humid air. Warm air can hold more moisture than cool air. Warm air entering a cool crawlspace can reach its dew point and give up its moisture as condensation. Relative humidity, dew point and the stack effect combine to make crawlspace vents more likely to compound a moisture problem than to alleviate it.

For these reasons, I close the vents outside and seal them from the inside with 2-in.-thick foam insulation and polyurethane caulk. And yes, I sleep well at night because I am doing the right thing for my clients.

Wet Crawlspaces Need Drainage

In addition to water vapor, many crawlspaces leak groundwater. Such cases require a drainage system appropriate to the details of the crawlspace. Outside, I make sure downspouts are directed away from the house. Inside, I grade to one corner and install a sump and a pump with a sealed lid. Groundwater that leaks in can make its way from the dirt floor into the sump and be pumped out (see "Got Water? Pump It Out" on the facing page).

If a lot of water is leaking in, I create a swale in the dirt at the perimeter to channel water into the sump more directly. As another option, I can trench in a perforated pipe around the perimeter pitched to the sump. To prevent the pipe from clogging with silt, I slip a filter-fabric sleeve over it. Except in cases where there's extreme flooding or where a concrete floor will be poured, I avoid using crushed stone on perimeter drains because it's heavy and it's hard to lug through small openings.

I do one more thing before installing the liner: clean the dirt. All sharp or large rocks are buried when I re-grade, thrown around the sump liner or removed along with any wood or other organic material.

Installing and Sealing the Liner

Once the crawlspace is cleaned out and drainage issues are solved, I install the liner. The liner material comes in a 24-ft. by 50-ft. accordion-folded roll. It's much easier to handle the 105-lb. roll outside than in the crawlspace, so I roll it out on the driveway to cut it to size (see the left photo on p. 152). I then fold and roll up the liner like a carpet, black side out, and bring it into the crawlspace.

I start with a piece of liner wide enough to cover the floor from the center row of piers to the perimeter, and up to the top of the wall. Next, I cover the other three walls, making sure the liner is long enough to overlap the floor by about 1 ft. Then I cut the remaining floor piece. After I roll out the liner, I take off my boots for the rest of the job to keep the liner clean.

Now, I turn back to the walls. I cut the liner 2 in. from the top of the wall (see the top left photo on p. 153) and fasten it with nylon expansion fasteners (Outwater Plastics; www.outwater.com) that press in ¼-in. holes that I drill every 3 ft. or 4 ft. along the top edge (see the bottom left photo on p. 153). I install the fasteners 3 in. down from the top of the liner (see the top right photo on p. 153) so that I can pull down the liner to seal it to the wall with polyurethane caulk (see the photo on p. 154). Polyurethane caulk is the only caulk I use on my projects; it sticks to anything and lasts for ages. I use Bostik 916 (www.bostik-sealants.com; 800-726-7845) or Vulkem® 116 (www.tremcosealants.com; 800-321-7906).

I never seal the liner to the sill plate because doing so gives water vapor a path to the wood and can be a route for termites and other insects to get to the house framing. Leaving the liner 2 in. down from the top of the wall allows for a routine termite inspection.

At wood posts, I lift the weight with a hydraulic jack, if possible, and slide the liner under. If I can lift the post only a bit, I slide a piece of aluminum flashing under the post and seal the liner to the edges of the flashing with caulk. At masonry piers or columns, I cut slits and wrap the liner up 6 in. or so,

GOT WATER? PUMP IT OUT

IF GUTTERS AND EXTERIOR GRADING won't stop water from coming in, a trench, perforated drainpipe, and a sump pump may be required to move it out. A water-removal strategy could be one of the following scenarios.

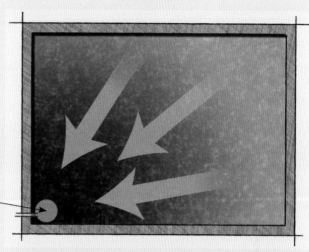

IF THE GROUND SLOPES TO ONE CORNER, install a sump in the lowest corner.

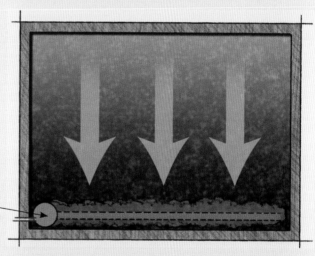

IF THE GROUND SLOPES TO ONE SIDE, dig a trench to channel water to the sump.

IF THE GROUND SLOPES MORE THAN ONE WAY, trench in a perforated pipe around the perimeter to carry water to the sump.

PLASTIC LINER IS MORE EASILY HANDLED IN THE DRIVEWAY. After the plastic is cut to size and rolled up, it can be installed in sections in the crawlspace. The author has liner material custom-made, but lighter plastic such as Tu-Tuf also can work.

then caulk. At seams, I caulk under the overlap and use a 4-in.-wide peel-and-stick tape made from a matching material, which makes the seams disappear. A high-quality builders' tape such as Tyvek® tape (www.dupont.com; 302-774-1000) also would work.

The finished system looks fantastic. My customers are pleasantly shocked when they see the end product. The white color reflects light, and it's clean and mold free. Indoor-air quality is improved, and the crawlspace can be used for storage.

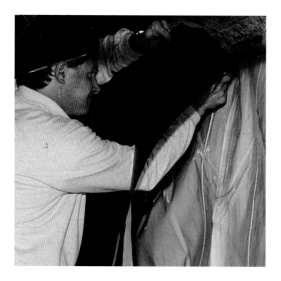

TO KEEP WATER AND INSECTS AWAY from floor framing, the liner is cut in place 2 in. below the top of the wall.

HOLES ARE DRILLED THROUGH THE LINER into the foundation (above), and nylon expansion fasteners are driven into the holes (top right).

SEEMS LIKE A SINGLE SHEET, BUT IT'S NOT. Overlapping seams of the liner sections are sealed with caulk and matching tape for a seamless barrier.

DAMP CRAWLSPACES CAN MAKE YOUR LIVING ROOM MOLDY

ALMOST WEEKLY, we see news stories about mold spores. Molds and individual tolerances to mold species vary. Some mold has little effect other than an unpleasant odor, but some can be toxic (most notably *Stachybotrys chartarum*).

Mold needs organic material, moderate temperatures, and moisture to grow. Remove one factor, and mold can't grow. Of these factors, moisture is the easiest to control. Mold thrives in damp environments. Using a hygrometer, we routinely find humidity readings well above 50% in dirt crawlspaces. Some are as high as 80%. This is compared with readings around 27% in conditioned space. According to the Environmental Protection Agency (EPA), relative humidity should be kept below 60% (ideally between 30% and 50%) to control mold. Properly sealing a damp crawlspace lowers relative humidity to within these levels.

For more information on mold prevention, visit the EPA website (www.epa.gov/mold/index.html).

POLYURETHANE CAULK AND PLASTIC TAPE SEAL THE DEAL

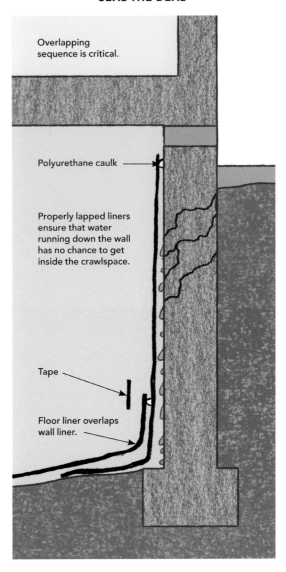

Overlapping sequence is critical.

Polyurethane caulk

Properly lapped liners ensure that water running down the wall has no chance to get inside the crawlspace.

Tape

Floor liner overlaps wall liner.

SEAL THE LINER to the foundation with polyurethane caulk.

PART 4

Retrofits and Add-Ons

The Stay-Dry, No-Mold Finished Basement

BY ANDY ENGEL

Finished-basement projects usually begin with visions of a game room for the kids or of a secluded spot for Dad to watch Sunday football games with his cronies. Just about as frequently, these projects end badly with black spots of mold, crumbling drywall, and a smell reminiscent of a dungeon. What goes wrong? In most cases, water becomes trapped behind a wood wall or floor and nurtures a bloom of rot.

However, it probably isn't a flood that causes the problem. Yes, bulk water, the kind that flows across the floor, needs to be eliminated before an attempt is made to finish a basement. (Some common measures include exterior waterproofing, functioning gutters, and/or an internal drain system.) But even if your basement looks dry, you easily can have problems when you enclose the concrete with a framed wall. The real villain here is water vapor, the invisible moisture that keeps concrete damp and makes cold-water pipes drip with condensation in the summer. This water is always present. To reduce mold growth, water's contact with cellulose (paper, wood, etc.) has to be limited, and the water has to be allowed to escape.

Through research published by Building Science Corporation (see "Sources" on p. 163), I've found

(Continued on p. 163)

BEFORE

AFTER

A REC ROOM THAT WILL LAST. Built with conventional wall framing, a plywood subfloor, and rigid-foam insulation, this basement remodel doesn't trap moisture that can cause problems later. (By the way, the stair railing isn't finished.)

UNDERSTANDING THE NATURE OF BASEMENTS AND WATER

MOISTURE MOVES FROM WET TO DRY and from warm to cool. In the summer, damp soils and warm air outside make the moisture drive mostly inward. Humid outside air enters the basement and condenses on anything below its dew point: cold-water pipes, concrete walls, and floors. In particular, carpeted concrete floors can be a problem because they easily can become wet enough to support mold and dust mites.

Most basements dry out only in the winter when interior heat sucks the available moisture out of the basement and drives some moisture outward through the exposed portion of the foundation. There's also some drive-out through the foundation itself because the basement is warmer than the surrounding soil. The trouble is that the soil tends to be wet, and so has a limited capacity for drying.

There's a significant energy cost in moving this water through the foundation. The traditional response has been to frame walls next to the foundation, fill them with fiberglass, and seal them with a plastic vapor barrier. But a basement vapor barrier can trap moisture and promote rot. Basement floors built with a similar system fare no better.

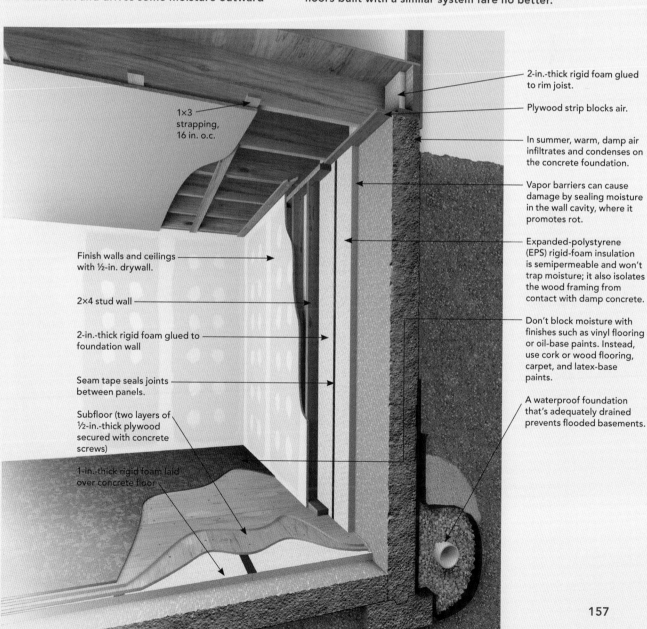

1×3 strapping, 16 in. o.c.

Finish walls and ceilings with ½-in. drywall.

2×4 stud wall

2-in.-thick rigid foam glued to foundation wall

Seam tape seals joints between panels.

Subfloor (two layers of ½-in.-thick plywood secured with concrete screws)

1-in.-thick rigid foam laid over concrete floor

2-in.-thick rigid foam glued to rim joist.

Plywood strip blocks air.

In summer, warm, damp air infiltrates and condenses on the concrete foundation.

Vapor barriers can cause damage by sealing moisture in the wall cavity, where it promotes rot.

Expanded-polystyrene (EPS) rigid-foam insulation is semipermeable and won't trap moisture; it also isolates the wood framing from contact with damp concrete.

Don't block moisture with finishes such as vinyl flooring or oil-base paints. Instead, use cork or wood flooring, carpet, and latex-base paints.

A waterproof foundation that's adequately drained prevents flooded basements.

PLYWOOD SUBFLOOR IS SUPPORTED AND INSULATED WITH RIGID FOAM

USE RIGID FOAM INSTEAD OF WOOD FOR SLEEPERS

To isolate the wood from moisture in the concrete, full sheets of EPS are laid on the concrete floor. Seam tape and expanding foam seal the seams against the infiltration of moist air.

TWO LAYERS OF PLYWOOD GO DOWN WITH SCREWS

After drilling and countersinking pilot holes $\boxed{1}$ $\boxed{2}$, the author attaches the first layer of 1/2-in.-thick plywood with 2½-in.-long concrete screws $\boxed{3}$. To allow for expansion, 1/8-in. gaps are left between each sheet and around the room's perimeter. Laid at right angles to the first layer, a second layer of plywood is fastened with 1⅝-in. drywall screws and spans the joints between sheets to make a stronger floor $\boxed{4}$.

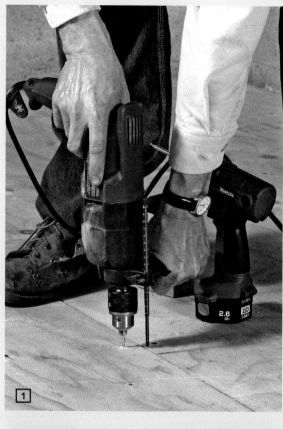

FRAMED WALLS ARE ISOLATED FROM THE FOUNDATION'S MOISTURE

AN INSULATED BAND JOIST STOPS THERMAL BRIDGING

Insulating the joist bays with 2-in.-thick EPS will keep air leaks and cold spots to a minimum. Minimal amounts of expanding foam applied around the edges of each piece act as both a sealant and an adhesive.

BLOCKING AIR INFILTRATION

A strip of plywood is screwed to the underside of the floor joists (photo below). Extending from the edge of the mudsill to the inside of the wall plate, this plywood creates an air barrier. Gaps are filled with expanding foam.

MAKE THE FOAM ON THE WALLS AS TIGHT AS POSSIBLE

After the floor is done, the walls are insulated with EPS sheets trimmed for a friction fit and glued to the foundation with expanding foam [1] [2]. Seams and gaps are filled with the foam and taped. Plywood scraps keep the sheets in place until the glue sets [3]. Unlike furring strips, a stud wall goes in plumb and straight, and allows room to run any utilities in the usual manner [4].

AIR QUALITY AND FIRE SAFETY IN THE BASEMENT

ONE OF THE EFFECTS of finishing a basement is to cut off leaks that may have been supplying combustion air for the boiler, furnace, or water heater. Failure to replace this air supply could contribute to backdrafting and the possible buildup of lethal amounts of carbon monoxide.

Unless the appliance manufacturer provides specs that say otherwise, the rule of thumb is to provide makeup-air ducts leading to the outside that are twice the size of the combined flues. In this basement, the boiler and water heater share a 6-in.-dia. flue. I provided two 6-in. supplies, one that ended at the ceiling level and one that ended near the floor in the mechanical room. To prevent these ducts from chimneying nice warm air to the outside, they were fitted with fabric dampers made for this low-pressure application (see the bottom photo below and "Sources" on the facing page).

One other safety consideration is basement egress. Most building codes require habitable basements to have two exits in case of fire. This basement already had two doors, so that requirement wasn't an issue. Lacking the second door, I'd have had to provide a code-approved egress window (a 5.2-sq.-ft. opening within 44 in. of the floor, leading to a 36-in. by 36-in. well with ladder rungs leading to grade). Last, if your home isn't already so equipped, install hard-wired smoke and carbon-monoxide detectors in the basement.

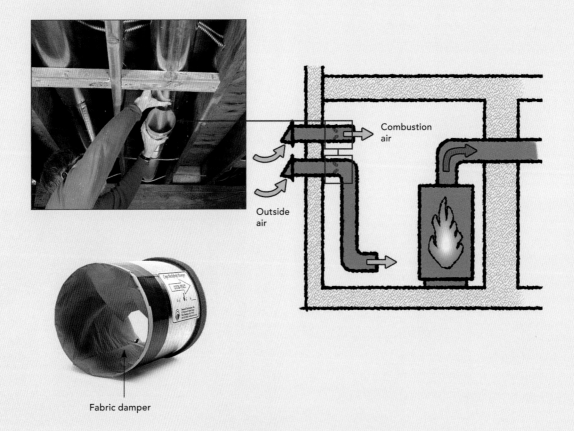

Combustion air

Outside air

Fabric damper

that rigid-foam insulation both thermally protects the basement and breaks the contact between framing and concrete. To avoid trapping moisture, I never install a vapor barrier. Instead, I use materials and finishes that allow moisture to diffuse. You can get rid of this diffused water by installing a dehumidifier or by extending the air-conditioning ductwork into the basement. I'm no expert in this area, so let an HVAC contractor figure out the specifics.

Isolate and Insulate the Concrete

I use 2-in.-thick expanded-polystyrene foam (EPS, or Styrofoam) on the walls and 1-in.-thick EPS below the plywood subfloor. This rigid-foam insulation is sufficient to make a noticeable temperature difference in the basement without crowding in the walls or the ceiling height. EPS is cheap, effective, and vapor permeable. Believe it or not, it also has the compressive strength to support a two-layer plywood subfloor without the use of sleepers.

After insulating the rim joist, I cover the floor with a layer of 1-in.-thick EPS. On top of this, I lay the subfloor, then build a regular stud wall against the foam on the walls.

Keeping wood from contacting concrete is critical. Fail here, and you're inviting water in through capillary action. You could use pressure-treated plywood and framing lumber, but I think that's false security and an unnecessary expense. If you've got enough moisture in the wall or the floor to cause rot, then you've also got the right conditions for mold growth, something that pressure-treated lumber won't prevent.

It's also possible to skip the stud wall and to screw furring strips to the concrete through the foam, but I don't like that approach for two reasons. First, I haven't seen many basement walls that are as plumb or as straight as I can build a stud wall. Unless you want to spend days playing with shims, the furring strips will mimic the defects of the foundation. Second, furring strips don't have the depth that allows easy installation of electrical boxes.

SOURCES

The foam gun, canisters of expanding-foam sealant, seam tape, and low-pressure dampers are available from the Energy Federation Inc. (800-876-0660; www.efi.org).

Expanded-polystyrene (EPS) rigid foam is available at most lumberyards and home centers.

Much of the information in this article was obtained from the consulting firm Building Science Corporation; its website (www.buildingscience.com) has a wealth of information on building technology.

Adding Insulation to Basement Walls

BY MARTIN HOLLADAY

If you live in South Carolina, Alabama, Oklahoma, southern California, or anywhere colder, your basement walls should be insulated. In climate zones 3 and higher, basement insulation is required by the 2012 International Residential Code as follows: R-5 in climate zone 3, R-10 in climate zone 4 (except marine zone 4), and R-15 in marine zone 4 and climate zones 5, 6, 7, and 8.

If your home lacks basement-wall insulation, it's much easier to install interior insulation than exterior insulation. Here's how to do it correctly.

Make Sure Your Basement Is Dry

Before installing any interior-wall insulation, verify that your basement doesn't have a water-entry problem. Diagnosing and fixing water-entry problems in existing basements is too big a topic to be discussed here. Suffice it to say that if your basement walls get wet every spring or every time you get a heavy rain, the walls should not be insulated until the water-entry problem is solved.

Use Foam Insulation

The best way to insulate the interior side of a basement wall is with foam insulation that is adhered to or sprayed directly on the concrete. Any of the following insulation materials are acceptable for this purpose: closed-cell spray polyurethane foam or either XPS, EPS, or polyisocyanurate rigid foam.

Rigid foam can be adhered to a poured-concrete or concrete-block wall with foam-compatible adhesive or with special plastic fasteners such as Hilti® IDPs or Rodenhouse Plasti-Grip® PMFs. To prevent interior air from reaching the cold concrete, seal the perimeter of each piece of rigid foam with adhesive, caulk, high-quality flashing tape, or canned spray foam.

Building codes require most types of foam insulation to be protected by a layer of gypsum drywall. Many builders put up a 2×4 wall on the interior side of the foam insulation; the studs provide a convenient wiring chase and make drywall installation simple. (If you frame a 2×4 wall, don't forget to install fire blocking at the top of the wall.)

If your basement has stone-and-mortar walls, you can't insulate them with rigid foam. The only type of insulation that makes sense for stone-and-mortar walls is closed-cell spray polyurethane foam.

If you plan to insulate your basement walls with spray foam, the best approach is to frame your 2×4 walls before the foam is sprayed, leaving a gap of 1½ in. to 2 in. between the back of the studs and the concrete wall. The gap will be filled later with spray foam.

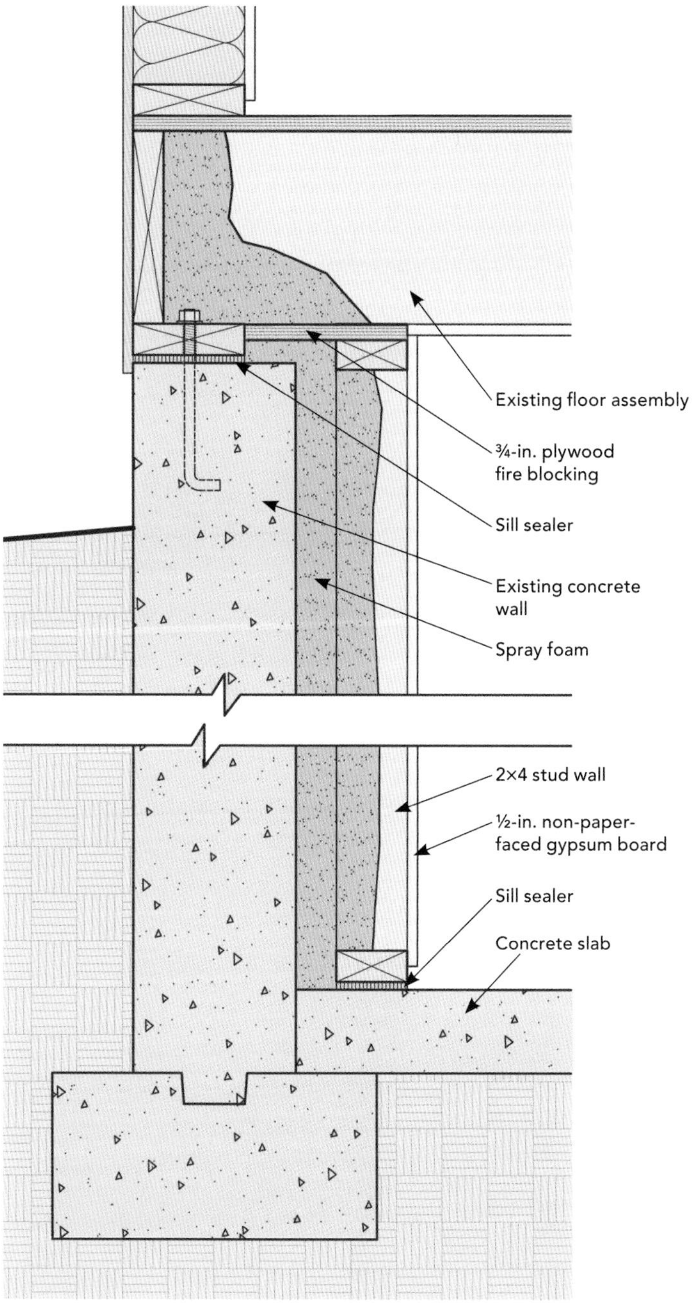

Existing floor assembly
¾-in. plywood fire blocking
Sill sealer
Existing concrete wall
Spray foam
2×4 stud wall
½-in. non-paper-faced gypsum board
Sill sealer
Concrete slab

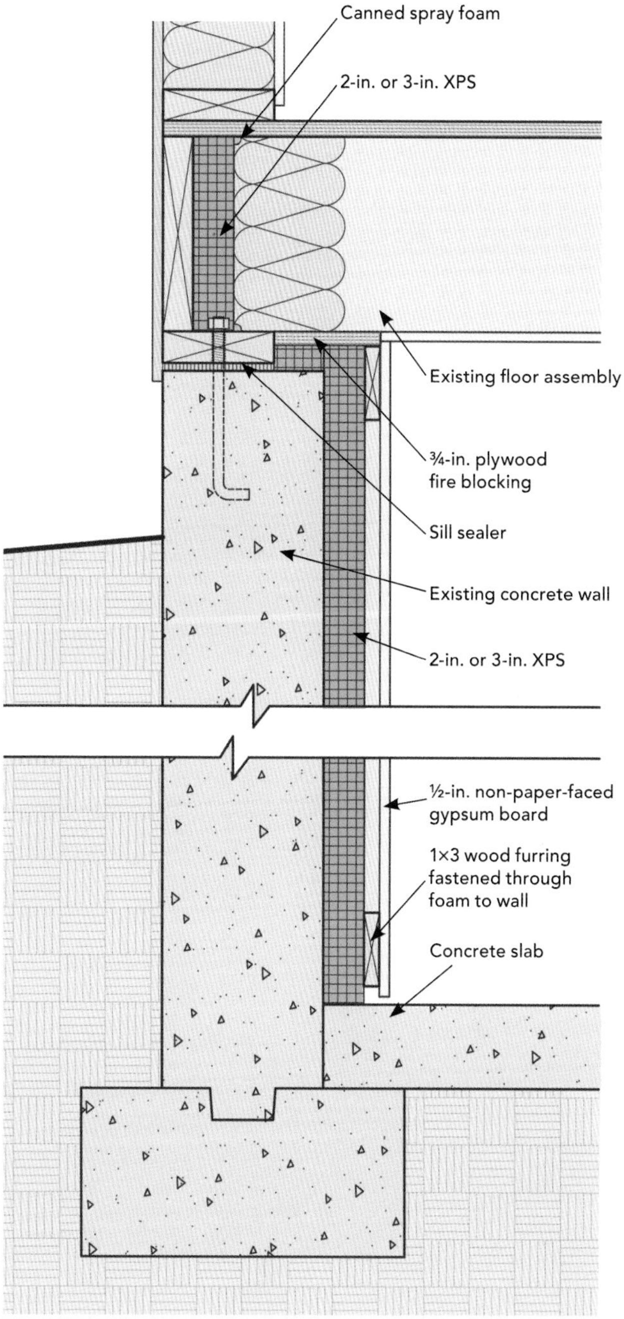

Canned spray foam
2-in. or 3-in. XPS
Existing floor assembly
¾-in. plywood fire blocking
Sill sealer
Existing concrete wall
2-in. or 3-in. XPS
½-in. non-paper-faced gypsum board
1×3 wood furring fastened through foam to wall
Concrete slab

CLOSED-CELL FOAM

If you want to insulate the interior of your basement wall with spray foam, specify closed-cell spray foam, not open-cell foam. Closed-cell foam does a better job of stopping the diffusion of moisture from the damp concrete to the interior. Frame the 2×4 wall before the spray foam is installed, with a gap of about 2 in. between the 2×4s and the concrete.

RIGID FOAM

A 2-in. layer of XPS foam (R-10) is adequate in most of climate zone 4. However, if you live in marine zone 4 or in climate zones 5, 6, 7, or 8, you need at least 3 in. of XPS or 4 in. of EPS to meet the minimum code requirement of R-15. Furring strips should be fastened to the concrete wall through the rigid foam.

If you live in an area where termites are a problem, your local building code may require that you leave a 3-in.-high termite-inspection strip of bare concrete near the top of your basement wall.

While reduced costs might tempt you to use fibrous insulation such as fiberglass batts, mineral-wool batts, or cellulose, these materials are air-permeable and should never be installed against a below-grade concrete wall. When this type of insulation is installed in contact with concrete, moisture in the interior air can condense against the cold concrete surface, potentially leading to mold and rot.

Don't Worry about Inward Drying

Some people mistakenly believe that a damp concrete wall should be able to dry toward the interior—in other words, that any insulation on the interior of a basement wall should be vapor-permeable. In fact, you don't want to encourage any moisture to enter your home by this route. Don't worry about your concrete wall; it can stay damp for a century without suffering any problems or deterioration.

Avoid Polyethylene Vapor Barriers

Basement wall systems should never include polyethylene. You don't need any poly between the concrete and the foam insulation, nor do you want poly between gypsum drywall and the insulation. If your wall assembly includes studs or furring strips, polyethylene can trap moisture, leading to mold or rot.

Basement Insulation Is Cost-Effective

If you live in climate zone 3 or anywhere colder, installing basement-wall insulation will almost always save you money through lower energy bills. It will also provide an important side benefit: Insulated walls are less susceptible to condensation and mold. This means that insulated basements stay drier and smell better than uninsulated basements.

Retrofitting a Foundation

BY BRIAN BROPHY

Replacing a house's foundation can be a daunting task, but the work can restore a home's structural integrity and make it last for another century or more. After having retrofitted several foundations, I've settled on doing as much of the work as I can. I've found the work to be easier than expected, and the more I do myself, the more I profit. That said, when the work exceeds my expertise or comfort level, I sub it out. In the end, a handful of subs work on each project, including an engineer, an HVAC contractor, and a house-lifting company. The contractor's job is to keep the job site safe and the work moving by hiring quality subs and communicating clearly with them.

Make the Choice to Retrofit

Most people would rather repair a foundation than replace it. However, certain situations call for a complete retrofit. In my experience, foundations fail mostly because they were not engineered properly for the soil conditions around the house. Common sources of failure include weak bearing soil, which is

RETROFITTING A FOUNDATION begins with the disconnection of all utilities and the installation of steel I-beams, on which the house will rest when lifted from the old foundation.

THIS FARMHOUSE sat in a 300-acre vine-yard 2 hours east of San Francisco for more than 100 years. It had been passed down through generations of grape growers. The original brick foundation finally reached critical failure. The brick itself was in decent shape, but all the mortar had disintegrated.

- Location: Lockeford, Calif.
- Foundation length: 140 lin. ft.
- Foundation height: 6 ft.
- Type: Concrete replacing brick
- Project length: 15 days
- Project cost: $45,000 (2011 prices)

GENERAL COST BREAKDOWN

- Engineer: 9% ($4,050)
- HVAC/plumbing sub: 5% ($2,250)
- Machinery rental: 10% ($4,500)
- Material: 10% ($4,500)
- House lift: 15% ($6,750)
- Crew labor: 20% ($9,000)
- Net income: 31% ($13,950)

THE BEAMS ROLLED UNDER THIS HOUSE were lifted with individual 30-ton jacks. Some outfits use a unified hydraulic-jack system that raises and lowers the house evenly in one shot. Those systems require less labor, but the individual jacks that were used on this job work well, too.

Project Journal

My greatest strengths as a contractor are my own crew and the relationships I have with my subs. Here is an outline of who completed each step of the project and when they were on site. A job of this scale hinges on a variety of site-specific factors, but by implementing a similar schedule in your own foundation-retrofit project, you will be more apt to stay on deadline and within your budget.

not capable of properly supporting the weight of the house, or poor soil compaction, which creates voids. (For more on soil problems and solutions, see "Soil: The Other Half of the Foundation" on p. 8.)

It is also important to pay attention to the foundation material itself. For instance, brick can deteriorate through a process known as spalling, and concrete can suffer sulfate attack, which can reduce its cohesion and strength.

Most of these failures can be detected visually, but I find it best to consult with an engineer whenever possible. An engineer can provide critical feedback that will steer the course of the work.

DAY 1

Disconnect all the ductwork tied to the furnace and air-conditioning units.

- *Who's responsible:* HVAC subcontractor
- *What to look for:* Be sure that the subcontractor temporarily seals all the ductwork openings before demo. This will keep the ducts—and the house—free of dirt, dust, and debris. In older homes, this is also a good opportunity to analyze the performance of the heating and cooling elements and to replace them with more efficient models.

Disconnect electrical and plumbing runs to the main floor.

- *Who's responsible:* Contractor's crew (electrical), plumbing subcontractor
- *What to look for:* All the plumbing lines and electrical runs should be disconnected and secured so that they will not be damaged and so that they will not hinder the work under the house. If need be, remove any plumbing that will interfere with getting the beams in place. Plan to replace the gas and septic lines when the foundation is removed. It is unlikely that there will ever be better access to these lines again, so take advantage of the opportunity to do the work. There will be lots of activity on the job during this phase of the project. The order in which the subs are called doesn't matter much, but be sure they're scheduled so they're not forced to interrupt each other's workflow.

Build the cribbing necessary to support the structure, and install the steel I-beams with a crane. Lift the house with jacks, and stabilize it on cribbing.

- *Who's responsible:* House lifters

- *What to look for:* Be sure that the beams are placed in the correct position and that the load-bearing points of the structure are well supported. If the engineer has offered recommendations on beam placement, be sure that the house lifters' installation is in sync with that plan.

DAY 2

Begin the excavation work around the house.

- *Who's responsible:* Contractor's crew
- *What to look for:* Crew members should be comfortable with and capable of operating a rented Bobcat® and mini-excavator. Someone should dig by hand around critical elements like gas and sewer lines. Create enough space between the foundation and the edge of the trench to work safely. Take measures to reduce erosion and prevent rainstorms washing dirt into the basement. Move excess soil away from the trench and place silt fence around each dirt pile.

DAY 3

Excavation work continues.

WE CREATE A TRENCH WIDE ENOUGH, about 6 ft., to allow the Bobcat to drive down to the grade of the slab. This makes removing the old foundation material a lot easier. It also creates a large, safe working zone for those building the new footings and foundation walls.

CONSULT AN ENGINEER

I ALWAYS CONSULT AN ENGINEER before I start foundation retrofit work. It would be easy enough to let local codes dictate the details of a project, but the codes in my part of the country are rather lax. I want to be sure that my job is done right and that my work reflects the specific demands of the site. An engineer helps me do that. My engineer offers guidance on everything from the temporary support-beam placement and footing construction to rebar and anchor-bolt placement.

Choosing the right engineer is imperative, but unfortunately, there isn't a formula to follow when deciding who is best. I've worked with the same engineer on every project, and the only recommendation I can offer is to find someone who has worked on house lifts before and whom you trust.

DAY 4

Begin foundation removal after all excavation is complete.

- *Who's responsible:* Contractor's crew
- *What to look for:* Use the bucket on the mini-excavator to pull down large sections. Use the Bobcat to haul away all the material and to make room for the new footings. Work carefully around any existing gas lines and sewer lines. Remove the bricks in these locations by hand with sledgehammers and wrecking bars, never with machinery.

DAY 5

Foundation removal continues.

DAY 6

Finish foundation removal and final cleanup of debris.

- *Who's responsible:* Contractor's crew
- *What to look for:* The job site should be clear of brick and any construction debris to make room for forming new footings.

IDEALLY, DAY 8 OF THE PROJECT WILL FALL ON A FRIDAY, as it did on this job, so that the footings can cure through the weekend.

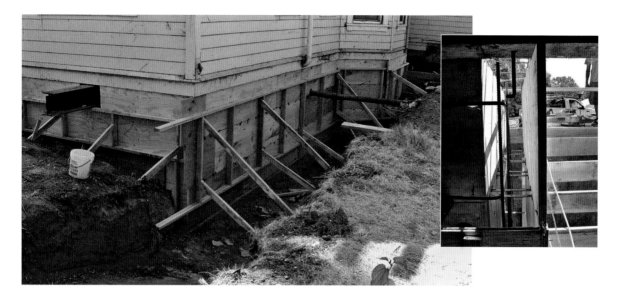

ON THIS PROJECT, WE BUILT 140 LIN. FT. OF FORM using 2×4s for walers, 1⅛-in. plywood, and snap ties. You can certainly sub out this work, but building forms goes quickly. I've found that building forms costs less than hiring a concrete subcontractor to do the work.

DAY 7

Dig and form the new footings for the foundation stemwalls.

- *Who's responsible:* Contractor's crew
- *What to look for:* Be sure that the overall dimensions of the footings are code compliant and in tune with the engineer's recommendations. These footings are 24 in. wide by 24 in. deep and are reinforced with ½-in. rebar placed horizontally 3 in. from the top and bottom of the forms and vertically every 18 in.

For more information on building square and level footings and walls, visit FineHomebuilding.com (search for "Site work and foundations").

DAY 8

Pour new footings.

- *Who's responsible:* Contractor's crew
- *What to look for:* The grade of the footings is determined and marked with a transit and chalkline when the forms are built. Be sure that the crew is following the proper grade. Also be sure that all the rebar is well supported; otherwise, it will sink to the bottom of the form when concrete is poured and reduce the strength of the footing. Rebar can be set atop metal chairs or dobies or be suspended from above by wrapping the rebar with wire and attaching the wire to a furring strip nailed to each side of the form.

DAY 9

Build the forms for the foundation stemwalls.

- *Who's responsible:* Contractor's crew
- *What to look for:* Check to be sure that all the walls are plumb, square, and level. All the rebar should be in place in accordance with the engineer's recommendations. Before the concrete truck's arrival, new anchor bolts should be hung from the mudsills by attaching a nut to each bolt.

DAY 10

Formwork continues.

DAY 11

Pour foundation stemwalls.

- *Who's responsible:* Contractor's crew
- *What to look for:* The concrete truck should have clear access to the foundation. Concrete trucks

I SPECIFY THE DRIEST CONCRETE MIX that my plant will supply for optimum strength and that will cure properly in my climate, which usually demands the use of additives. Drier concrete, however, sometimes leads to small voids in the wall after the forms are stripped.

THIS WALL WAS DAMPPROOFED using a spray-on product called Pene-Krete® (www.super-krete.com). If using a dampproofing membrane, stop it 4 in. below final grade. Reduce installation errors by snapping a chalkline on the foundation wall at this height.

weigh a lot and have the ability to cause substantial damage to driveways, buried sewer pipes, and septic tanks. Keep the truck on solid ground. Spray all the forms with a release agent. Minimize voids in the wall by ensuring that the concrete hose is at the bottom of the form, and by filling the form from the bottom up instead of letting concrete fall from the top. During the pour, shake the forms with a vibrating rod to help settle the concrete.

DAY 12

Strip the forms, and fill voids.

- *Who's responsible:* Contractor's crew
- *What to look for:* Use a trowel and masonry mortar to fill any honeycombing, or small voids between the aggregate. If larger voids form, patch them with a 3,000-psi concrete mix. The holes in the foundation that are left for beam removal will be patched later with a similar mix.

DAY 13

Lower the house onto the new foundation walls.

- *Who's responsible:* House lifters
- *What to look for:* The most critical error that can occur when retrofitting a foundation is having the house lifters transfer the weight of the house from the beams to the new foundation too quickly. Let

the foundation cure properly before the house is lowered, which may demand supplemental wetting over the course of a week if admixtures weren't used.

DAY 14

Patch access holes and reconnect all the mechanical, plumbing, and electrical systems.

- *Who's responsible:* HVAC subcontractor and contractor's crew
- *What to look for:* Assess the condition of all ductwork, plumbing lines, and electrical wires. This is the time to replace any damaged, dated, or questionable materials.

DAY 15

Backfill, compact, and regrade the soil surrounding the new foundation.

- *Who's responsible:* Contractor's crew
- *What to look for:* The final grade of the site should slope down and away from the new foundation. This ensures that surface water will drain away from the foundation instead of settling alongside it.

Creating a Sealed Crawlspace

BY MARTIN HOLLADAY

I f you live in the eastern half of the United States and want a damp, moldy crawlspace, just make sure that it is vented to the exterior. Within a few short years, the fiberglass batts installed in the crawlspace ceiling will become so damp that they'll hang down like stalactites. You'll end up with a classic moldy crawlspace—one that represents a significant source of moisture for the house above.

During the summer months, warm outdoor air holds more moisture than cooler crawlspace air. When that humid outdoor air enters the crawlspace vents, it hits cool surfaces—concrete, water pipes, and air-conditioning ducts—and condensation forms and begins to drip. One remedy that is sometimes attempted is to add a fan to the space, but that just increases the occurrence of condensation. The more you ventilate, the wetter the crawlspace gets. Crawlspace vents also can cause problems during the winter by introducing frigid outdoor air into the space, which can cause pipes to freeze.

Properly designed unvented (sealed) crawlspaces stay drier than vented crawlspaces, the pipes within them are protected from wintertime freeze–thaw cycles, and they require less insulation than vented crawlspaces (because the area of the perimeter walls is less than the area of the crawlspace ceiling). They also bring any ducts running through the crawl-space into the conditioned envelope of the house—an improvement that usually results in energy savings.

New-construction crawlspaces may require temporary dehumidification to remove construction moisture. Once the home is dried in, it's a good idea to install a dehumidifier in the crawlspace and run it for 3 months or 4 months until the interior relative humidity stabilizes. Also, remember that any combustion appliance (for example, a water heater or furnace) in an unvented crawlspace should be a sealed-combustion unit.

Detailing an Unvented Crawlspace

If you want to build an unvented crawlspace, follow these recommendations.

- To help keep the crawlspace dry, make sure the exterior grade slopes away from the foundation.
- Remove all rocks and debris from the crawlspace floor, and rake the dirt smooth. In new construction, it's best for the crawlspace floor to be higher than the exterior grade.

- If the crawlspace is subject to water entry, slope the floor to a sump equipped with a drain or a sump pump.
- Install a durable vapor barrier—for example, a 20-mil pool liner or Tu-Tuf poly—over the floor. Extend it up the crawlspace walls, leaving 3 in. uncovered at the top to create a termite-inspection strip.
- Attach the top of the vapor barrier to the wall with horizontal battens secured with masonry fasteners.
- Seal the seams of the vapor barrier with a compatible tape or mastic. Many builders use duct mastic embedded in fiberglass-mesh tape.
- Install a 2-in.- or 3-in.-thick concrete slab to protect the vapor barrier, or install a sacrificial layer of 6-mil poly on top of the permanent vapor barrier to protect it from damage during installation of mechanicals and insulation.
- If testing shows high radon levels, install a passive radon-collection system below the crawlspace floor.
- Insulate the interior of the walls and rim joists with rigid foam or spray polyurethane foam. Many builders use Thermax™, a polyisocyanurate foam that in most jurisdictions does not require a thermal barrier or ignition barrier. (Alternatively, you can insulate the exterior of the walls.) If your crawlspace has stone-and-mortar walls, you must use closed-cell spray polyurethane foam. Install at least as much insulation as required by the 2012 IRC for basement walls: R-5 for climate zone 3; R-10 for climate zone 4 (except marine zone 4); and R-15 for marine zone 4 and climate zones 5, 6, 7, and 8.
- Install an exhaust fan or a forced-air register as required by code (see "Code Requirements for Unvented Crawlspaces" at right). Be sure that the fan does not exceed airflow requirements for the size of the crawlspace, because exhaust fans always carry an energy penalty.

CODE REQUIREMENTS FOR UNVENTED CRAWLSPACES

MOST BUILDING CODES PERMIT the construction of unvented crawlspaces. In recent versions of the International Residential Code, requirements for unvented crawlspaces can be found in section R408.3. If an unvented crawlspace has a dirt floor, the code requires exposed earth to be covered with a continuous vapor retarder with taped seams: "The edges of the vapor retarder shall extend at least 6 in. up the stem wall and shall be attached and sealed to the stem wall."

In addition to the requirement of a duct or floor grille connecting the crawlspace to the conditioned space above, the code lists two options for conditioning unvented crawlspaces.

Option 1 (see right drawing on the facing page): Install a continuously operating exhaust fan in the crawlspace that blows through a hole in the rim joist or an exterior wall. Make sure that the fan isn't too powerful (1 cfm for each 50 sq. ft. of crawlspace floor area), because the makeup air entering the crawlspace is conditioned air from the house.

Option 2 (see left drawing on the facing page): Install a forced-air register to deliver supply air from the furnace or air handler to the crawlspace (again, 1 cfm for each 50 sq. ft.). Assuming the house has air-conditioning, this introduction of cool, dry air during the summer keeps the crawlspace dry.

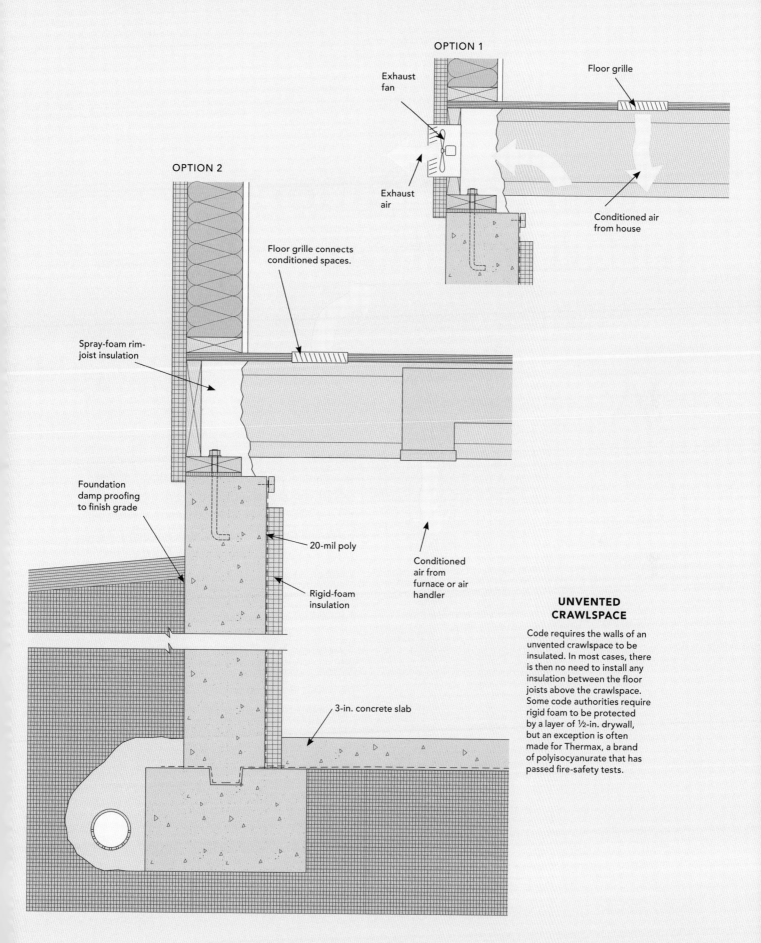

OPTION 1

Exhaust
fan

Floor grille

Exhaust
air

Conditioned air
from house

OPTION 2

Floor grille connects
conditioned spaces.

Spray-foam rim-
joist insulation

Foundation
damp proofing
to finish grade

20-mil poly

Rigid-foam
insulation

Conditioned
air from
furnace or air
handler

3-in. concrete slab

UNVENTED CRAWLSPACE

Code requires the walls of an unvented crawlspace to be insulated. In most cases, there is then no need to install any insulation between the floor joists above the crawlspace. Some code authorities require rigid foam to be protected by a layer of ½-in. drywall, but an exception is often made for Thermax, a brand of polyisocyanurate that has passed fire-safety tests.

A Fast Foundation for an Addition

BY RICK ARNOLD

A few years ago, a builder asked me to form and pour a crawlspace foundation for a small addition using insulating concrete forms (ICFs). I had never worked with ICFs before. He was a good customer, though, so I rolled my eyes and agreed. I grabbed my friend and fellow contributing editor Mike Guertin, figuring we could muddle our way through just about anything. Less than two hours later, we were ready to pour, and I was sold.

Since then, I have used ICFs to form everything from full basements to two-story houses. Along the way, I've discovered many benefits of building with ICFs (see "Building with ICFs" on p. 178), but I especially like them for small-addition foundations, like the 18-ft. by 18-ft. foundation featured here, because they can be installed so quickly. In fact, I've talked contractors and homeowners through the process over the phone.

Because ICFs are so easy to install, I can save a lot of money in labor by doing the job myself rather than paying a subcontractor. For instance, this job cost a bit more than $1,400: $900 for the blocks, and about $550 for the 7½ yd. of concrete (2005 prices). ICFs are available in several styles, each suited for different types of walls. I prefer the flat-wall type,

even though it requires more concrete than other styles, because it emulates the more familiar poured-concrete wall.

To estimate the number of blocks needed for a job, I start by dividing the length of each wall by the length of a single block. When added together, this tells me how many blocks I need in each course. Next, I divide the required height of the wall by the height of one block; this tells me how many courses I will need. When multiplied together, these two numbers give me the total blocks needed. I also like to add one extra block for each side of the foundation in case I run into problems.

Establish a Dead-Level First Course

To start, I sweep the standard concrete footing clean and snap chalklines representing the outside perimeter of the foundation (see "Forming and Pouring Footings" on p. 67). Next, I cut 2½-in. light-gauge steel-stud track to length and fasten it along the chalklines with masonry nails (see the top photo on p. 179). The metal track, which normally is sold as top and bottom plates for steel-stud wall systems, just happens to be the right width to hold the iForm blocks firmly in place.

THANKS TO INTERLOCKING FOAM FORMS, you can form, pour, and insulate any small foundation in a single day.

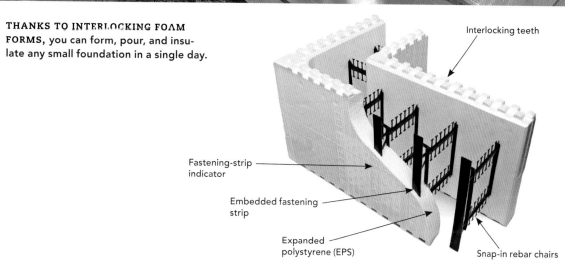

Interlocking teeth

Fastening-strip indicator

Embedded fastening strip

Expanded polystyrene (EPS)

Snap-in rebar chairs

PROS

- Unlike conventional concrete foundations, ICFs require no special tools or training. Basic carpentry skills are about all that is needed.
- The expanded-polystyrene (EPS) blocks are light, easy to cut and place, and permanent.
- There is no hassle of stripping forms after the pour.
- Fabrication around difficult areas like live sewer pipes and electrical conduit is easy.
- When concrete is poured inside ICF blocks, a negligible amount of water evaporation occurs, which is crucial to proper curing. Most contractors strip conventional forms a day or two after the pour, which increases evaporation and interferes with the curing process.
- Pouring concrete in cold weather is not a problem because the curing concrete generates heat that's retained by the insulation.
- If a conditioned crawlspace is part of the building-envelope strategy, the ICFs provide a well-insulated and air-sealed barrier.
- Basements built with ICFs are less prone to moisture problems than are poured-concrete walls.

CONS

- Exposed exteriors require a protective finish. I use an exterior insulation and finish system (EIFS) coating called Dryvit® (www.dryvit.com) or ¼-in. cementitious panels (www.jameshardie.com).
- The outer 2½ in. of the finished foundation is not load bearing, so I use a larger sill plate (2×8 instead of 2×6); I always double the plate anyway.
- Building officials may require the inside wall of an ICF crawlspace to be covered with a fire-retardant material.
- ICFs offer no means of visual inspection for insects. Some brands of ICFs are treated for insects, but termite shields and ground treatment are good ideas.

Before I start installing the blocks, I check the footing for level. The key to a quick, accurate installation is a dead-level first course. If the footing is more than ¼ in. out of level, I have some adjusting to do. This can be done by trimming the bottom of the blocks or by lifting them with shims, and later filling in any gaps with expanding foam.

Because each block is 16 in. tall and the overall foundation height often isn't a multiple of 16, I usually have to trim one course to get the correct finished height. If this is the case, I prefer to cut the bottom of the first course so that the top course is a full-height block. The blocks can be cut quickly to a uniform height on the tablesaw, using the rip fence as a guide.

Corners Come First

Because the corners are the weakest points in the foundation, they are the first blocks to be installed on each course. This ensures that I won't have to compromise their strength by cutting them to fit the rest of the blocks. After I lay the corners, I fill in with straight blocks.

As I work my way out of each corner, I usually have to trim one block on each side of the foundation to get the right fit. The iForm blocks have vertical lines at 1-in. increments on the sides, so I can take my jigsaw and cut by eye, using the nearest inch line as a guide. It's best to cut a little short rather than a little long; any extra length will push the corners out of square.

Block by block, I work my way toward the existing foundation. Butting the ICFs against a flat surface (poured concrete or concrete block) simply involves cutting the last blocks to the correct length and inserting rebar into the existing wall. But on this job, the existing foundation was fieldstone that had a very irregular surface. Thanks to the easy-working properties of the ICFs, I was able to scribe the blocks to fit against the old foundation (see the left photo on p. 181). I didn't need any rebar anchoring the new wall to the old because the rough

THE FIRST COURSE IS MOST IMPORTANT

Anchor the first course of ICF blocks by fastening steel track along the chalklines with 1-in. masonry nails spaced 2 ft. to 3 ft. o.c. (left). I set the corners of each course first to eliminate any need to cut, and thereby weaken, this structurally vital part of the foundation (below).

ZIP TIES SECURE THE CORNERS. Because the corners are the weakest points in the form assembly, it's important to secure corner blocks to adjacent straight blocks with plastic zip ties.

REBAR STRENGTHENS THE CONCRETE

PLASTIC ZIP TIES and internal webbing hold vertical and horizontal rebar in place.

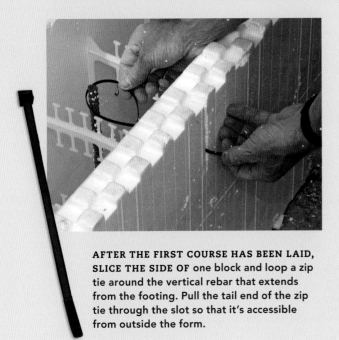

AFTER THE FIRST COURSE HAS BEEN LAID, SLICE THE SIDE OF one block and loop a zip tie around the vertical rebar that extends from the footing. Pull the tail end of the zip tie through the slot so that it's accessible from outside the form.

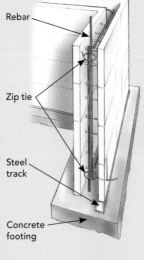

Rebar

Zip tie

Steel track

Concrete footing

WHEN THE AUTHOR DROPS IN ANOTHER LENGTH OF VERTICAL REBAR from above, it is carefully threaded into the looped zip tie, which then is pulled tight with a pair of pliers to tie the rebar together.

fieldstone offers a strong bonding surface, which poured-concrete and block walls do not.

Reinforce the Forms with Plastic and Steel

Once the first course is laid, I reinforce the corners by securing the corner blocks to adjacent straight blocks with zip ties (see the bottom photo on p. 179). Available at any hardware store, zip ties are thin plastic straps used for bundling cables and wires. I also use zip ties to tie together the two blocks that form the vertical seam. Then I snap in a row of $\frac{1}{2}$-in. rebar and overlap it by at least 18 in. in the corners. The rebar chairs of the block I use are formed to allow two pieces of rebar (up to $\frac{5}{8}$ in. dia. each) to be snapped together, one on top of the other, eliminating the need for wire ties. That's a real time-saver.

On the next course, I flip the corner blocks end for end so that the seams will stagger. I build up the corners pyramid style, making sure to attach the corner blocks to adjacent straight blocks with zip ties before stacking the next unit.

After measuring the diagonals of the foundation to make sure it's still square, I lay the rest of the straight blocks in place, reinforce the vertical seams, and scribe the ends as before. Staggering the cut seams in successive courses is not an option because ICFs with interlocking teeth almost never line up correctly; therefore, one of the two rows of teeth would have to be cut off to get the forms to seat properly.

Handling Vents and Openings

To create a hole for crawlspace access, I build a permanent frame using pressure-treated lumber. The bottom of the frame is separated into two halves with a gap in the middle so that I can watch for voids underneath during the pour.

When I use steel vents meant for poured-concrete walls, I run into two problems. The first is that traditional vents are made for 12-in.-wide walls, but the ICF walls I use are 13 in. wide. This means the vent has to be recessed 1 in. on the inside of the crawlspace. Also, there is no easy way to secure vents during the pour. I've managed to solve this problem by placing a heavy rock on top until the pour is finished.

Getting Ready for the Pour

I straighten the top of the walls with steel track, which keeps the interlocking teeth from clogging with concrete. I also string up a dry line 1 in. to 2 in. above the outside perimeter of the walls. After snapping in the top row of rebar, I reinforce the vertical cut seams in the blocks by gluing them together with foam and screwing plywood scabs into the embed-

ded fastening strips across both sides (see the right photo below).

It doesn't take much concrete to move an unbraced wall, but it doesn't take much time to brace it either. As concrete is poured into the wall, it tends to push the blocks away from the existing foundation. To prevent this, I brace the ends of the wall opposite the existing foundation. Because the blocks I use lock together so tightly, bracing the sides of the foundation isn't necessary. However, if you use another brand of ICFs, check the instructions.

TIE UP LOOSE ENDS BEFORE THE POUR

EVEN THOUGH THE ICF FOUNDATION is strong and stable, I always reinforce large seams with a combination of plywood and foam, and I brace the outside corners to ensure a trouble-free pour.

FOAM FILLS THE GAPS. Expanding foam can be used to seal seams, plug holes, and tighten rough scribe work.

THERE'S NO SUCH THING AS TOO MUCH BRACING. It may be overkill, but always brace the corners securely to prevent the blocks from pushing away from the existing foundation.

PLYWOOD BANDAGES. After gluing large vertical seams with foam, reinforce them with plywood scabs screwed to the embedded fastening strips found on both sides of the seams.

POUR THE CONCRETE

THE POUR REQUIRES CLOSE ATTENTION. It's best to pour the walls in 2-ft.- to 3-ft.-high sections called "lifts." Start with the corners before proceeding to the straight sections, making sure to watch carefully for a void-free pour. I use rocks to hold down the vents, and a dry line lets me double-check that the walls stay true.

SMOOTH THE SURFACE. Once the walls have been topped off, use steel track as a guide to remove excess concrete and to smooth out the surface before inserting anchor bolts.

The Pour Is the Trickiest Part

Most ICF manufacturers list how many blocks can be filled by 1 cu. yd. of concrete. For instance, 1 cu. yd. of concrete fills seven and a half 13-in.-wide iForm blocks. So I simply count the number of blocks in the foundation, divide it by 7½, then round up to the nearest half yard.

The design and engineering of ICF blocks are based on a 3,000-psi concrete strength, but double-check your local code and the ICF manufacturer's specs to make sure you pour the right type of concrete in the foundation. I usually order 3,000-psi concrete with ¼-in. to ⅜-in. peastone aggregate. I've found that concrete with aggregate larger than ⅜ in. is difficult to pour and consolidate in the ICFs.

Pouring the concrete is the trickiest part of the process. Because the concrete needs to flow between the webbing of each ICF block, the consistency of the concrete is important. The lower the slump, the less water is mixed with the concrete, and the stiffer it will be. But a higher slump of 6 or 7 may result in substandard strength.

As with all three-wall foundations, I first anchor the corner blocks by filling them about halfway with concrete. Keeping the concrete at a 4 slump, I continue pouring the rest of the walls to the halfway mark. Then I have the truck driver loosen the concrete to about a 5 slump, start back at the corners again, and continue with the top half of the pour.

During the pour I constantly watch for voids forming, walls bowing, or gaps and seams opening up between the forms. I just use a stick to poke the concrete beneath the vents because I don't like to use a vibrator unless absolutely necessary. If gaps or seams open up, I stop the pour and reinforce the area with plywood scabs. Then I give the concrete a little time to set up, usually by continuing the pour in another area.

SOURCES

Founded in 1995, the EPS-Industry Alliance (IA) is a growing group of professionals ranging from manufacturers to ready-mix suppliers, all focused on educating builders about the benefits of ICFs. Visit them online at www.forms.org.

The International Residential Code (IRC) has a section covering ICFs, complete with rebar tables. The source document for the code is "The Prescriptive Method for Insulating Concrete Forms in Residential Construction," published by the Department of Housing and Urban Development (www.hud.gov) and available as a PDF from www.huduser.gov.

Once the wall has been topped off, I float it level with a trowel, using the steel track as a guide (see the bottom photo on the facing page). Then I install the anchor bolts. One last adjustment can be made simply by pushing or leaning on the wall to tweak it straight—and my foundation is formed, insulated, and poured in record time.

Basement Insulation Retrofits

BY DANIEL S. MORRISON

Finished basements are a great way to add living space to a house without adding on. You often can add almost as much living space as the main floor offers. Before thinking about flooring choices and paint colors, though, think about the basics. Moisture, insulation, and air infiltration must be tackled before any finish materials are installed. In new construction, these issues are addressed from the outside before the basement is backfilled. Retrofits mean that you have to work from the inside. In either case, it is important to consider the climate before work begins.

Start with Water Management

Because basements are mostly buried in the ground, they are sometimes wet, are usually damp, and are seldom dry. Rarely do old houses have perimeter-drainage systems, insulation, or capillary breaks. When converting a basement to living space, the basement must manage moisture better than it did before the insulating and air-sealing because a tighter basement is less able to dry out when it becomes wet.

You can use grading to manage bulk groundwater on the outside, but foundations also have to disrupt capillarity. Water in the soil can and will wick up to the roof framing if you let it. Capillary breaks such as brush-on damp-proofing, sill sealer, and rigid insulation block this process.

Air Sealing Saves Energy and Stops Moisture

The connection between concrete foundations and wood framing is almost always leaky because wood is often warped and concrete is rarely flat. Air leaks waste energy and cause moisture problems. Most basement air leaks occur between the top of the concrete wall and the bottom of the subfloor, where there are many joints and connections. The easiest way to seal and insulate the rim-joist area is with spray foam, but blocks of rigid foam sealed in place can work well too.

Insulation: More Is Better

Rigid-foam insulation in a basement eliminates condensation by keeping the interior surface of the foundation warm. How much insulation you need depends on your climate zone, though energy-conscious builders strive to exceed code minimums. While it's possible to meet code minimums with rigid foam alone, you also can use a combination of rigid foam and cavity insulation.

R-VALUE MINIMUMS BY CODE AND CLIMATE ZONE

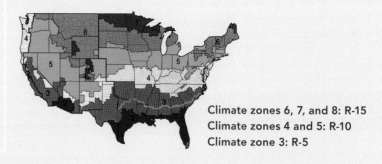

Climate zones 6, 7, and 8: R-15
Climate zones 4 and 5: R-10
Climate zone 3: R-5

WHICH RIGID INSULATION SHOULD I USE?

EXPANDED POLYSTYRENE

The least-expensive choice, EPS is manufactured in different densities. EPS (typically white in color) is not as strong as XPS and is susceptible to crumbling at the edges. EPS is the most vapor-permeable type of rigid foam.

R-value: About 4 per inch
Perm rating: 2 to 5.8 for 1 in., depending on density

POLYISOCYANURATE

Polyiso has a higher R-value per inch than EPS or XPS. Many building officials allow foil-faced polyiso to be installed in basements without any protective drywall, making it the preferred foam for basements without stud walls.

R-value: up to 6.5 per inch
Perm rating: 0.03 for 1 in. (with foil facing)

EXTRUDED POLYSTYRENE

Because of its high strength and low permeance, XPS (often blue or pink in color) is the most commonly used type of rigid foam for basement walls.

R-value: About 5 per inch
Perm rating: 0.4 to 1.6 for 1 in., depending on density

MINERAL WOOL

Although many energy experts advise against using fibrous materials to insulate basement walls, some builders may want to consider using mineral-wool batts because they are less susceptible to water damage. Manufacturers include Thermafiber® and Roxul®.

R-value: 3.7 per inch
Perm rating: Hasn't been tested, but highly permeable

INSULATION AMOUNT DEPENDS ON LOCATION

THE INTERNATIONAL RESIDENTIAL CODE (IRC) specifies particular R-values for each climate zone; how you get there is up to you. For very cold climates, you may need to add extrathick rigid insulation or fill the stud cavities. Don't, however, treat a below-grade wall like a regular wall. Expect bulk-water problems, and choose insulation that can handle it. Never include a plastic vapor barrier when insulating a basement wall, because it will trap moisture.

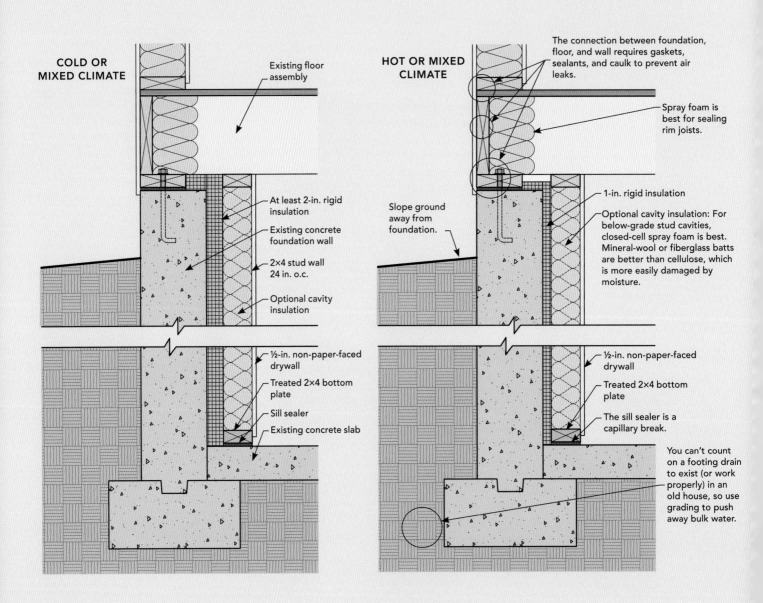

COLD OR MIXED CLIMATE

Existing floor assembly

At least 2-in. rigid insulation

Existing concrete foundation wall

2×4 stud wall 24 in. o.c.

Optional cavity insulation

½-in. non-paper-faced drywall

Treated 2×4 bottom plate

Sill sealer

Existing concrete slab

HOT OR MIXED CLIMATE

The connection between foundation, floor, and wall requires gaskets, sealants, and caulk to prevent air leaks.

Spray foam is best for sealing rim joists.

1-in. rigid insulation

Optional cavity insulation: For below-grade stud cavities, closed-cell spray foam is best. Mineral-wool or fiberglass batts are better than cellulose, which is more easily damaged by moisture.

Slope ground away from foundation.

½-in. non-paper-faced drywall

Treated 2×4 bottom plate

The sill sealer is a capillary break.

You can't count on a footing drain to exist (or work properly) in an old house, so use grading to push away bulk water.

Air-Sealing a Basement

BY MARTIN HOLLADAY

Once you've sealed the air leaks in your attic floor—the cracks where warm air escapes from your house during the winter—it's time to turn your attention to the basement or crawlspace, where cold air leaks in. If you turn off the basement lights and look for daylight, you might be surprised to find some large holes.

Weatherization contractors often use a blower-door test to help pinpoint leaks in the building envelope. Once your house is depressurized, you can use your bare hands to feel for air infiltration. The most common places to find air entering basements are around windows and doors and between the concrete foundation and the mudsill. But some air-leakage paths may surprise you: Air can even seep through the crack at the perimeter of your basement slab or through a sump in the basement floor. Here are five places to check for air leaks in your basement and some advice on how best to seal them.

Foundation Walls

Walls made of poured concrete or concrete blocks are usually fairly tight. However, if your basement walls have any obvious cracks, fill them with silicone caulk. If the walls are made of stone and mortar, don't use canned spray foam or caulk to seal cracks.

Instead, remove any loose material from these areas, and repair them with mortar and small stones.

Use caulk or canned spray foam to seal leaks near wall penetrations for your electrical service, water service, cable service, or natural-gas service. Your home also may have penetrations for a fuel-oil filler pipe, an oil-tank vent, or a clothes-dryer vent. If basement access is awkward, some cracks may be easier to seal from the exterior.

Rim Joists

Air can leak through the crack between the top of the foundation wall and the mudsill, the crack between the mudsill and the rim joist, and the crack between the rim joist and the subfloor. The best way to seal leaks in the rim-joist area is with a high-quality caulk.

Once these cracks are caulked, you may want to reduce air leaks further by installing a layer of closed-cell spray foam at the rim-joist area using a two-component spray-foam kit.

Although spray foam is effective, it is expensive and sometimes messy. If you would rather not use it, you can insulate rim joists with rectangles of 2-in.-thick rigid foam (polyisocyanurate or extruded polystyrene). Seal the perimeter of each foam rectangle with caulk or canned spray foam. Don't use fiberglass batts; they do nothing to slow airflow.

Windows and Doors

If your basement has old single-pane windows, they may need new glazing compound and weather-stripping. If the windows are in bad shape, consider replacing them with new double-glazed units.

If you rarely open your basement windows, consider sealing them shut with screws and caulk or even covering them with rigid foam. (Of course, this advice applies only to small basement windows, not to any egress windows in a basement bedroom.)

Don't forget to caulk between the window frame and the concrete.

Every bulkhead entry needs a tight, weather-stripped exterior door at the base of the stairs. Be sure to caulk or to foam the gap between the door jamb and the foundation. If the door is warped or difficult to weatherstrip, it's time to replace it. Most lumber-yards can order a custom insulated entry door to fit any size opening. If you're framing the rough opening, use pressure-treated lumber, and seal the frame to the concrete with canned spray foam.

Basement Floors

After a new foundation is backfilled, the fill often shrinks away from the foundation, leaving a gap next to the basement wall that allows outdoor air to reach the footings. That's one way for outdoor air to enter a home through cracks in the basement floor or sump pit. Even if a home has no shrinkage gap, air can still reach the footings, especially in areas with porous soil.

If there's a crack at the perimeter of your basement slab, clean the crack with compressed air or a vacuum cleaner, and then fill it with caulk. If you have a sump pit without a tight lid, replace it with a new airtight lid. Sumps that have airtight lids are available from Jackel (www.jackelinc.com).

Basement Ceilings

Chases and chimneys that extend from the basement to the attic should certainly be capped at the top, but the bottom of these chases should be sealed as well. After all, once air gets into a chase, it can move side-ways into joist bays and partition walls until it finds an exit crack. This belt-and-suspenders approach is the best way to prevent the stack effect from stealing your home's heat.

Cover large ceiling holes with plywood, drywall, or rigid foam and seal the edges with caulk, spray foam, or housewrap tape. While you're at it, check for holes under first-floor bathtubs or showers. Plumbers typically cut out a big piece of the subfloor to accommodate drain lines and traps; these air pathways should be sealed.

COMBUSTION SAFETY IN A TIGHT BASEMENT

ATMOSPHERICALLY VENTED appliances —for example, water heaters, furnaces, or boilers attached to old-fashioned brick or metal chimneys—depend on air leaking through cracks in your walls to supply com-bustion air. If your basement is very tight, atmospherically vented appliances could be starved for air, and exhaust gases may struggle to exit through the chimney. That's why the best appliances for tight homes are sealed-combustion appliances equipped with ducts that supply outdoor air directly to the burners.

Because flue gases sometimes include carbon monoxide, it's always important to be sure that your combustion appliances have adequate combustion air and that your chimneys draw well. If you plan to seal cracks in your basement, arrange for a combustion-safety test of any atmospheri-cally vented appliances once air-sealing work is complete. Contact your gas utility or a home-performance contractor certified by RESNET or BPI for more information on combustion-safety testing.

TWO WAYS TO AIR-SEAL AND INSULATE A RIM JOIST

RIM JOISTS ARE A COMMON SOURCE of air leakage in basements and are often left uninsulated. The first step toward an energy-smart rim joist is to caulk gaps between the foundation wall and the mudsill, the mudsill and the rim joist, and the rim joist and the subfloor. As seen in the details shown here, you then can use rigid foam or spray foam to add another layer of air-sealing and to insulate the area.

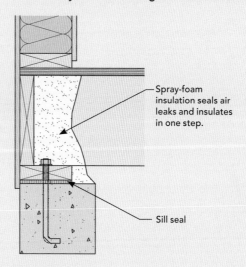

Existing floor assembly

Optional cavity insulation

1½-in. rigid insulation

Expanding foam around the perimeter of loosely cut rigid insulation

Seal mudsill to foundation with silicone caulk.

Spray-foam insulation seals air leaks and insulates in one step.

Sill seal

RIGID FOAM
You can cut the pieces of rigid foam roughly and somewhat undersize because the perimeter of each rectangle should be sealed in place with canned spray foam. With the rim joist air-sealed and covered with rigid foam, you can now add cavity insulation like fiberglass batts or, better yet, a second layer of rigid foam.

SPRAY FOAM
Extend spray foam from the top of the foundation wall to the underside of the subfloor above. In addition to sealing leaks, 2 in. of cured foam will insulate to R-13. Most building codes, including the International Residential Code, allow spray foam installed at rim joists to remain exposed—without protection from a thermal barrier like drywall—as long as the foam is no thicker than 3¼ in.

TEST FOR RADON

RADON IS A COLORLESS, odorless, naturally occurring gas that can seep through soil into your basement. High radon levels can damage human health. While most homes have relatively low radon levels, some have dangerously high levels.

Sealing cracks in your basement can affect radon levels in your home, either for better or worse, depending on several factors. If necessary, a radon-remediation contractor can install plastic pipes under your basement slab to lower the radon to safe levels.

The best way to determine whether your home needs radon-remediation work is to test the air in your home. For more information on radon testing and remediation, visit http://epa.gov/radon.

Insulating a Slab on Grade

BY MARTIN HOLLADAY

What's the best way to insulate a slab-on-grade foundation? The answer depends on at least four factors: the climate, the type of foundation, whether the slab includes hydronic tubing for radiant heat, and the severity of the local termite problem.

The most important factor is climate. In climate zones 1, 2, and 3, most builders don't bother to install any insulation. While it could be argued that insulation might be useful in climate zone 3, it really isn't needed in warmer climates, where an uninsulated slab helps lower air-conditioning bills compared to an insulated slab.

In climate zones 4 through 8, the most common locations for insulation are at the perimeter of the slab (installed vertically) and under the slab (installed horizontally). Less common is a third method: buried horizontal or sloped "wing" insulation installed around the exterior perimeter of the building to raise soil temperature.

Two types of rigid-foam insulation—expanded polystyrene (EPS) and extruded polystyrene (XPS)—are suitable for use in these positions. (Make sure EPS is rated for ground contact.)

During the winter, when the temperature of the outdoor air is colder than the soil temperature, the coldest part of a slab on grade is always the perimeter.

Stemwalls

In cold climates, most slab-on-grade foundations include perimeter stemwalls (or frost walls) that extend 3 ft. or 4 ft. below grade. The area between the stemwalls is usually filled with compacted gravel to support the slab. Because they are easier to insulate, slab foundations with stemwalls are preferable to monolithic slabs.

At a minimum, this type of foundation requires vertical perimeter insulation to separate the slab from the stemwall. Most builders install 2 in. of XPS or EPS insulation at this location. Thicker insulation is better, of course, as long as the builder can come up with a detail that allows finish flooring to be installed easily near the exterior walls—a task that can be difficult if the foam insulation is exposed at this location. Many builders bevel the top of the vertical insulation so that none of the rigid foam is visible after the concrete slab is placed.

In cold climates (climate zones 4 and higher), it's important to install vertical insulation on the interior side of the stemwall all the way down to the footing.

Insulation Requirements

In climate zones 4 and higher, it's also a good idea to install some horizontal insulation under a slab on grade. If you want to save money, you can install a

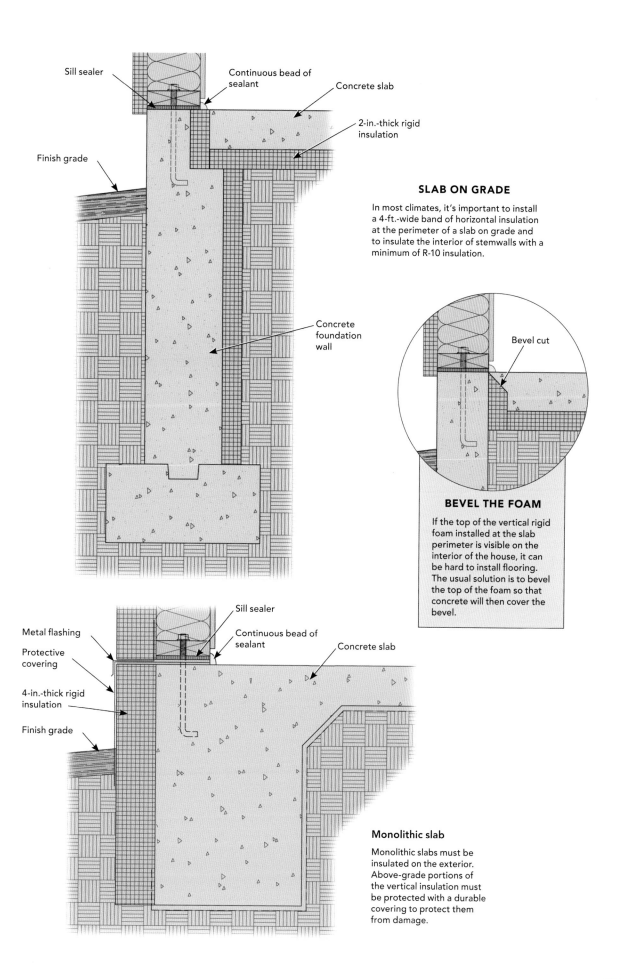

Sill sealer

Continuous bead of sealant

Concrete slab

2-in.-thick rigid insulation

Finish grade

Concrete foundation wall

SLAB ON GRADE

In most climates, it's important to install a 4-ft.-wide band of horizontal insulation at the perimeter of a slab on grade and to insulate the interior of stemwalls with a minimum of R-10 insulation.

Bevel cut

BEVEL THE FOAM

If the top of the vertical rigid foam installed at the slab perimeter is visible on the interior of the house, it can be hard to install flooring. The usual solution is to bevel the top of the foam so that concrete will then cover the bevel.

Sill sealer

Continuous bead of sealant

Concrete slab

Metal flashing

Protective covering

4-in.-thick rigid insulation

Finish grade

Monolithic slab

Monolithic slabs must be insulated on the exterior. Above-grade portions of the vertical insulation must be protected with a durable covering to protect them from damage.

4-ft.-wide band of horizontal R-10 (or higher) insulation at the perimeter of the slab in a picture-frame configuration.

Builders with a bigger budget, especially those in cold climates, should consider installing continuous horizontal insulation under the entire slab. A continuous layer of horizontal insulation reduces heat loss in the winter and reduces condensation of humid air on the slab during the summer.

Slabs that include embedded hydronic tubing for radiant heat always need a continuous layer of horizontal insulation under the entire slab. If your slab is heated, it's a good idea to increase the R-value of the vertical and the horizontal insulation to at least R-20.

Monolithic Slabs

Monolithic, or thickened-edge, slabs can be insulated only on the exterior. In climate zones 4 and 5, building codes require a minimum of R-10 vertical insulation that extends down 2 ft. In climate zones 6, 7, and 8, it must extend down 4 ft.

The main disadvantage of exterior foundation insulation is that the above-grade portion needs to be protected from physical damage. Materials options include a cementitious coating (ideally, one with chopped fiberglass), cement backerboard, pressure-treated plywood, metal flashing, or a proprietary plastic or peel-and-stick covering.

What about Termites?

Unless you live in a very cold climate, you probably have to consider termites. Most experts advise builders to treat the ground under slabs and near foundations with an insecticide that includes fipronil (for example, Termidor®) and to install a termite shield, set in mastic, under sill plates. Requirements for protection vary widely from state to state, so consult your local building department to verify requirements before beginning construction.

THE CODE IS UNCLEAR

INSULATION REQUIREMENTS for slab-on-grade floors can be found in section R402.2.9 of the 2012 IECC and section N1102.2.9 of the 2012 IRC. Both codes state, "Slab-edge insulation is not required in jurisdictions designated by the building official as having a very heavy termite infestation." Otherwise, both codes require that "slab-on-grade floors with a floor surface less than 12 in. below grade" need vertical insulation at the slab perimeter. These codes do not require any insulation for slabs that are more than 12 in. below grade. The codes are silent about whether above-grade slabs need to be insulated.

This omission is curious because most slab-on-grade homes have above-grade slabs. Most inspectors, however, require above-grade slabs to be insulated in the same way as below-grade slabs. In climate zones 1, 2, and 3, slabs are not required to be insulated unless they include hydronic tubing, in which case they are required to have R-5 vertical insulation extending downward from the top of the slab to the footing.

In climate zones 4 and 5, the code requires certain slabs (below-grade slabs that are less than 12 in. below grade) to have R-10 vertical insulation at the slab perimeter, extending downward from the top of the slab to a depth of at least 2 ft. If the slab has hydronic tubing, the minimum R-value of this insulation increases to R-15. The same R-value requirements apply in climate zones 6, 7, and 8, but the insulation must extend to a depth of at least 4 ft.

There are no requirements for horizontal insulation under slabs, but the requirements for perimeter insulation can be met partially with horizontal insulation. This compliance option is explained this way: "Insulation located below grade shall be extended the distance provided in Table N1102.1.1 [namely, 2 ft. in climates zones 4 and 5, and 4 ft. in climate zones 6, 7, and 8] by any combination of vertical insulation, insulation extending under the slab, or insulation extending out from the building."

Replacing a Rotten Lally Column

BY EMANUEL SILVA

As a restoration and remodeling carpenter in and around Boston, I get to work on a lot of old homes. The years have not been good to many of these old structures. Over the past 15 years, I've been called to address sagging floor joists and their support beams so often that shoring them up has almost become routine. Many of these older floor systems were supported by inferior, hollow Lally columns—steel pipes typically filled with concrete for increased durability and load-bearing capacity—temporary jack posts, and even tree trunks. To make matters worse, they were typically set atop equally inferior footings or on no footing at all.

By temporarily supporting and jacking up the beam just enough to loosen the existing column, I can create enough workspace to install a proper footing and Lally column. I don't attempt to fix sagging or otherwise unlevel floors (see "Why Shouldn't I Level the Beam?" on p. 197). My goal is simply to prevent further settling.

The house shown here has moisture problems as well, thanks to surrounding properties that channel rainwater toward its foundation. While the concrete Lally columns will likely survive occasional flooding, I decided to anchor them atop small piers for longevity. The process is roughly the same whether you want columns raised or set flush to the slab.

SAGGING FLOORS may be due to a failing column or the lack of a proper footing. In either case, you must temporarily support the beam and remove the old column.

A PROPER FOOTING AND POST add floor support that will never fail again.

Build Cribbing to Support Temporary Posts

When removing an existing column, it's imperative that the temporary supports are as strong as the new columns being installed. Because most of the homes I work on have slabs that are in poor condition, I try to spread the load by building cribbing. The cribbing serves as a strong, level base in which I can place screw jacks. With the jacks in place, I can use 4×4 pressure-treated posts to raise the beam safely. It's best to install these supports roughly 1½ ft. from the location of the new footing. This lends the support you need and allows comfortable working room.

START LEVEL, STAY STRAIGHT. Use small scraps of lumber to bring two 3-ft.-long 4×4 pieces of pressure-treated lumber to level. The next two pieces are stacked perpendicular to the first two. The top layer then is screwed to the bottom.

TWIST TO LIFT. Before cranking on the jacks, plumb the post and secure it to the beam with toenailed screws. If someone accidentally bumps into a post, it will stay put. Raise the jacks to relieve enough pressure on the old posts so they can be removed easily, but no higher.

MEASURE OUT, PLUMB DOWN, AND DIG. According to code, there must be a support column along this beam every 8 ft. Take measurements from the foundation wall, and mark them in the center of the beam. Then plumb down from each mark to locate the center of the footings. From this point on the slab, measure 1 ft. out in four directions. With a framing square, connect the points to create a 2-ft. by 2-ft. square. Use a cold chisel to score the perimeter line, and then use a jackhammer or a sledgehammer to break through the slab. Dig down 1 ft.

Punch a Square Hole in the Old Slab

This slab was in bad shape and, at 2½ in. thick, it was thinner than the slabs poured nowadays. From my experience, I knew that if a footing existed, it would be little more than stones thrown in a hole. I was right. Not all footings have to be rebuilt, though. Assess the condition of the slab, and look for signs that the home was built to high standards. When in complete doubt, dig.

WOOD, DRYWALL, AND PLASTER ARE viscoelastic. (Think of Silly Putty® as an extreme case.) They act elastically under short-duration loads and act plastically under sustained, long-term loads. As such, it is difficult to jack all of the sag out of a beam that has crept over the years unless it is done slowly over time.

Although it may be possible to bring a beam back to level, the question of whether sag should be jacked out of a beam is difficult to answer. It depends largely on the framing above the floor. If there are plaster or drywall walls above, then it may be possible to remove only a small amount of sag from the beam. Drywall and plaster creep over time and do not like to be moved. I have seen contractors literally jack a house off its foundation before getting any sag out of a beam.

If the beam is in an open expanse of floor, then raising it is an easier proposition. I have even recommended that contractors kerf stubborn beams in several locations. The beam, and subsequently the floor, then can be raised easily. The beam itself can be sistered up with additional lumber to restore its integrity.

—Rob Munach is a professional engineer in Carrboro, N.C.

Pour a Bombproof Footing

Because we wanted to elevate the new column's base above the slab, I incorporated a builder's tube into the footing to create a pier. I reinforced the pier with six pieces of #4 rebar. You can bypass this step if you'd like and install the posts so they're flush with the slab. To do that, simply lay a grid of rebar 3 in. from the bottom of the footing, and install another grid 3 in. from the top of the footing.

ADD CONCRETE. Make sure the soil is compacted. Then cover the bottom of the hole with 3 in. of concrete rated for 4,000 psi. Place two pieces of rebar parallel to each other on top of the wet concrete and 6 in. from each wall of the hole.

CREATE THE PIER SUPPORT. Into the wet concrete, set a 16-in.-long, 12-in.-wide builder's tube fitted with two pieces of rebar that protrude 6 in. from each side, and level it. The exposed rebar, which sits a few inches below the height of the slab surface, helps tie the pier to the rest of the footing.

FILL IT UP, AND SCREED IT AWAY. Pour concrete in and around the builder's tube until the concrete is slightly proud of the slab and the lip of the builder's tube. Push two 16-in.-long pieces of rebar into the pier—so that their top end is 2 in. to 3 in. below the finished concrete—before screeding off the excess concrete and feathering the surrounding concrete into the slab. During the pour, make sure you're maintaining center by checking the pier location with a plumb bob.

Install the New Column

I like to use 3½-in. concrete-filled Lally columns. Manufacturers say that the color—red or gray—is no indication of performance or application differences. A variety of cap and base plates is available. I use the standard plates that come with the columns from the lumberyard.

TIP: Hang a retractable plumb bob, such as this one made by Tajima (www.tajimatool.com), from the beam to mark the center of the footing. It can be raised when it gets in the way and lowered regularly to check center.

TAP IT INTO PLACE. After cutting the column to length (be sure to consider the thickness of the plates when measuring for length), place the column on the bottom plate. Add the top plate to the column, and tap the assembly into place with a sledge-hammer. Check to be sure the column is plumb.

SECURE THE PLATES. Drill pilot holes through the screw holes of the bottom plate, and secure the plate with 3-in. Tapcon® screws or concrete anchors. Attach the top plate to the beam with 2½-in. lags, never with nails.

FINISH THE PIER. Remove the exposed builder's tube by scoring it with a utility knife where it meets the slab. Masonry caulk, such as Quikrete® concrete repair (www.quikrete.com), cleans up and protects the seam.

TIP: You can cut a lally column with a specialty column cutter. However, I find it easier to hold the column in place with a large pipe wrench and cut it with a pipe cutter that has the capacity to cut 4-in. pipe. I clean up the cut edge by chipping away any concrete with a cold chisel.

PART 5

Concrete in the Landscape

Broom-Finished Concrete Flatwork

BY RICK ARNOLD

Good concrete starts with a sturdy base. For example, for a front walk, once I've removed the topsoil and confirmed the remaining soil is freedraining and well compacted, I mark the location of the walk on the house and use these marks to place 18-in. stakes that receive the 2×4 formboards. At the opposite end of the walk, I spread the forms to the correct width and attach a formboard for the end of the walk. Then I pull diagonal measurements to square the corners and use a level to slope the walk away from the house ¼ in. per foot. Once everything is square, I drive the rest of the form stakes and attach the formboards with 2-in. screws.

As I'm pouring the walk, I lift the reinforcing mesh and rebar into the middle of the concrete and screed the concrete flush with the top of the forms. Then I use a bull float to smooth the surface and to force the aggregate down into the concrete. Bull-floating brings up bleed water that must evaporate before finishing can continue. When the bleed water is gone and a footprint leaves a ¼-in. impression in the surface, it's time to start finishing with a mag float. The mag float brings up a layer of water and cement particles known as cream. Once there's a nice layer of cream, the edges can be rounded with an edge tool, and the control joints can be made with a groover.

After a pass or two with a steel finishing trowel, the walk can be finished with a stiff-bristle broom pulled across its width. Rinse off the bristles after every pass for distinct ridges that provide maximum traction.

1 **SQUARE THE FORMS.** With a formboard on the end of the side forms (opposite the house) establishing the width of the walk, shift the formwork left or right until measurements from opposite corners are equal, which means the forms are square. Drive in stakes on both sides to keep the forms from shifting, but don't attach the screws just yet.

2 **STRAIGHTEN THE SIDES.** Use a taut string to straighten the sides of the formwork. Drive in stakes every 2 ft., and screw through them into the sides of the form. Backfill against the forms with soil or gravel to prevent bulging.

3 **ADD STEEL FOR STRENGTH.** Three rows of 3/8-in. rebar and a grid of 4-in. reinforcing mesh add strength and help to control shrinkage. Rebar dowels inserted into the foundation prevent the walk from sinking near the house. Make the holes with a rotary hammer.

A KIT FOR CONCRETE

CONCRETE WORK REQUIRES some special gear, but you can outfit yourself with all the good-quality tools you need for less than $300. The biggest-ticket item is a bull float, but you can rent one for about $16 a day.

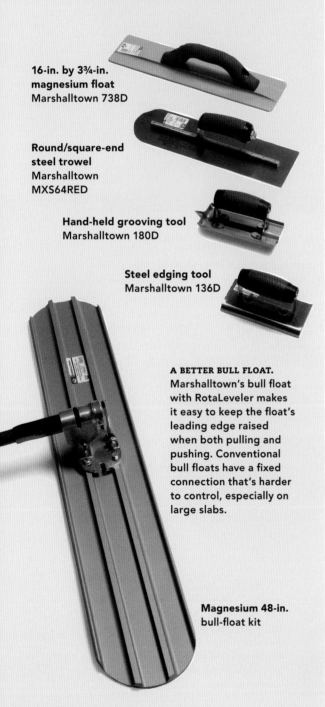

16-in. by 3¾-in. magnesium float
Marshalltown 738D

Round/square-end steel trowel
Marshalltown MXS64RED

Hand-held grooving tool
Marshalltown 180D

Steel edging tool
Marshalltown 136D

A BETTER BULL FLOAT. Marshalltown's bull float with RotaLeveler makes it easy to keep the float's leading edge raised when both pulling and pushing. Conventional bull floats have a fixed connection that's harder to control, especially on large slabs.

Magnesium 48-in. bull-float kit

4 | FILL AND SCREED. Fill the forms so that the wet concrete is just over the tops of the forms, then screed off the excess, using the forms as a guide. A helper or two moving concrete ahead of the screed makes this process easier.

5 | BREAK OUT THE BULL FLOAT. Level the surface, and force the aggregate into the mix with a bull float. Keep the leading edge raised as you push or pull to avoid digging into the surface. Two or three passes is enough.

6 | MAKE CREAM WITH A MAG FLOAT. After the bleed water has evaporated, use a magnesium float to bring up the layer of water and cement particles called cream. Then round the corners with the edging tool, and make control joints every 5 ft. with a 2×4 and a groover.

7 | USE A STEEL TROWEL FOR A SMOOTH FINISH. With the grooves cut and the corners rounded, use overlapping arcs with a steel finish trowel to tighten up the surface before brooming.

8 | BROOM FINISH FOR TRACTION. Special concrete brooms exist, but a regular push broom with stiff bristles works fine too. Keep the texture perpendicular to the traffic direction. Once you've finished brooming, go over the corners and control joints again.

Build a Sturdy Stone Sitting Wall

BY BRENDAN MOSTECKI

I used to get annoyed when I heard people compare building a stone wall to assembling a jigsaw puzzle. Stone walls have no precut pieces, and they certainly don't come with a picture. Then one day I sat down with my two sons to put together a jigsaw puzzle. As these things often go, they quickly ran off with the box, and I was left with a pile of pieces but no road map. That's when I realized that a stone wall wasn't so different from a puzzle after all. I start each wall by emptying and sorting a pallet of stone into four categories: base pieces, face pieces, cornerstones, and caps. I lay out the first row, establish the corners, then work in toward the middle, just like a puzzle but without the picture, of course.

I could write an entire book about different ways to build stone walls. They can be dry-stack or wet-tack (set in mortar with or without visible joints) and built either freestanding or with stone applied to the face of concrete blocks. The stones can be round or flat, natural or chiseled, rough or smooth, and random or uniform.

For the project shown here, my crew and I built a small retaining wall that doubles as extra seating around the perimeter of a patio. Sitting walls can be topped with large flat stones that match the face of the wall but I prefer to cap these walls with custom slabs, in this case bluestone.

Size the Base, and Consider the Drainage

Stone walls can be built atop a well-compacted gravel base or atop a poured concrete footing. Personally, the only time I choose a gravel base is if I'm building a dry-stack farmer's wall. For most situations, substituting the gravel base with a rebar-reinforced concrete pad allows you to cut the base depth in half. A concrete pad also helps unify the assembly, allowing the wall to rise and fall as one unit when the ground freezes and thaws.

In most cases, a poured footing can be formed just by digging a trench, adding rebar, pouring the concrete, and letting everything set. Straight footings are the easiest, but curved footings aren't much extra work. Once I have the area cleared and leveled, I scribe the curve in the dirt, playing around with the layout until I'm happy with the shape and the flow of the wall. Then digging can begin.

If patio pavers are going to abut the stone wall, I like to form the edges of the footing with ¼-in. or ½-in. plywood, which I remove once the wall is built. This creates a smoother surface so that in winter months, the patio pavers will be less likely to collide with the wall footing and heave; it's the same principle as using cardboard Sonotubes® for pier footings.

DRY-STACK,
BUT WET IN BACK

Although it has a classic dry-stack look, each stone in
this wall is actually set in mortar. Because the back of
the wall is hidden, it is built with inexpensive rock and
coated with a slick of cement to provide strength and
to help control drainage.

Mulch

2-in.-thick
bluestone cap

Filler rock set in
ample mortar

Face stones

Cement slick to
divert bulk water

Decorative-rock
drip gutter

Thick bed of
mortar under
first course

Concrete pad

#4 rebar

Patio pavers

Drainage and hydraulic pressure are also concerns when I'm designing a wall. I wish there were a rule of thumb for this issue, but every installation is different. The stone wall featured here was set at the foot of a short hill; the soil both below it and behind it had lots of gravel mixed in to provide excellent natural drainage. In this case, no other drainpipes were necessary, but if a retaining wall is at the bottom of a long downward-sloping hill and doesn't have at least a perforated drainpipe set similar to a typical footing drain on a house, the buildup of water behind the stone will force the wall forward (see "Tall Walls Need Drainage" at right). It's also sometimes necessary to install small-diameter PVC pipes through the wall to allow water to drain from behind the stones. If you are unsure of your site conditions, I suggest calling a qualified contractor to help you assess the soil, drainage, and other factors. The same is true if you are building a wall that will be taller than 4 ft. or that will support a structure or a driveway; consult a structural engineer. These walls often need additional reinforcement and are best left to professionals.

The First Course Is the Easiest

Once the footings have cured, I like to spread the pallets out and pick through all the stone to find cornerstones and, if necessary, capstones. Cornerstones should have at least one 90° angle; capstones should be relatively large and flat on one side. When I find a stone that looks appropriate for the face of the wall, I use my bricklayer's hammer to chip off unwanted tapers and nonusable corners until the stone is ready to go. Doing this work at the pallet also keeps most of the waste away from the wall, which makes it easier to work.

I put the usable stones in a wheelbarrow and move them to the working area near the wall. I place the undesirable stones and broken leftovers in buckets to be used as backfill, as shims to prop up the main stones during installation, and later as chinking to fill gaps.

TALL WALLS NEED DRAINAGE

BECAUSE THE WALL in this project was only about 2 ft. tall and was surrounded by soil with a high gravel content and lots of thirsty vegetation, we didn't need a massive amount of reinforcement or additional drainage behind it. Extra drainage is, however, a good idea for walls that are taller, built over clay soil, or located in an area that sees lots of runoff. If you are unsure, don't wing it. Contact a qualified contractor or mason to help assess the site conditions.

The standard approach to drainage is a perforated drainpipe set at the bottom edge of the concrete pad and surrounded by free-draining gravel, with the whole assembly wrapped in filter fabric. Short lengths of 1-in.-dia. PVC pipe also can be placed among the stones to let out water from behind the wall.

If the wall is taller than 4 ft., it's often a good idea to incorporate drainage at the footing and at the upper part of the wall as well (see the drawing below). I also like to pitch tall walls backward about ¾ in. for every 3 ft. of vertical rise.

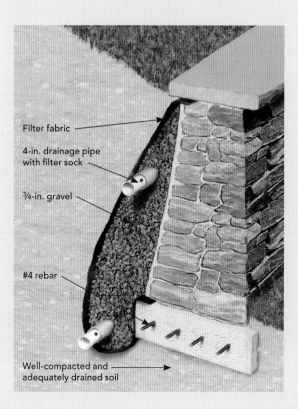

Filter fabric

4-in. drainage pipe with filter sock

¾-in. gravel

#4 rebar

Well-compacted and adequately drained soil

LAYING THE FIRST COURSES

THE CONCRETE PAD will be wider than the finished wall, so it's important to double-check that the wall sits at the right spot on the pad by dry-laying the first course. Once I'm happy with the curve, I trace a line along the front face of the stones 1 , then pick up the stones one at a time and set them in a thick bed of mortar.

Using the first course of stones as a guide, I drive wooden stakes into the ground at each corner and transition point, and I tie and level guide strings tautly to each stake 2 . I prefer to tie the strings with loops so I can move the string up as work on the wall progresses.

The flat surface of cornerstones makes it easier to stack courses neatly and ensures that the end of the wall is both strong and attractive 3 . I like to establish the corners early because they require stones with at

least two flat faces that are square to each other, and finding these stones takes time.

Once the first course is set, I place the rest of the stones, keeping the mortar toward the back where it won't be visible 4 .

Stone walls set on top of stepped pads are a bit less forgiving in terms of layout. Almost as important as setting the corners, the height changes must be laid out carefully to keep subsequent courses level 5 .

2

Keep it in line with string.

1

The first course sets the curve of the wall.

Corners anchor the wall.

Aim for a dry-stack look.

Pay attention to changes in height.

The first course of stones in this type of wall is actually the easiest because you don't have to think about the bottom of each stone; you need to worry only about the sides and the top because a healthy bed of mortar evens out the bottom. For this first course, I choose stones that vary in height and size, but I make sure they are flat on top. Any stones that have a flare or a slope will be difficult to build on top of, so make sure to put that side of the stone face-down. I like to lay out the whole first course before applying any mortar, which allows me to double-check my work. After adjusting any stones I'm not happy with, I mix the mortar and set the first course.

String Lines Help Guide the Installation

String lines (mason twine) are essential for helping me keep each course of stone level and plumb. The string line should be set even with the front face of the first course of stones and moved up on the wooden stakes as the courses progress. I periodically check that the wall is plumb by standing above the string line and looking down toward the base of the wall (see photo 2 on the facing page). This string-sighting method doesn't work as well on curved walls as it does on straight walls, so make sure also to check the curved sections with a level as the wall is built.

With the string lines in place, I begin work on the corners and transition points of the wall, building them up to the desired finish height, then filling in toward the middle.

My last piece of advice: Don't work in one spot on the wall. Instead, grab one stone at a time, and bring it to an appropriate spot on the wall. The stones might need to be tweaked with a few blows from a bricklayer's hammer before being placed on the wall, but if you pick up a stone, install it somewhere.

After all the courses have been set, the capstones can be fabricated and installed. I prefer to leave backfilling and landscaping until after the capstones have set up completely. This allows me to run the backfill right up to the back edge of the bluestone for a smooth transition.

MATCH THE MIX TO THE TASK

THE BASIC INGREDIENTS in a batch of mortar are portland cement, hydrated lime (typically labeled as type-S or type-N mortar), and sand mixed with water. I vary the mix proportions depending on the task. Here are the different mixes I used for this stone wall.

Portland cement   +   Hydrated lime   +   Sand   =   Mortar

FACE/FILLER STONES
- 1 bag type-2 portland cement
- ½ bag type-N or type-S mortar
- 18 to 20 shovelfuls of sand
- About 5 gal. of water
- Adjust amount of sand until the mix looks smooth and fluffy.

CAPSTONE AND SLICK ON BACK SIDE OF WALL
- ½ bag type-2 portland cement
- ½ bag type-N or type-S mortar
- 14 shovelfuls of sand
- 3 gal. to 4 gal. of water
- Mix to a thick, peanut butter–like consistency.

BUILD UP THE BACK SIDE. After setting a few courses of stone on the face of the wall, the author builds up the back side with less expensive blasted ledge stone set in plenty of mortar.

Customize the Cap with a Rock and Thermal Finish

Because this wall borders a patio and is meant to be a place to sit, I chose an 18-in.-deep bluestone cap. To dress up the edges, I did a "rock and thermal" finish. These finished caps can be ordered from a masonry supplier, but this service is not cheap, especially on curved caps, which require some additional steps. I prefer to do the work myself, starting with 24-in.-wide by 4-ft.-long slabs. I recommend practicing the cutting, chiseling, and torch work on a scrap before taking on the full slabs; each type of stone behaves differently. Also this work involves lots of dust, heat, and flying shards of rock, so wear a respirator when making cuts, safety glasses when chiseling, and a full face mask and gloves when using the torch.

GAPS GET SCRAPS. To help create a true dry-stack look, the crew uses the chipped-off chunks and slivers from the rock hammering to fill the spaces between stones. Ideally, these small stones will slide in deep enough to be held in place by the mortar. If not, we add a bit of mortar before inserting.

STEP 1

After I've laid out the slabs and cut the joints with a diamond-blade wet saw, I decide on an appropriate overhang for the front edge, typically 1¼ in. to 1½ in. so that water running off the cap won't drip onto the face of the wall. Next, I use a flexible piece of vinyl molding to transfer the curve of the wall to the capstone.

STEP 2

After making a shallow cut along the line with my angle grinder and a diamond blade, I then transfer the curve to the back of the capstones and cut both edges using a wet saw. If the curve is too tight for the saw, get close, then finish with an angle grinder. Don't worry if your cuts aren't perfect; just make sure they are square and not tapered in or out vertically.

STEP 3

The chisel work, also known as "rocking," comes next. I set one of the slabs in a bed of sand, making sure that it's fully supported to prevent cracks from the force of the chisel and hammer. I scribe a guideline about ¼ in. from the outside edge of the stone, place a chisel on the line, then strike it with the sledge in a firm outward motion. I move the chisel over, and repeat. Once all the edges are rocked, I place the slabs back on the wall, using cutoffs as shims to keep them level front to back.

STEP 4

I complete the look by "thermaling" the chiseled edge of the stone to make it appear natural. First, I soak the edge of the slab with water, and then follow along with a torch to make the surface pop off. I prefer to use an oxygen-propane torch with a

Determine the overhang.

Cut the curve.

rosebud tip and grade-T hose (www.airgas.com). A small propane torch kit (www.bernzomatic.com) can also be used for small jobs, but don't expect to get much run time out of these smaller cylinders. The key is the right amount of heat. The torch should be hot enough that you hear the surface of the stone pop off within seconds of being touched with the tip of the flame.

To set the caps, I pour a crumbly, dry mixture of mortar on the top course of the wall, and then brush a thick, gooey mixture of mortar and water on the back side of each slab before placing it on the wall. This combination of wet and dry mortar forms a durable bond. After the cap has set for 24 hours, the joints between each slab can be cut to the desired width and taped off with painters tape in preparation for jointing. Mortar is a good choice for joints in masonry surfaces that will see lots of foot traffic, but a sitting wall won't get much traffic. The wall I built for this project will be fully exposed to the harsh New England ice and snow, so I used a flexible silicone sealant.

Chisel the outside edge.

Torch the chiseled edge.

Four Retaining Wall Choices

BY ERIC NELSON

A homeowner once approached me as I stood, hammer in hand, working on a stone retaining wall, and asked, "Is that it? You just knock the rocks into place?" I wish it were that simple. Stacking natural stone or concrete pavers or spiking together timbers may look easy, but I've replaced or rebuilt enough walls to know how often it is done incorrectly. The trick is to pick the material that best suits your landscape, your budget, and your ability (if you plan to tackle the project yourself).

I usually build fieldstone or timber walls because they are the most popular materials in my area, but modular-block and poured-concrete (or concrete-block) walls also are excellent options. Each type of wall requires a different set of tools and building skills. For instance, timber landscape ties are a good, inexpensive material for someone comfortable building with wood. A poured-concrete wall is likely the strongest choice, but the installation is probably best left to professionals.

Choosing the most appropriate material is the first decision you need to make when starting a retaining-wall project. Before you begin building a wall, you also need to consider the elevations of the new finished grades, the appropriate base and backfill, and the question of whether an engineer should design the wall.

Modular Block

If you want the look of a natural-stone wall but lack the skill to build one, a modular-block wall might be the answer. These wall systems come in a variety of styles, patterns, and colors. There are tumbled blocks of uniform size that simulate the look of quarried granite, blocks of varying sizes that form patterns to look like natural stone, and split-faced blocks that look like what they are: concrete. In fact, these blocks are made from really strong concrete; most have a compressive strength of 5,000 psi.

Modular-block retaining-wall systems are available from a number of manufacturers. Prices vary between manufacturers and styles. Each company—sometimes each style—has its own building system. Most systems are made up of a few different components, including the basic wall blocks, corner blocks, and cap pieces. The good news is that none of the systems is too complicated, and the walls go up quickly.

The trick is to get the first course level. Then it is mostly a matter of stacking blocks and backfilling. Many systems even incorporate a setback into the design so that as you build up, the wall automatically pitches back into the retained earth behind. It is hard to avoid cutting blocks, but the only specialty tools you'll need are a masonry or diamond blade for your circular saw and a mason's chisel.

MODULAR BLOCK is versatile in design and interlocks for strength.

RANDOM PATTERNS LOOK NATURAL.
Allan Block's Ashlar Blend™ is a combination of three different blocks that can be mixed and matched (www.allanblock. com; 952-835-5309).

MODULAR BLOCK RETAINING WALL

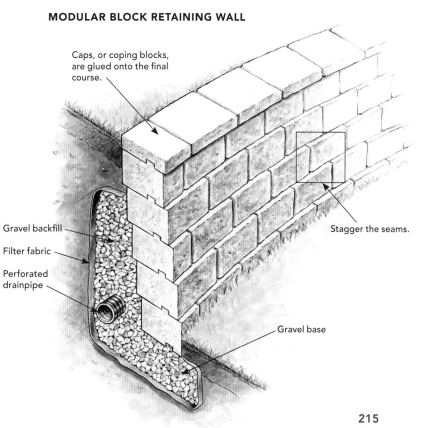

Caps, or coping blocks, are glued onto the final course.

Gravel backfill

Filter fabric

Perforated drainpipe

Stagger the seams.

Gravel base

215

INTERLOCKING BLOCKS

WITH PINS OR RIDGES, blocks lock together for strength.

UNILOCK ROMANPISA®. A ridge on the top of one course fits into a groove on the bottom of the next (www.unilock.com; 800-864-5625).

VERSA-LOK® MOSAIC. A top-down pinning system lets you push a pin through a hole in one course and into a groove in the course below (www.versa-lok.com; 651-770-3166).

KEYSTONE COUNTRY MANOR®. Pins are placed into the top of one course, and the next course is positioned on the protruding pins (www.keystonewalls.com; 800-747-8971).

These interlocking systems are versatile enough for most designs. Curved walls can be built, and matching steps and walks can be incorporated. Some manufacturers will send a representative to help you figure out just what you need for your project.

Concrete

Poured-concrete and concrete-block, or concrete-masonry-unit (CMU), walls are the most complicated, most expensive, and least attractive retaining walls. If they're engineered well, though, they're probably the strongest. And veneers can take the curse off how they look.

These heavy walls always should be designed by a professional who will test the soil conditions and draw plans for the project. Because they demand extensive excavation for the footing and mate-

rial to build the forms, the pour is also best left to professionals. CMU walls require a footing engineered similarly to poured-concrete walls, and their strength depends on the right mortar mix and reinforcement. If you need retaining walls near a house under construction, consider having them poured at the same time as the foundation.

Laying up veneer can be tackled by a first-timer. Although the process is slow and the materials expensive, the wall's structural integrity won't be threatened by mistakes.

There are a variety of veneer materials to choose from. Natural stone is popular, but thin stone veneer is more expensive than most wall stone. Cultured, or artificial, stone is less expensive and has the advantage of uniform thickness. Of course, in the right landscape, brick veneer and stucco are good choices, too.

CONCRETE is a strong material with many looks.

CONCRETE WALLS TAKE ON THE LOOK of the surface treatment: here, stucco (left) and brick (right).

CONCRETE RETAINING WALL

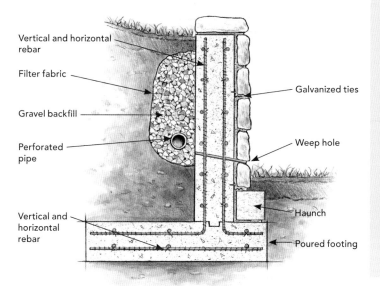

Vertical and horizontal rebar

Filter fabric

Gravel backfill

Perforated pipe

Galvanized ties

Weep hole

Vertical and horizontal rebar

Haunch

Poured footing

CONSIDER TERRACING

EVEN THE MOST ATTRACTIVE retaining wall can lose its charm if the wall is too massive for its surroundings. If there is enough area to divide the change in grade into multiple stepped walls, a series of small walls might be more visually appealing. Terraced walls also may avoid the need for permits, engineers, and complicated construction details. The area between terraced retaining walls does not have to be level and can be used for lawn or gardens.

Building two or more small walls also may be easier on your back because you don't have to lift the stone, block, or timbers too high, or set up staging. If you decide to build a terraced retaining wall, start with the lowest wall: You'll create flat areas to stand on while working on the upper walls, and you can incorporate steps, which have to be built from the bottom up.

TIMBER IS LESS DURABLE, but easy to build.

Timber

For most folks, timber retaining walls are the easiest type to build. And in most cases, they are the least expensive option (8-ft. pressure-treated 6×6s start at $16). If you are comfortable with basic carpentry, you shouldn't have a problem building a timber retaining wall. In a dry area, a timber wall can be built without a base or tricky backfill. Steps can be made by joining two 6×6 timbers and are incorporated easily into these walls. It is simple to make 90° and 45° corners, though curves are tricky.

Timbers range from used railroad ties to planed lumber. If you can find them, used railroad ties are fairly inexpensive, but they're often treated with creosote. They also may be inconsistent in dimension and not very straight. This combination can make for tricky building.

The most commonly used material is pressure-treated 6×6 landscape timbers. You can use a rough-sawn, dimensional 6×6 for a rustic look, or a planed 6×6 (actually 5½ in.) for a more-finished look. For shorter walls, a 4×6 timber also can be used.

The length of the ties also varies. A 12-ft. or 16-ft. tie can cover a lot of ground but is difficult to handle alone. An 8-ft. tie is more manageable for one person.

The obvious drawback to timber walls is that they eventually rot. Pressure-treated timbers will last longer than untreated timbers, but be aware that the manufacturer's warranty on new pressure-treated timbers may not be honored if the tie is cut.

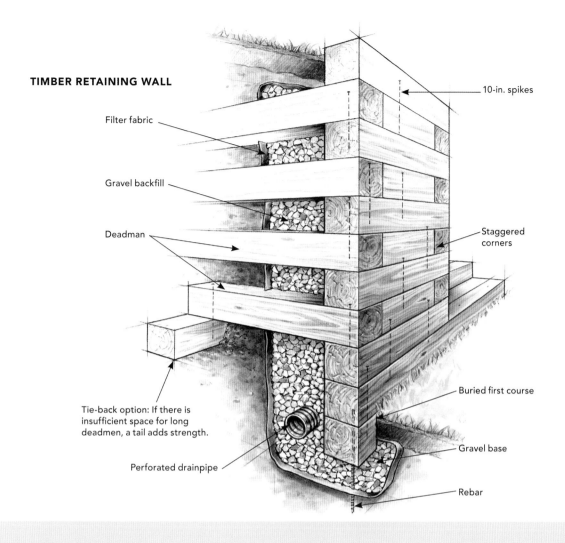

TIMBER RETAINING WALL

Filter fabric

Gravel backfill

Deadman

Tie-back option: If there is insufficient space for long deadmen, a tail adds strength.

Perforated drainpipe

10-in. spikes

Staggered corners

Buried first course

Gravel base

Rebar

THE BASIC STEPS OF TIMBER-WALL CONSTRUCTION

Cut timbers with a chainsaw, or with a circular saw and a handsaw.

Drill pilot holes so that spikes or rebar can be driven easily, with less chance of splitting.

Tie courses together by driving spikes with a 12-lb. hammer or 20-lb. sledgehammer

Stone

Stone walls may be the best choice for a natural-looking landscape. Natural stone offers limitless design possibilities, including curves, and stone walls can be built to follow a sloping grade. Steps can be incorporated into stone walls, though stone treads often are too heavy to handle without a machine. The price, type, and availability of stone vary from one area to the next, but natural stone is almost always one of the more expensive retaining-wall materials.

Along with pricey material costs, stone walls bring high labor costs. It takes practice to learn to build with the irregularities of natural stone, and even for an experienced mason, building a stone wall takes longer than building the same wall with another material. Still, stone walls can be a rewarding project for patient first-timers. In most areas, you can have pallets of stone delivered. And a few inexpensive tools, such as a mason's hammer, will make the work go more smoothly.

STONE WALLS CAN BE DECEIVING. From a distance, this stone retaining wall appears dry-stacked. A closer look reveals that the stones actually are mortared. Mortared backfill is a good idea for taller walls or walls that will be walked on or sat on.

THE MANY FACES OF NATURAL STONE. The availability and type of stone vary from one area to the next. Fieldstone is easy to find in the Northeast (facing page). Quarried Niagra boulders (left) and limestone (above) are common in the Midwest.

Stone walls can be stacked dry using stone and rubble for backfill. Dry walls are built on a base of compacted gravel. It's important for hidden backfill stones to be stacked just as securely as visible "face" stones. All voids inside the wall should be filled with rubble.

Another option is to stack the face stones dry, then backfill with stone and mortar. This type of construction requires a deeper (24 in.) compacted-gravel base. Finally, you can mortar the joints between stones. These walls should be built on a poured-concrete footing with rebar placed horizontally in the footing and vertically to extend through the wall as it is built up. All "wet" walls need a drain in the backfill or weep holes to relieve pressure from water that seeps behind the wall.

Base and Backfill

One truth about all retaining walls is that they are only as good as the base they are built on. The right depth and type of base depends on the material and the landscape. The base and backfill in the drawings

THREE WAYS TO STACK A STONE RETAINING WALL

1. Dry-stacked walls are backfilled with rubble

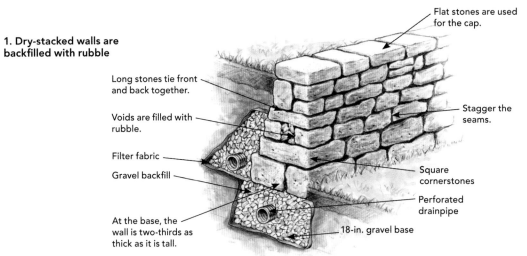

Flat stones are used for the cap.

Long stones tie front and back together.

Voids are filled with rubble.

Filter fabric

Gravel backfill

At the base, the wall is two-thirds as thick as it is tall.

Stagger the seams.

Square cornerstones

Perforated drainpipe

18-in. gravel base

2. The dry look, with the strength of cement

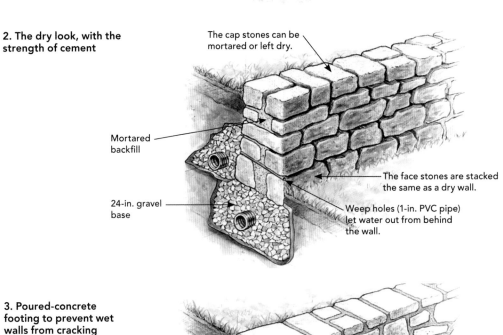

The cap stones can be mortared or left dry.

Mortared backfill

24-in. gravel base

The face stones are stacked the same as a dry wall.

Weep holes (1-in. PVC pipe) let water out from behind the wall.

3. Poured-concrete footing to prevent wet walls from cracking

Vertical rebar

Poured footing

Mortared joints

Horizontal rebar

shown on the facing page represent best practices. In other words, this is how I would build each of these walls in wet or uncertain conditions. In dry areas, I build timber walls right on the ground. And although I always build stone and modular-block walls on at least an 18-in. gravel base, I put a drain in the base only in wet areas. Any time a perforated pipe is used in the base, the gravel must be separated from the earth with filter fabric.

Backfill is equally important. Dry-laid stone walls usually are backfilled with large stones, and the voids are filled with rubble. If the wall is separated from the earth with filter fabric, drainage behind the wall often is unnecessary. Modular-block walls should be backfilled with gravel and a perforated drainpipe and separated from the earth with filter fabric. This method also can be used for a timber wall in a wet area, a wet-stacked stone wall, or a poured-concrete wall. Weep holes are another option for poured-concrete walls and wet stone walls.

For some projects, excavating for the base and backfill is the most laborious part of the job. If this is the case, it might be worthwhile to hire an excavator or to rent a backhoe for a day.

The last thing I do before I begin a wall is to determine the height of the top of the wall and the finished grade at the bottom of the wall. This way, I can make sure the top of the base is set a few inches below the finish grade (lawn or garden) to keep it hidden when the project is complete. Don't trust your eye when determining elevations. Use a site level to avoid mistakes.

WHEN DO YOU NEED AN ENGINEER?

YOU'LL HAVE TO CHECK with your local building department to find out if you need a permit and engineer's approval to build a retaining wall. The International Residential Code regulates the construction of walls more than 4 ft. tall. Likewise, most manufacturers of modular-block wall systems recommend that any wall over 4 ft. be designed, or at least approved, by a professional engineer. I agree that there is little danger in a homeowner or contractor tackling a project less than 4 ft. tall. I also agree that it is a good idea to speak with an expert before attempting to build a retaining wall over 5 ft., even if your local code doesn't require that you do. In many cases, two small walls look better than one tall wall anyway.

Dress Up a Block Wall with a Rock Wall

BY CODY MACFIE

In the old days, foundations of rock or brick were the norm. They looked good and were fairly easy to build. Nowadays, concrete block or poured concrete is the foundation method of choice because they're much faster to build. This newfound speed, however, comes at an aesthetic cost: Concrete is ugly. But you can make a plain-looking block wall into a great-looking rock wall by veneering it with field-stone. The tools and materials needed are few, and the payoff is huge.

The techniques for veneering are the same for block, poured concrete, or even a wood-frame wall, as are the requirements. Make sure you have sufficient support below the stone (a solid footing), and attach the veneer to the wall with wall ties. If the veneer is a retrofit, you may need to pour an additional footing, usually about 6 in. wide. And for wood-frame walls, you need to add a moisture barrier, such as peel-and-stick roofing membrane or #30 felt paper, to the wood. Wall ties are easy to install if you're laying up a new block wall. For concrete walls or existing block walls, the ties can be attached with a powder-actuated nail gun or with masonry screws.

Although veneering an entire house is best left to a professional, a short foundation veneer, such as the one featured here, is certainly bite-size enough for a non-mason to attempt.

Tight-Fitting, Yet Natural

There are as many varieties of stonework as there are stonemasons, but most can be lumped into a few patterns (see "Rubble Patterns" on the facing page). Much of my work is in a style called dry stack, which resembles a traditional no-mortar rock wall. When veneered in the dry-stack style, mortar is packed behind the stones as well as in a thin layer around the stones, but the mortar is not visible. While dry-stack veneer looks rough and tumble, it's rather precise. The stones fit together tightly yet do not look manipulated. With jointed-style stonework, you don't have to be as particular because the visible mortar around the stones absorbs the bumps and irregularities.

Good-looking dry-stack veneer is all about tight joints that look natural. You can close gaps between stones by chipping away bumps, by using plugs, or by manipulating the shape of the stone with a hammer and a blunt chisel. Large gaps not only look unnatural but also can allow stones to shift, which creates a weak spot in the wall.

The Most Important Tool Is Space

Being able to look at all the stones to choose the best size, shape, or face for each particular spot—especially the corners—is critical. Because stonework

RUBBLE PATTERNS

RUBBLE PATTERNS REFER TO STONEWORK that doesn't look manipulated (cut or chiseled). Whether the mortar is visible or not, there are a few common patterns for laying up stone.

1 Random rubble has no visible continuous course or bed lines. The stones may fit together tightly but randomly, as featured in the photo on p. 226.

2 Coursed rubble has a somewhat level bed line with every course. The stones are of varying sizes, but each large stone defines a level bed line.

3 Squared rubble has a level bed line every third or fourth course.

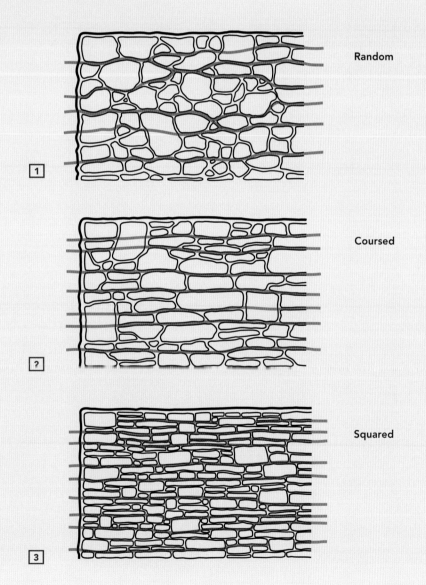

1

Random

?

Coursed

3

Squared

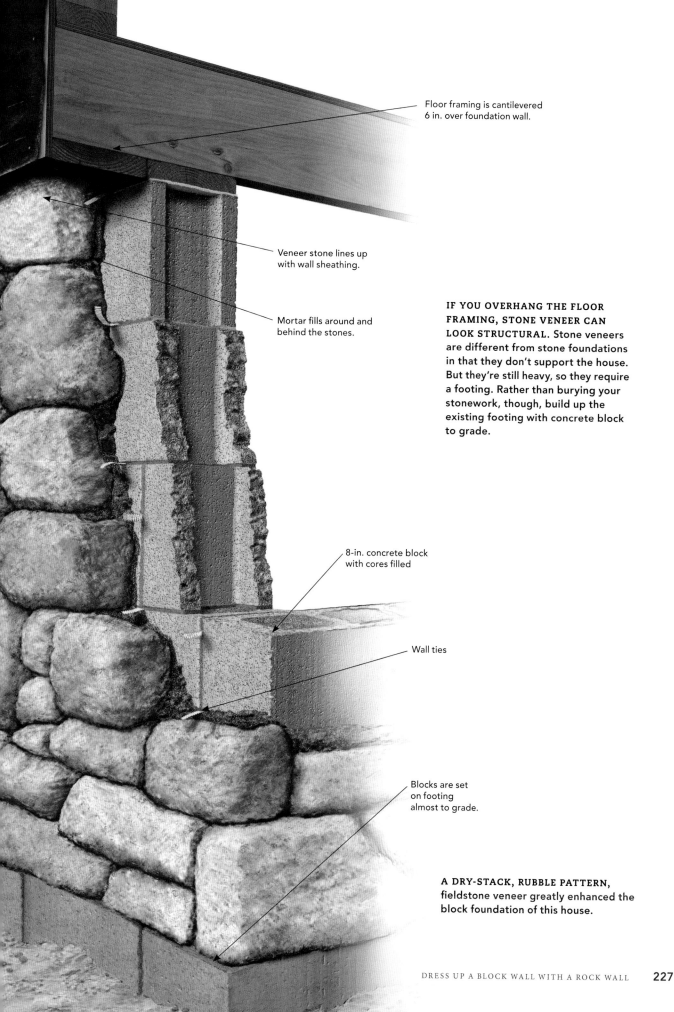

Floor framing is cantilevered 6 in. over foundation wall.

Veneer stone lines up with wall sheathing.

Mortar fills around and behind the stones.

IF YOU OVERHANG THE FLOOR FRAMING, STONE VENEER CAN LOOK STRUCTURAL. Stone veneers are different from stone foundations in that they don't support the house. But they're still heavy, so they require a footing. Rather than burying your stonework, though, build up the existing footing with concrete block to grade.

8-in. concrete block with cores filled

Wall ties

Blocks are set on footing almost to grade.

A DRY-STACK, RUBBLE PATTERN, fieldstone veneer greatly enhanced the block foundation of this house.

is a mixture of art and grunt labor, plenty of space allows you to take inventory and set aside key stones, such as corners and caps, so that you won't have to switch gears as often. Stopping the process of laying up stone to haul another load can be frustrating.

Start by dumping the stone into a large space near the work area, and shuttle small piles to the wall in a wheelbarrow. The other tools you'll need are a square shovel, a pointing trowel, a mason's trowel, a 4-ft. level, a brick hammer, a 4-lb. rock hammer, a blunt chisel, a plumb bob, a tape measure, and a garden sprayer. If the job is large, rent a cement mixer.

Before You Start, Look Up and Down

Although stone veneer doesn't support weight, a footing must support it. Because the footing is below final grade, stacking 6-in. or 8-in. concrete blocks to just below the final grade line and laying stones on the blocks makes sense. Blocks need to be secure to make a solid seat for the first course of stones, so set them in mortar. If dirt has covered the footing, dig it out until the footing is exposed.

Verify that the wall to which you are veneering is plumb. A plumb wall speeds the veneering process because you can simply measure the same distance from the wall to the face of the stone as you lay them. If the wall is not plumb, then use a level to make sure the stone faces are plumb.

4-FT. LEVEL

You can make a plain-looking block wall into a great-looking rock wall by veneering it with fieldstone.

THE TOOLS OF THE TRADE

CARPENTER'S DOG

MASON'S TROWEL

4-LB. ROCK HAMMER

POINTING TROWEL

BLUNT CHISEL

BRICK HAMMER

MORTAR BINDS THE WALL

LAY STONE ON A BED OF MORTAR and pack more behind. The unseen mortar below, beside, and behind the stone holds the wall together, but visible mortar in front will be scratched out.

USE SHIMS TO SET THE STONES MORE SECURELY. The rock-fragment shims can be used in one of two ways: either as temporary shims until the mortar sets up or as permanent plugs to fill gaps between stones, giving a tighter appearance.

TRIM ROCK WITH A BLUNT HAMMER. Break bumps off the back and bottom to improve fit and to reduce the chances that the stone will move as rocks are piled on top of each other.

PACK MORTAR BEHIND THE STONES. Mortar holds the stone in place, and wall ties embedded into the mortar tie the stone veneer to the block wall. Lay a mortar bed on top of each stone course for the next course.

Mortar Holds the Stone Together

I measure mortar in batches, or the amount that my mixer can mix, that my wheelbarrow can hold, and that I can maneuver around the site. A full batch fills my mixer. I mix either a full batch or a half batch depending on the weather, my crew size, and proximity to quittin' time. Regardless of whether you use a mixer or a wheelbarrow, the recipe is the same: a 3-to-1 mixture of sand to portland cement. A full batch in my mixer is a half bag of portland cement and 14 shovelfuls of sand. If you mix in a wheelbarrow, small batches make the mixing much easier. Whether mixer or wheelbarrow, mix the dry ingredients well before adding the water.

Dry-stack mortar can be mixed a bit wetter than jointed style; it should be slightly sticky. To test, take a handful, form it into a loose ball, and throw it into the air. If it stays in a ball, you're ready to go. If it crumbles and doesn't stay in a ball, slowly add water. Be conservative. There is probably more water in the mix than you realize, and if the mix becomes too soupy, you'll need to add more sand and cement. On hot days, mix the mortar a little wet because it tends to dry quickly, especially when sitting in the sun.

A fast-drying variation of this 3-to-1 recipe is to change the cement mix from 100% portland to half portland and half type S. Type-S cement is stickier and sets up faster. I use this recipe when I need to be able to build a wall higher than 4 ft. or 5 ft. in a single day. The stickier mortar adheres well to the stone, and it dries within a couple of hours.

TIP: I never build more than 4 ft. or 5 ft. high in one day without using fast-setting (type-S) mortar. Portland cement–based mortar won't cure fast enough to hold the weight.

The Craft of Stonework: Cutting and Shaping

The difference between a good-looking wall and a monster has a lot to do with your ability to manipulate a rock. The tighter the stones fit together, the neater the overall wall will look. Good masons know how and where to hit a stone, then where to place it.

To trim the edges of large stones, use a blunt chisel; keep the brick hammer sharp for trimming the edges of smaller stones. If you are unhappy with how the stone looks on the wall, take it down and trim it the way you want it, or simply find another stone.

For a rustic look, minimize surface chiseling; don't trim the textured faces you want exposed. On this job, the homeowners wanted an organic, native stone with a lot of texture, natural weathered color, rigid lines, and shadowed indentations, so I left the faces alone. The sides and tops of the rocks, however, aren't exposed, so I was fairly liberal in trimming around the edges.

Without surface chiseling, the face of the wall will vary somewhat. I set the face of each stone roughly 6 in. from the block wall. Some surface lumps or dimples will be closer or farther. The main body of the stone aligns, and the surface irregularities provide texture.

Because cornerstones have two exposed faces, it's a good idea to choose them first. And because the corners dictate the course lines, that's where I start. After setting a couple of alternating cornerstones, I lay a long base of horizontal stones before building up. I never build more than 4 ft. or 5 ft. high in one day without using fast-setting (type-S) mortar. Portland cement–based mortar won't cure enough to hold the weight. When placing each stone, orient it so that the thickest part is on the bottom, which keeps it from kicking out when weight is stacked on top. Make sure the stone doesn't shift before you fill in with cement. And don't trim rocks while they are resting on the wall; trimming can loosen surrounding stones before they are set.

ALTERNATE THE CORNERSTONES

BECAUSE CORNERSTONES have two faces exposed, pick them carefully. To make a corner strong, the stones should alternate directions. Build up the corners, then work sideways into the field.

KEEP THE ROCKS PLUMB. Regardless of how thick the rocks are, the faces should be in the same plane. If the foundation wall is plumb, you can measure to the face of the rocks consistently.

THE CAPSTONE TAKES A LITTLE PLANNING. Select the capstones before you place the preceding course. Because the siding will hang down an inch or so, there's some wiggle room that can be filled with mortar.

RAKE OUT THE SEMIDRY MORTAR. After a few hours, the mortar is dry enough to remove all that is visible. Use a pointing trowel and go deep. There should be no visible mortar in a dry-stack veneer wall.

Long Stones Make the Wall Look Stronger

Stones often are packaged in similar shapes: long horizontal stones, nuggets, rounded fieldstones, etc. A pattern that I like is a mixture of 20% to 40% fieldstones and 60% to 80% horizontal stones, but the final pattern depends somewhat on how the stone yard packages the stone. For this job, I bought the stone for the project in bulk to get a more random selection of rock shapes because the homeowners didn't want the wall to have a formal pattern. Even for a random pattern, though, I follow a couple of rules.

- *Rule #1:* Always bridge vertical joints with the stones in the next course. Running vertical joints are not pleasing to the eye and eventually can crack if the foundation settles or shifts.
- *Rule #2:* Alternate corners to the left and right as you set each course. Even with a rustic pattern such as this one, structure demands that the quoins, or large cornerstones, alternate. Although I didn't pull strings from the wall ends for a straight corner, I did take care to choose cornerstones with faces at right angles to one another.

Cap the Wall

Because this veneering project tucks under cantilevered framing, a perfect cap isn't as critical. However, if a veneer projects beyond the siding, a flat cap with the same type of stone gives the wall a finished look and allows it to shed water.

If you know the veneer will need a finished cap, make sure you leave enough room for it. Up to 2 in. more than the thickness of the capstones is enough

space to angle the stone away from the house to shed water. Tap capstones with a rubber mallet to set them in position. Make sure the capstones are level. One easy way is to snap a chalkline across the wall before you set the last course of stone.

Finish with a Brush and a Sealer

As you lay the stones, packing mortar behind them to set each one and to hold the wall ties, some mortar will make its way to the surface cracks. After allowing a couple of hours for it to cure, scrape away this excess with a small pointing trowel. The mortar should crumble and fall out. Scraping too soon may smear cement on the edges of the stones or compromise the integral structure of the hidden mortar bed. With dry-stack veneering, you don't need to finish the joints, so after scraping out excess mortar, brush the joints with a small broom.

After a few days, the mortar should be cured fully and ready for a waterproofing sealer. I like Sure Klean® Weather Seal Siloxane PD (www.prosoco.com; 800-255-4255). Waterproofing keeps moisture out of the basement and also prevents efflorescence. Apply sealant to the stone with a garden sprayer. The most important place to seal is the top of the wall (the cap) because this spot gets the most water.

TIP: Don't trim rocks while they are resting on the wall; trimming can loosen surrounding stones before they are set.

Creating a Curved Concrete Walkway

BY RICK ARNOLD

While the work might seem intimidating, installing a curved concrete sidewalk is a surprisingly easy project that most anyone with a few friends and a day of good weather can handle.

The first step is preparing the base. In general, the base needs to be free of organic material, well compacted, and free draining. For this walk, I excavated the topsoil, then placed and tamped down a layer of gravel and dirt so that the top of the base material was 4 in. below the final elevation of the walkway.

I also pitched the section near the house about ⅛ in. per ft. to direct water away from the house. Although the minimum width of a sidewalk is 3 ft., I made this walk 4 ft., which is more comfortable to use. Because this walk needed to turn 90° toward the house, I included a curve for extra interest.

Plan the Path

If you're working around established landscaping, you can stretch out a garden hose or two to visualize the path. Because this simple design was built on bare soil, I outlined one side of the path with a can of marking paint and then used a 4-ft. stick to space and mark the other side evenly. With conventional ⅜-in. plywood forms, a 2-ft. radius is the tightest turn you can make, but tighter turns are possible with plastic forms, which are available at concrete-supply houses.

Reinforcement Is a Must

All concrete needs reinforcement to prevent cracks. For this sidewalk, I used 6-in. wire mesh and #3 (⅜-in.-thick) rebar. To bend the rebar to fit the curves, have a helper lift up the end while you walk down its length. When placing it, be sure to overlap the bars by at least 12 in., and secure the joint with tie wire (or plastic zip ties) in two places. The steel should be near the middle of the concrete depth (about 2 in. from the bottom). You can either place the reinforcement on supports (called *chairs*), or you can pull it up as the concrete is being placed.

Order Concrete Like a Pro

Place your order two or three days ahead of time for a better chance of getting the concrete when you want it. Be prepared to give the dispatcher directions to the job and answers to the questions below. When you're done placing the order, ask the dispatcher to read back the specs and to give the total price. The total should include the price per yard as well as any extras for fuel, Saturday deliveries, or small loads. Ask about the standard unload time. Some suppliers charge extra when their trucks are on site longer than normal.

FORMING, POURING, AND STAMPING a concrete walkway creates an inviting path to any front door.

WHAT STRENGTH AND SLUMP?

Residential concrete is generally rated from 2,000 psi to 3,000 psi. Used for exterior flat work, a 2,500-psi air-entrained mix is common in sidewalks and patios, but check with your building inspector for local requirements. Measured on a scale from 1 in. to 10 in., slump describes the stiffness of wet concrete. The lower the number, the stiffer the mix. Walks and patios should be placed at a 5-in. slump, whereas steps should be at a 3-in. slump. Water weakens the mix, so place concrete as stiff as possible.

HOW MANY CUBIC YARDS?

Dispatchers often help you figure out how much concrete you need, but this should be a way to double-check a figure you've already come up with.

For sidewalks, multiply length by width (in feet) by thickness (4 in. = 0.33 ft.), and divide by 27. For curving walks, use a 50-ft. or 100-ft. measure (they're more flexible) to follow one side of the walk's curving formwork. Double-check your math, and add 10% to compensate for spillage and an uneven grade.

HOW MUCH TIME BETWEEN TRUCKS?

If your order requires multiple loads (a full-size mixer holds between 9 yd. and 11 yd.), consider how long you need to empty each truck. Because the concrete will start to cure, you don't want a truck waiting, and you'll also have less time to pour and finish. If you're using a wheelbarrow to move wet concrete, plan to have three or more going at once.

(Continued on p. 242)

LAY OUT AND FORM

A **CURVING WALKWAY** starts with a stable subgrade of well-compacted, free-draining material. The design is planned either with a garden hose or by eye and is transferred to the soil with marking paint. Curving forms are made from 4-in. strips of $^3/_8$-in. plywood screwed to stakes so that the tops of the plywood and the stakes are flush. Straight forms made from 2× stock are placed similarly. Inside the forms, a grid of reinforcement helps prevent cracks and control shrinkage.

DRIVE THE STAKES. Space the stakes every 1 ft. in the curved sections and every 2 ft. in straight sections. Then, using a rotary laser equipped with a receiver (a water or spirit level works, too), mark the stakes no less than 4 in. above finished grade. Once they're marked, cut them off with a circular or reciprocating saw so that the screed board can pass easily.

ADD REINFORCEMENT. Place sections of reinforcing mesh so that the panels overlap by 6 in., and cut away the excess so that the wire is about 2 in. away from the sides of the form. Then put in rows of $\frac{3}{8}$-in. rebar spaced about 1 ft. apart. Overlap the bars by 1 ft. and tie them together at both ends of the overlap.

WET THE GROUND. Concrete needs adequate water to cure properly. Prevent water from being drawn out of the concrete by thoroughly wetting the ground just before you start pouring.

POUR AND FINISH

THE MAIN WORKER SCREEDS the concrete level with the forms while helpers rake out the concrete and raise the reinforcement so that it's in the center of the slab. Finishing starts with a magnesium bull float to bring up bleed water and force the aggregate into the mix. After the bleed water has evaporated, start troweling, first with a magnesium float, then with a steel finishing trowel.

PULL UP THE REINFORCEMENT. You can place rebar and reinforcing mesh on small metal stands, called chairs, ahead of time or you can raise them as you spread the wet concrete.

BULL FLOAT FIRST. Take two or three passes with a magnesium bull float to level the surface and to push the aggregate into the mix. Raising the leading edge of the float will prevent it from digging into the surface. Additional handle sections provide extra reach on large pours.

BRING UP THE CREAM. A smaller float made of magnesium, aluminum, or wood brings cement particles and fine aggregate to the surface. The resulting cream fills small voids and smooths the surface.

EDGE THE CORNERS. After mag floating, use an edging tool on the slab corners. Rounded edges resist weather better than do sharp corners.

FINISH WITH A STEEL TROWEL. The final finishing tool is a large steel trowel, which forces the cream back down into the surface for a smooth, durable finish. Trowels with curved corners are less likely to leave tracks.

STAMP THE SURFACE

AFTER FINISHING WITH A STEEL TROWEL, cover the surface with a powdered release agent (www.advancedsurfaces.com), which allows the stamp mats to be removed without damaging the textured surface. Arrange the mats in running-bond pattern, and start stamping. At first, stamping is easy, but it gets more difficult as the concrete firms up. Stamp mats are expensive, costing between $100 to $200 each, but they can be rented at many concrete-supply yards.

TRANSITION AT CURVES. A stripe with a simple contrasting pattern provides a convenient place to hide control joints and to eliminate odd transitions where the walk changes direction.

APPLY RELEASE AGENT. Before stamping, cover the entire surface with a release agent. Shaking it on with a broom is fast and easy, but be careful not to hit the wet concrete with the bristles.

ARRANGE THE STAMPS. Place the first row of stamp mats parallel to the form's end board, and stagger subsequent rows to create a running-bond look. Tamp the form straight down. Be careful not to overstamp, or you may leave small cracks in the surface. You may have to vary the order you stamp, depending on the pattern.

IS THIS A FIRM ORDER?

When the weather is iffy, some suppliers take a will-call order, meaning that the concrete will be sent only if you call ahead of time (usually 2 hours) to confirm. This contrasts with a firm order, which means that your concrete will be delivered at the agreed-on time unless you cancel. If you need to postpone, call the dispatcher right away.

Get Extra Help for the Pour

When it's time to place the concrete, it helps to have at least three people on hand. The most important job is getting the concrete flat with a screed board. A screed board is a 2×4 long enough to span the formboards on both sides of the walkway. It scrapes away excess concrete and highlights low spots so that the forms are filled to the perfect level. You also need people with rakes to move the concrete around. Their job is to place the right amount of concrete in front of the screed and to lift the wire and rebar into the middle of the concrete as the pour progresses.

Concrete has a limited working time. When temperatures are in the high 70s or warmer, you may have only 30 minutes before the concrete is too hard to finish and stamp, but in cooler temperatures, especially below 65°F, you may have to wait an extra hour or two before you can start finishing. Note: projects in direct sun will set up faster than those in shady areas.

As you stamp the concrete, it will get harder. But be careful not to pound too heavily, which will create small cracks in the surface. Once you've finished stamping, check the edges and transitions for any places that need to be touched up.

Apply a Sealer

After about 24 hours, wash off the release agent with a garden hose. Once the surface is dry, apply a good sealer with a thick-nap paint roller or a garden sprayer. I like to use Renew-Crete® sealer (www.renewcrete.net) because it usually covers in a single application. A walk like this costs about $8 per sq. ft. in my area, which is a bargain compared to the $12 per sq. ft. a walk with real cobbles would cost.

Stone Walls that Stay Built

BY BRIAN POST

I began my professional training as a waller working under certified craftsmen in Great Britain, a country whose landscape is laced with stone walls that date back millennia. In New England, where I live, two-century-old walls are common. While this may come as a surprise, that's far longer than most mortared walls last. If you learn to properly lay dry stone, you can build walls that will outlast your great-grandchildren.

Mortar Hurts More Than It Helps

While it can take years of practice to efficiently build a near-perfect wall, building a good dry stone wall is quite easy. The process starts with forgetting what you think you know about the importance of mortar. One reason for their longevity is that properly laid dry stone walls flex as the ground moves, whereas a mortared wall will crack. This flexibility often allows dry stone walls to be built directly on the native soil, while mortared work requires a concrete foundation below the frost line. And while a dry stone wall allows water to pass through harmlessly, mortared walls can trap moisture that will destroy the wall when it freezes.

In a dry stone wall, the aim is to use gravity to maximize friction. Friction keeps the stones from sliding apart, and their weight increases the friction.

But even the best built wall can fail if it is poorly designed.

Base the Design on the Site and Stone

When siting, think about what can damage a wall. In northern areas, set walls back from roads and driveways so that plows won't push snow against them. Trees growing in girth can put pressure on walls, and roots can shift or lift when a tree blows in the wind, pushing a wall up from underneath. A good practice is to stay back at least 10 ft. from trees and roads.

The foundation is the earth or gravel the stones rest on, and it should be dug so that it is level from side to side. If you are building on a slope with less than a 1-ft. elevation change in 20 ft., just run the wall parallel to the ground. On steeper slopes, dig the foundation in level steps like stairs. Otherwise, the stones will gradually slide downhill and cause the wall to fail.

For stability, walls should be wider at the bottom than at the top. This taper is called batter. Expressed as a ratio of run to rise, batter typically ranges from 1:6 to 1:10. A 1:6 batter means that for every 6 in. of height, the wall narrows 1 in. on each side. So, a 3-ft.-tall wall with a batter of 1:6 would be 12 in.

ESSENTIAL RULES

ALTHOUGH THERE ARE many mor techniques that can help you build a better-looking wall or work more efficiently, those are grace notes to these five rules. Following these tips will lead to walls that last centuries.

1. Set the stones so their lengths go into the wall, not along it. Like stacked firewood, only the ends of the stones will show. Placing the stones this way maximizes the friction and puts their centers of mass closer to the wall's core. Placing stones counter to this rule is called tracing, and is a primary reason walls fail.

2. Heart tightly. Hearting is key to a strong wall because it adds many points of contact between stones to increase friction and keep them from moving independently. Fill the voids with the biggest pieces you can. Gravel or anything you could readily shovel is too small for hearting and will act like ball bearings in the wall.

3. Cross the joints. Like brickwork, each stone should span the joint in the course below and sit firmly on the two stones on either side of that joint. Vertical joints that break this rule and run through multiple courses are called *running joints*.

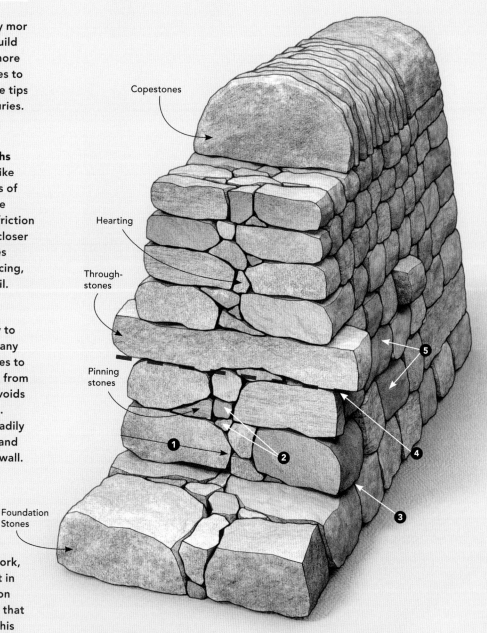

Copestones

Hearting

Through-stones

Pinning stones

Foundation Stones

4. Set stones level. Each stone needs to be able to support the stones above. The simplest way to achieve this is to set each stone so its top is level.

5. Build with the wall's plane. Set stones so their faces line up on the outside face of the wall to create a smooth, even plane without hollows or overhangs, which can cause stones to tip.

ESSENTIAL TOOLS
- Braided mason's string
- Batter frames, made from wood or rebar
- Shovel

- Tape measure
- 2-ft. level
- 6-ft. prybar
- 22-oz. brick or mason's hammer

- 3-lb. hammer
- 6-lb. to 10-lb. sledgehammer

LEFT: TIE STRINGS TO THE FRAMES. Set strings level with each other, just above course height. Sight between the string and batter frame to locate the edges.

BELOW: BATTER FRAMES SHAPE THE WALL. This frame for a 1:6 batter is being set with a level and an angled wedge. A rotary hammer with an electrician's ground-rod driver pounds rebar several feet deep to ensure stability.

narrower (6 in. on each side) at its top. With flatter stones, a steeper batter like 1:10 may be appropriate, while a batter of 1:6 makes a wider base that's better for more irregular stone.

The width of a wall's base depends on its height, the width of the top, and the batter. Walls lower than 3 ft. lack enough area for the unevenness of individual stones to blend visually into a smooth face. Narrower walls use less stone, while wider walls make it easier to use larger stones and tend to be sturdier. With these factors in mind, the top is typically 14 in. to 18 in. wide. With smaller stones or flatter stones, you can make the wall closer to 14 in. at the top. With larger or rounder stones, make the wall closer to 18 in. at the top. The size of available capstones may also influence the top's width.

Choosing the Right Stone

A 4-ft.-high wall takes about 1,000 lb. of stone per linear foot, and the options vary by region. First, look for stones of a size you can move, and keep in mind that those with one longer dimension work better. Flat stones don't necessarily equal good stones, and round or irregular stones don't equal bad stones. Flat stones can make working with thickness variations between adjacent stones harder; plus, they're often thin, meaning lots of courses and slower building. Rounded stones make it easier to work with thickness variations, and each course tends to be thicker, so building goes faster. With irregular stones, build a wall whose face stones fit more loosely. With flatter stones or ones that are easy to shape, build a tighter wall.

Stone from the ground right by the wall is the traditional material to use. Old piles that were collected but never built into walls and debris from construction sites can also be good sources. For reasons of historical preservation, even with permission, harvesting stones from old walls or structures is frowned on and may be illegal. But taking stones from walls in poor condition that aren't visible from a road and don't mark property boundaries is more of an ethically gray area.

Crushed stone quarries often produce an 18-in. and smaller size (referred to as "18 minus") that can be used quite effectively. Gravel-pit leftovers or tailings can also work well. Stone from these sources may include a lot of unusable shapes, but it is often available for as little as $20 per ton. Another option is palletized stone from landscape yards, but it often costs over $200 per ton. Usually meant for use as veneer, it tends to have either long side faces or large flat surfaces rather than the end faces best for dry-laid walls.

People Worry Too Much about the Foundation

With well-drained soil, foundation preparation can be as simple as removing the topsoil and compacting the grade below. If the soil is prone to settling or holding water—for example, clay or silt—put in a foundation of ¾ in. to 2½ in. of clean, crushed stone. The smaller stone shovels more easily, but larger stone tends to be more stable. Crushed stone has sharp, angular shapes that knit together and work much better than rounded gravel. A 6-in. to 18-in. foundation about a foot wider than the wall is typical, with dense clay and other poorly drained soils at the upper end of that range. Water that collects in the crushed stone needs a 4-in. perforated pipe pitched to daylight for drainage. Otherwise, you've just made a pond under your wall.

Compact the foundation using a jumping-jack compactor or by driving back and forth over it a few times with a loaded pickup truck or tractor. A walk-behind vibratory plate compactor does virtually nothing and is not worth using.

Before starting to lay stone, get organized. Walls should be built with larger stones at the base, graduating to courses of smaller stones near the top. Sorting the stones by thickness beforehand will increase your speed and help to ensure that each stone is used to its maximum benefit. Sort the stones into big, medium, and small sizes. Place an equal amount of stones on each side of the wall, leaving 18 in. of clear walking space, with the thickest stones near the foundation and smaller stones farther out.

Set pieces of the size and shape needed for through-stones and cap- or copestones aside, as well as any stones that have even a possibility of being useful in a wall end. Ends are tricky, and a large selection of stones is important. Pile hearting near the wall every 6 ft. or so, moving it around in 5-gal. buckets.

Although professional wallers can usually build 20 sq. ft. or more per day, as you start out, aim to build 5 sq. ft. to 15 sq. ft. per day. If you're slower than that, you are likely being too fussy. If you're faster than that, you're likely not being careful enough.

Completing shorter sections of wall at a time is more efficient. Step back the ends of each section so the next section of wall ties into the area you've just finished. Define these sections by setting up sturdy batter frames 5 ft. to 20 ft. apart. String is used as a guide to keep walls straight and level or parallel to the ground. Tie strings to the inside edge of the batter frames on each side of the wall, level with each other and just higher than the course you're laying.

Set foundation stones so that the top edges of their faces align with the string (bumps may protrude past the string on this course). When sighting stones, line the string up to the inside edge of the batter frame, or use two string lines on each side of the wall, one about 8 in. higher than the other, and sight down between the two. It's usually easier to place the foundation stones along one side at a time, and quicker to set stones from one end to the other rather than working in from two ends and filling the middle with stone of an exact width. It's best to place stones so any sloped faces match the batter. A stone face that angles down will cast shadows that make the wall look rougher.

Try to find stones whose faces mate with their neighbors, but don't be too fussy. Large stones tend to meet with larger gaps, and when looking at a finished wall your eye will focus on its top half, which will be built with smaller stones that tend to fit more tightly.

Thicker foundation stones can be dug into the foundation so they sit securely. Eyeball the stones so their tops are as level as possible, and keep the tops of adjacent stones even. If the top of a stone must slope, slope it toward a neighboring stone. Sloping it toward the face will cause stones placed atop it to slide out, and sloping it toward the core will push the wall apart over time. Stabilize stones as needed with wedge-shaped pinning stones placed from within the wall, leaving no large voids.

Don't worry too much about how the stones fit inside the wall, just pack voids tightly with hearting. Stones that wobble are not properly hearted. A mouse might be able to work its way through a well-hearted wall, but a squirrel will definitely not.

Building Upward, Course by Course

After finishing one course, move the strings up by the thickness of the next. Ensure each stone meets the five rules of walling, keeping the points of contact near the stone's face. If a stone tips when you push down near its face, the contact points are too far back. Focus more on following the five rules than fitting the stones' faces like puzzle pieces. A strong wall will look good, but an incorrectly built wall, no matter how tight-looking it starts out, will fall down. Experience will develop your ability to fit the stones tightly while still following the rules.

Once you've placed a few feet of stones on both sides of a course, fill any voids between them up to the top of the stones. Set hearting so it won't move when the next course's weight is added.

Unlike the foundation course, only the farthest point of each stone from the second course to the top of the wall should align with the string. Keep the strings just above the course you are working on so stones won't push on the string. When working with smaller stones, set a few on the wall and move them until you find a place for each rather than looking for stones to fit specific spots.

The exception to the rule about every stone sitting on the two below: A smaller stone may sit entirely on a larger one. Two stones may be needed to equal the thickness of a neighbor. This is acceptable and creates a way of changing thicknesses within a course.

ABOVE: START BIG. Roll foundation stones into place and level their tops by digging into the soil or gravel below.

LEFT: THERE WILL BE VOIDS. Face stones don't have to meet tightly inside the wall. Just pack the spaces full of hearting stones.

The Faces Need a Strong Connection

It's vital to a wall's structure to tie its sides together with through-stones placed at mid-height. Arrange through-stones no more than 3 ft. apart along the length of the wall and in good contact with the stones below, being careful not to create running joints. Heart under each through-stone so no daylight comes through or they may break from weight placed above. Walls over 5 ft. tall require additional rows of through-stones spaced no more than 2 ft. apart vertically.

Ends must tie the two sides together and tie back into the wall (corners are built much the same way). Ends are traditionally plumb to meet a gatepost, but a slight batter such as 1:48 on the end face will increase the strength.

TOP: TIE THE SIDES TOGETHER. It's typical to let through-stones extend 1½ in. past the wall face to allow for flexibility in their length and for the wall to settle without slipping off them.

BOTTOM: PIN FROM WITHIN. Pinning stones shim the face stones level and solidify their placement. Never pin from the face of the wall because it will just fall out over time.

The best stones for ends are long and large with flat and parallel top and bottom surfaces. Cube-shaped stones won't tie back and will force the creation of a running joint in at least one direction on the next course. The contact points below each stone should be close to the outside corners. You will likely need to shape stones used in wall ends and corners, so plan to spend time on these features.

The Top Stones Help Hold the Wall Together

Walls are topped with either capstones or coping to give it a finished look, to knit the sides together, and to protect the stones below. Thick and flat, capstones are laid across the width of the wall. Coping consists of flat stones set on edge like books on a shelf and is structurally the best way to top a wall. Coping provides the equivalent weight of very thick capstones without the hassle of lifting massive stones to the wall top. They provide many points of contact with the last course, anchoring it with lots of weight and friction. And because of their height, copestones can substitute for one or more upper courses.

Keep copestones as vertical as you can, make the end pieces as big as possible so they won't be pushed off, and make sure they don't rock. For a refined

LEFT: BUILD ENDS AND CORNERS LIKE LOG CABINS. Shaping is often needed to fit end stones. Alternate stones that span the wall width with long stones that tie back into each course.

ABOVE: COPESTONES PROTECT THE WALL TOP. Placed on end like books on a shelf, copestones add height and weight to the wall and tie the top together.

finish, shape them uniformly before setting them on the wall. To get the tops even, tie a string at the top height of the copes on either side of the wall. Tighten the coping by hammering small wedges of stone between the copestones at the top, and hammer pinning stones into any large gaps at the bottom corners. This will build up a tremendous amount of friction between the copestones. When finished, they shouldn't wiggle at all.

Laying Concrete Pavers

BY JOSEPH CRACCO

M y company, Modern Yankee Builders, specializes in remodeling. We end up doing
all sorts of work, from framing to high-
quality trim. Sometimes we even get to spend nice
days outdoors, working on landscaping projects.
This particular job was typical for us. It included a
small kitchen addition and replacement of the old
asphalt driveway with a new one made of concrete
pavers. (A backyard patio or a sidewalk would
use the same techniques.)

Concrete pavers offer a bunch of advantages for driveways and patios: A wide
variety of styles and colors is available,
uniform sizing eases installation, and
aside from the excavation (which we
subcontract), the few special tools
needed are readily rented.

Designing for the Site

Because the number of paver styles available is vast, visiting supply yards to review
the possibilities and obtain samples is a good
idea. A decent supply yard should be able to
help with design and with determining how many
of each size of paver are needed. A word of caution:
Some pavers can be ordered only by the full pallet.
So if I require a third of a pallet of, say, small squares

PAVERS NEED LAYERS

The showy part of the driveway is the pavers on top, but
what's below matters just as much. Choose the right
materials, and compact them correctly for a flat, durable
installation.

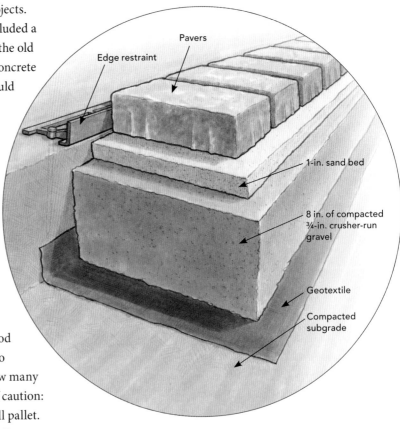

Edge restraint

Pavers

1-in. sand bed

8 in. of compacted
¾-in. crusher-run
gravel

Geotextile

Compacted
subgrade

GET THE BASE RIGHT. A good excavator is crucial. When digging down to the required depth of the base stone, be sure that the subgrade is flat so that the succeeding layers are of a consistent depth.

GEOTEXTILE SEPARATES THE LAYERS. The main purpose of geotextile is to prevent the crusher run from mixing into the subgrade over time and losing its bearing capability.

SPREAD THE CRUSHER RUN. A mix of stone from ¾ in. to dust, the crusher run helps to spread the loads from the pavers above to the subgrade below.

TAMP TO PREVENT SETTLING. Place the crusher run in two 4-in.-deep lifts. Compact the first lift, then place and compact the second.

instead of three pallets of rectangles, I'm out of luck. If my supplier quoted a price based on a per-paver basis, I may find out that what I thought was a $150 purchase now costs $450 because of that two-thirds of a pallet of small squares I don't want. I need to find a place for those extra small squares or change my pattern.

Where I work, patios usually don't require a building permit; for driveways, however, some towns require the local public-works department to do an existing-conditions survey (sometimes they just snap a photo) before issuing a certificate allowing the work to proceed. When the new driveway is complete, someone returns to verify that you didn't alter the size or location of the driveway's intersection with the street. Other jurisdictions are much more restrictive, particularly for the first 20 ft. or so where a driveway meets the street. I always check local requirements before commencing work, and I start with a site survey if I'm going to be anywhere near the property lines.

Planning the excavation and fill depth was critical for making sure that the new driveway shown here matched the height of the neighbor's driveway. To have a clean edge to butt our pavers against, we needed to cut a straight line through the neighbor's asphalt driveway and along the edge of the street. Two things were critical in cutting the asphalt. First, the cuts needed to penetrate the existing pavement completely or the excavator would hook the uncut asphalt and rip up big sections beyond the cut. Even after patching, this never looks right. Second, the cuts needed to be dead straight as well as perpendicular to each other or the job would look bad, forcing us to waste time trimming the full pavers to fit.

We could have made the cuts ourselves, but when we added up the time to rent the saw, cut 60 ft. of asphalt, and return the saw, and then factored in the rental rate, the cost to hire a specialized contractor to cut a dead-straight line was only a little more.

Base Prep Is Key

No matter the kind of paver project, success depends on installing the base correctly. Pavers require a sand setting bed atop a base of crushed stone for drainage and support as well as underlying subsoil that can handle the loads. Each paver manufacturer has specific requirements, but the ones here are fairly typical.

Elevation restrictions on all sides controlled the depth of our excavation. The driveway had to end up flush with or just a bit higher than the road and the neighbor's driveway. The edge near the front of the house needed to meet the front walk. The back had to rise slightly to eliminate what would have been a difference in height between the driveway and the client's planting bed. Ultimately, the adjacent asphalt driveway and the road were the critical control points. For the height to work out, the final elevation of the 1-in.-deep sand bed directly below the pavers would need to be 3 in. lower than the neighbor's driveway and the street. On other jobs, we might be looking for a crown to drain water off each side, or maybe a dead-flat, pitched base to send water in one direction. Over a 10-ft. span, the base has to be graded to within ¼ in. of flat. (Flat doesn't mean level, just planar.) The goal is to make adjustments by adding or subtracting from the crushed-stone base so that the sand setting bed ends up a uniform depth.

On any paver job, the excavation and the base materials that follow have to extend at least 8 in. beyond the edge of the pavers so that the edge of the base doesn't crumble under load. In this case, that didn't apply to the side that abutted the neighbor's drive because there was an existing compacted base there. Fortunately, the subsoil was suitable. If the soil had had significant amounts of clay or organic matter (both of which can hold a great deal of water, causing frost heave in cold climates), we would have had to excavate to good soil and to use more crushed-stone fill, driving up the cost of the project.

After Don Lemonde, our excavation contractor, removed the old asphalt driveway and hauled it to

DESIGN POSSIBILITIES

THERE ARE SEVERAL CONCRETE-PAVER manufacturers, each with its own product line. Offerings vary by region as well, so you'll have to shop around.

a recycling facility, he dug out all the soil down to a little more than 12 in. below what would be the final elevation of the pavers. After grading the subsoil to eliminate pockets, which retain water, Don compacted the excavation with a 4,000-lb. walk-behind vibrating compactor, running over it twice in perpendicular directions. Compactor weight refers to the force the compactor exerts as it vibrates, not the machine's actual weight. These walk-behind machines weigh a little more than 200 lb. and are readily rented.

Fill the Excavation Back Up

The next step was to install a layer of geotextile, a synthetic fabric that increases the stability of the soil and the aggregate base. Geotextiles keep fine soil particles from migrating into the aggregate, which helps maintain its drainage capacity. This becomes even more important when the base assembly is below a permeable pavement.

Above the geotextile, Unilock, the paver manufacturer, required 8 in. of compacted ¾-in. crusher-run gravel, a blend of crushed stone ranging in size from ¾ in. down to dust. Manufacturers specify how big a lift (or layer) of gravel can be installed at one time, based on the size of the compactor. A 4,000-lb. vibrating compactor allows for 4-in. lifts.

After Don finished, we had the pavers delivered. The pattern called for three different paver sizes, plus another for a border. We had the pallets placed as close as possible to the work area to save time and labor. We try to stage the correct quantity of each size paver so that the first ones to be used are close at hand and the others become more accessible as the work progresses. With the limited space here, we ended up locating a third of the pallets on the front lawn and the remaining pallets at the back of the property.

Create a Sand Setting Bed

The crusher run was to be topped with ¾ in. to 1 in. of coarse, angular sand (concrete sand, as opposed to mortar sand or play sand) in which to bed the pavers. Before my helper Kevin and I tackled that step, however, we verified Don's grade. He had it perfect, but if he'd been off, we'd have adjusted it by adding or subtracting crusher run with shovels and rakes, then compacting again.

To make the setting bed a uniform depth, we set 1-in.-dia. EMT-conduit guides at the correct height, filled around them with sand, and used a straightedge to screed off the excess. There are a number of methods for setting the exact level of the screed guides. A simple way is to set a string ½ in. higher than where you want the tops of the pavers to end up. The extra ½ in. allows for the pavers to be compacted into the sand bed. Set the screed guides on the subbase, and place pavers on each end. Adjust the guides up or down by adding or removing material below them until the pavers are even with the strings. If the base is right, little adjustment should be needed. In this case, because the neighbors' asphalt controlled our elevation, we simply set a ½-in. spacer on their driveway and used a 10-ft. piece of conduit in place of the strings.

A large magnesium screed typically used for concrete flatwork is ideal for flattening the sand, but a straight 2×4 or even a level also will work. Keeping some sand in front of the screed as you go will help to fill low spots, but letting too much build up can bow the screed and throw off the grade. Once the sand bed is flat, we gently pull out the guides and sprinkle sand into the depressions. I'm looking for a variation in the sand bed of no more than ⅛ in. in 10 ft. More than this means that you'll end up with dips that hold puddles. Over time, these areas will sink even more because the water will wash the fines out of the soil below the low spot in a vicious circle. We build the sand setting bed in 10-ft. sections, the length of the screed guides, laying pavers over each section before building the next. You could do the entire sand bed at once, but if you end up not laying pavers over an area, odds are that you'll come back to find that kids, dogs, or cats have destroyed your work. Once the sand is down and screeded, don't walk on it, or you'll create divots.

MAKE A FLAT SAND BED. First, determine the elevation. A piece of conduit resting atop a few pavers determines the height of the sand bed. The partially buried pieces of conduit are used as screed guides. Set them ½ in. high to allow for compaction.

START IN A SQUARE CORNER. This helps create two straight edges to work from, easing the balance of the installation. The mitered corner blocks are a simple custom touch.

LAY THE PAVERS. Place the pavers carefully so that they maintain proper contact with each other. Standing on boards spreads out your weight and prevents the set pavers from tipping.

Setting the Pavers

If you don't count how your back feels by the end of the day, setting pavers is the easy part. We usually start at a corner, guided by an existing fixture such as a foundation wall, or in this case, the neighbor's driveway and the street, and then fill in the field using a picture of the pattern as our guide. Without such an edge, we'd create a square starting corner by installing heavy plastic angles called edge restraints atop the base, fastening them with long galvanized spikes per the paver-manufacturer's requirements.

It's important to keep the pattern running straight and true. On this project, we had a 67-ft.-long straight line for one edge and only a 9-ft.-wide driveway, so we didn't need additional benchmarks. In other situations, we set up a centerline to guide the layout. To establish a centerline, you can set a stringline, which often gets in the way, or you can snap a chalkline on the sand setting bed, which is my preferred method.

It's important to set pavers flat, making sure not to dig a corner into the sand bed. When the pavers are compacted, the disturbed sand may even out, but I don't leave this to chance. It's easy to hold the paver about 1 in. above the setting bed, move it in contact with one or, preferably, two sides of the adjacent pavers, then slide it straight down onto the sand.

The pavers used here are made with ribs that bear on neighboring pavers to maintain a consistent gap. Without this contact, the entire assembly would be compromised. Each paver's ability to withstand vertical loads depends on its resisting lateral loads while pushing straight down on the underlying base. If a paver can rock under load, it will eventually fail. (Imagine a tire rolling over a single paver; first one edge and then the other would be pushed into the sand.) Each paver's ability to withstand lateral loads depends on its distributing the load to the pavers around it. If you have 8 ft. of pavers but 8 ft. 1 in. of

SCREED THE SAND FLAT. A level or other straightedge rides on the conduit guides (later removed) to screed the sand.

INSTALL EDGING. Spike plastic edge restraints to the ground as the job progresses.

A CIRCULAR SAW WITH A DIAMOND BLADE CUTS PAVERS EASILY. A light water mist cools the blade, extending its life and preventing it from warping due to heat, and it keeps the silica-laden dust down. Make sure to be plugged into a GFCI-protected outlet.

DON'T PLAY AROUND WITH SAND

FOR BEDDING, we use concrete sand (also known as coarse sand or sharp sand). Unlike play sand, whose grains are smooth and round, concrete sand is angular. Its flat sides engage each other, creating a solid bed. In comparison, play sand's grains move around like ball bearings. If you drove over pavers set in play sand, they would rotate, digging in on one side and lifting on the other as the play sand moved. Concrete sand's stability minimizes this motion. Ultimately, this means that the pavers will remain flat much longer.

Before compaction

After compaction

POUND 'EM DOWN. With a layer of plywood as protection, use a plate compactor to set the pavers firmly in the sand bed.

space to fill, don't gap each of the pavers a little bit to take up the extra space. You must either cut fillers or move the edge in 1 in.

Similarly, before the pavers are compacted into the sand bed, they are susceptible to rolling if you step on the edge instead of the middle. I lay walk boards on the pavers I've just set and move the boards as the setting progresses. Not only can I walk across the planks and not worry about rolling the pavers but the planks also act as a great place to stage the next row without the risk of chipping the set pavers.

We picked from several pallets at once to ensure an even distribution of any color variation. Once we distributed the pavers, Kevin and I laid them as a team. Each paver went from the pile to Kevin's hands to mine, and then to the sand bed without having to be put down and picked back up again.

On the house side, we placed edge restraints as we installed the pavers. Long galvanized spikes secure the edging to the base.

Cutting Pavers

Edges often mean cutting pavers. I use a wet saw to minimize dust, which is laden with silica and is a real health hazard. On a project with a lot of cuts, I set up my tile saw on a stand. We set all of the full pavers, then my helper marks the cuts and brings them to me at the saw. While I'm cutting the paver he just marked, he takes the paver I just cut, places it where it belongs, then marks the next paver to be cut.

FILL THE JOINTS. Sweep a graded material such as fine stone dust over the pavers until the joints are full.

FILL THE JOINTS AGAIN. Sweep in more joint filler after compaction to bring it up to the level of the pavers.

FINALLY FILLED. When done, the filler should end just below the level of the pavers.

For efficiency, I plan the job to make as few cuts as possible. There were only eight on this entire driveway. When there are few cuts to make, I don't drag out the tile saw. Instead, I use an old circular saw with a diamond blade. The pavers on this job had distressed edges, so I roughed up the cut edges with a hammer. The final step in setting the pavers was to backfill against the edge restraints with soil.

Finishing Up

With all the pavers laid, we were ready to compact them into the base and to fill the joints. It's important to compact as soon as possible after setting is complete. Wait too long, and rain or traffic can tilt pavers out of alignment. If heavy rain hits before we can compact, we wait a day for the sand to dry out a little. We closely inspect the pavers before compacting, replacing any damaged ones. Once compacted, heaven and earth need to be moved to get a paver back out.

Pavers should be isolated from the compactor to prevent damage to their surface. Special "paver saver" pads can do this, but our rental yard doesn't have them. Instead, we used scrap sheets of ¼-in. lauan plywood.

Compacting is done in two steps. The first compaction drives the pavers down into the sand and levels each paver to the adjacent ones. This operation also drives some of the sand up between the pavers. After running the compactor in two passes over an area determined by how much plywood we had, I moved up the driveway while Kevin started filling the joints with graded joint material. Using a stiff-bristle broom on the area I had just compacted, he swept off the excess so that it wouldn't be ground into the paver surface with the second compaction.

When I reached the driveway's end, I doubled back to begin compacting the areas Kevin had filled. This second compaction vibrated the joint filler and settled it well below the surface of the pavers. Kevin then swept in more filler to top off the joints.

A CASE FOR PERMEABLE PAVERS

UNLIKE TRADITIONAL CONCRETE-SLAB or asphalt driveways, paver driveways can be permeable, as is the one in the project shown here. This means that rather than increasing runoff, rainwater can soak through these pavers into the ground.

Storm-water runoff is an environmental problem. When water can't soak into the ground where it falls, the runoff can cause damaging erosion and carry sediments and pollutants into waterways. Humans exacerbate this problem by constructing buildings and paving over the ground. When water can soak into the ground directly, pollutants such as motor oil are retained at the point of origin, where they can be digested by naturally occurring microorganisms.

Densely populated municipalities usually limit the percentage of a lot that can be covered with impermeable structures, such as roofs or traditional pavement. This means, for example, that you might not be able to build as large an addition as you'd like. Here, because we replaced an impermeable concrete driveway with permeable pavers, the percentage of impermeable coverage on the lot shrank, even though we had just built an addition.

It's not just the pavers that must be permeable but the filler as well. On this job, we filled the joints with Aqua Rock, a granite product made specifically for permeable-paver joints. It fulfills the requirements for lateral-load transfer as well as the appropriate flow of water.

CONTRIBUTORS

Rick Arnold is a veteran builder and contributing editor to *Fine Homebuilding*. He is the author of *Working With Concrete* (The Taunton Press, 2003).

Steve Baczek is an architect in Reading, Mass.

Jim Blodgett is a carpenter in Roy, Wash.

Brian Brophy runs New Creation Construction in Lockeford, Calif.

John Carroll is a mason and builder in Durham, N.C. He's the author of several books, including *The Complete Visual Guide to Building a House* (The Taunton Press, 2014).

Joseph Cracco is a remodeling contractor from Cumberland, R.I.

Andy Engel is a senior editor with *Fine Homebuilding*.

Robert M. Felton is a consulting geotechnical engineer and free-lance writer in Wake Forest, N.C.

Scott Grice is a fence and deck specialist in Portland, Ore.

Mike Guertin, *Fine Homebuilding*'s editorial advisor, is a custom-home builder and remodeling contractor in East Greenwich, Rhode Island.

Carl Hagstrom is a builder in Montrose, Pa., and vice-president at WOODWEB.com, an online resource for the professional woodworking industry.

Jeremy Hess is a contractor in Elizabethtown, Pa.

Martin Holladay is a senior editor with *Fine Homebuilding*.

Larry Janesky is president of Basement Systems Inc. in Seymour, Conn.

Cody Macfie, a second-generation stonemason and freelance writer, owns Steep Creek Stoneworks and French Broad Stone Supply both in Brevard, N.C. He is the author of *Masonry Complete* (Taunton Press, 2012).

Daniel S. Morrison is the former managing editor of GreenBuildingAdvisor.com and a former *Fine Homebuilding* editor.

Brendan Mostecki is a mason in Leominster, Mass. His website is www.culturedmasonry.com.

Rob Munach, P.E., operates a structural-engineering firm in Chatham County, N.C., that specializes in residential and light-commercial environments (www.robmunachpe.com).

Eric Nelson owns Garden Paths, a landscape contracting and design business in Bethlehem, Conn.

Brian Post is a landscape architect and a DSWA-GB certified Master Craftsman. He is the executive director of The Stone Trust in Dummerston, Vt.

Tim Robinson and his wife, Anna, own HOMEWORKS, a construction company in Brevard, N.C.

William B. Rose is senior research architect at the Illinois Sustainable Technology Center of the University of Illinois at Urbana-Champaign.

Howard Stein was a builder in Townsend, Mass.

Rob Yagid is the Editorial Director of *Fine Homebuilding*.

CREDITS

All photos are courtesy of *Fine Homebuilding* magazine © The Taunton Press, Inc., except as noted below.

Front cover: Photo by Justin Fink

The articles in this book appeared in the following issues of *Fine Homebuilding*:

pp. 5–7: Understanding Building Loads by Rob Munach, issue 212. Drawings by Chris Mills.

pp. 8–15: Soil: The Other Half of the Foundation by Robert M. Felton, issue 136. Photo p. 9 by Tim O'Brien, photo p. 12 courtesy of S&ME, Raleigh, N.C., photo p. 15 courtesy of Avongard. Maps p. 10 U. S. Dept. of Agriculture (left), U.S. Geological Survey (right). Drawings by Christopher Clapp.

pp. 16–24: Getting the Right Concrete by Rick Arnold, issue 228. Photos by Rodney Diaz, except photo p. 17 by Roe A. Osborn, photos pp. 20–21 by Justin Fink, photo p. 23 by Carol Collins, and photos p. 24 by Chris Ermides.

pp. 25–27: How it Works: Efflorescence and spalling by Rob Yagid, issue 234. Photo by *Fine Homebuilding* Staff. Drawings by Christopher Mills.

pp. 28–36: Working with Rebar by Howard Stein, issue 137. Photos by Charles Bickford, except bottom photo p. 29 and photo p. 33 by Howard Stein, product photos p. 35 by Dan Thornton, top photo p. 35 by Roe A. Osborn. Drawing by Christopher Clapp.

pp. 37–40: Start with Batter Boards by Jim Blodgett, issue 169. Photos by Hugh Lentz. Drawing by Dan Thornton.

pp. 41–49: A Solid Deck Begins with Concrete Piers by Rick Arnold, issue 180. Photos by Christopher Ermides, except bottom right photo p. 47 courtesy of Ardisam Inc. Drawings by Dan Thornton.

pp. 50–52: Mix Concrete by the Bag by Scott Grice, issue 186. Photos by John Ross, except left photo p. 51 courtesy of Jackson Professional Tools.

pp. 54–56: Building Skills: Placing a small concrete slab by Andy Engel, issue 259. Photos by Patrick McCombe, except for the tool photos p. 56 by Rodney Diaz.

pp. 57–66: Pouring Concrete Slabs by Carl Hagstrom, issue 83. Photos by Rich Ziegner.

pp. 67–74: Forming and Pouring Footings by Rick Arnold and Mike Guertin, issue 120. Photos by Roe A. Osborn.

pp. 75–86: Forming and Pouring Foundations by Rick Arnold and Mike Guertin, issue 119. Photos by Roe A. Osborn except photos p. 72 by Justin Fink.

pp. 87–92: Air-Sealed Mudsill Assembly by Steve Baczek, issue 241. Photos by Justin Fink, except for product photos pp. 90–91 by Dan Thornton. Drawing by John Hartman.

pp. 93–98: An Energy-Smart Foundation in Two Days by Tim Robinson, issue 186. Photos by Daniel S. Morrison, except bottom right photo p. 98 by Anna Robinson. Drawing by Don Mannes.

pp. 99–106: Slab Foundation for Cold Climates by Andy Engel, issue 262. Photos courtesy of Patricia Steed. Drawings by Christopher Mills.

pp. 107–112: Superinsulated Slab by Steve Baczek, issue 242. Photos by Justin Fink. Drawings by John Hartman.

pp. 113–120: It's Time to Consider Helical-Pile Footings by Jeremy Hess, issue 260. Photos by Andy Engel, except for photos pp. 118–119 and bottom photos p. 120 courtesy of TechnoMetalPost.com. Drawing by Don Mannes.

pp. 122–124: Keep Your Basement Dry with a Curtain Drain by Eric Nelson, issue 189. Photos by Eric Nelson, except for product photos p. 123 by Krysta S. Doerfler. Drawings by Martha Garstang Hill.

CREDITS

pp. 125–135: Details for a Dry Foundation by William B. Rose, issue 111. Drawings by Christopher Clapp.

pp. 136–146: Keeping a Basement Dry by Larry Janesky, issue 140. Photos by Tom O'Brien, except photo p. 139 by Larry Janesky and photos p. 144 by Harold Shapiro. Drawings by Rick Daskam.

pp. 147–154: Sealing a Crawl Space by Larry Janesky, issue 153. Photos Harold Shapiro, except for fastener photo p. 153 by Roe A. Osborn. Drawings by Mark Hannon.

pp. 156–163: The Stay-Dry, No-Mold Finished Basement by Andy Engel, issue 169. Photos by Charles Bickford. Drawings by Toby Welles @ Design Core.

pp. 164–166: Energy Smart Details: Adding insulation to basement walls by Martin Holladay, issue 253. Drawings by Steve Baczek.

pp. 167–172: Retrofitting a Foundation by Brian Brophy, issue 217. Photos by Brian Brophy, except photo p. 167 and left photo p. 169 by Rob Yagid and photos p. 172 by Rick Arnold.

pp. 173–175: Energy Smart Details: Creating a Sealed Crawlspace by Martin Holladay, issue 252. Drawings by Dan Thornton.

pp. 176–183: A Fast Foundation for an Addition by Rick Arnold, issue 170. Photos by Roe A. Osborn, except bottom photo p. 177 by Brian Pontolilo and center photo p. 179, photos p. 181, and top photo p. 182 by Justin Fink. Drawing by Dan Thornton.

pp. 184–186: Energy Smart Details: Basement Insulation Retrofits by Daniel S. Morrison, issue 210. Photos by Dan Thornton, except for the bottom right photo p. 185 courtesy of Roxul. Drawings by Steve Baczek.

pp. 187–189: Energy Smart Details: Air-Sealing a Basement by Martin Holladay, issue 224. Drawings by Steve Baczek.

pp. 190–192: Energy Smart Details: Insulating a Slab on Grade by Martin Holladay, issue 245. Drawings by Steve Baczek.

pp. 193–200: Replace a Rotten Lally Column by Emanuel Silva, issue 209. Photos by Rob Yagid.

pp. 202–204: Building Skills: Broom-Finished Concrete Flatwork by Rick Arnold, issue 221. Photos by John Ross, except left photos p. 204 by Dan Thornton.

pp. 205–213: Build a Sturdy Stone Sitting Wall by Brendan Mostecki, issue 204. Photos by Justin Fink. Drawing by Toby Welles/Wow-House.

pp. 214–223: Four Retaining Wall Choices by Eric Nelson, issue 173. Photos by Brian Pontolilo, except top photo p. 215 courtesy of Versa-Lok, bottom left photo p. 215 courtesy of Allan Block, top and center right photo p. 217 courtesy of Walton & Sons Masonry Inc., Mountain View, Calif., center left photo p. 215 by Gary M. Katz, and photos p. 221 courtesy of Ted Lane Design/Build, Des Moines, Iowa. Drawings by Don Mannes.

pp. 224–233: Dress Up a Block Wall with a Rock Wall by Cody Macfie, issue 177. Photos by Daniel S. Morrison. Drawings by Toby Welles.

pp. 234–224: Creating a Curved Concrete Walkway by Rick Arnold, issue 221. Photos by John Ross.

pp. 243–251: Stone Walls that Stay Built by Brian Post, issue 266. Photos by Andy Engel. Drawing by Christopher Mills.

pp. 252–263: Laying Concrete Pavers by Joseph Cracco, issue 248. Photos by Andy Engel, except for photos p. 256 courtesy of Unilock and left photo p. 260 courtesy of Joseph Cracco. Drawing by Dan Thornton.

INDEX